Acting the Truth:
The Acting Principles of Constantin Stanislavski and Exercises

---

A Handbook for Actors, Directors, and Instructors of Theatre

---

by

Albert Pia

Bloomington, IN Milton Keynes, UK

authorHOUSE™

AuthorHouse™
1663 Liberty Drive, Suite 200
Bloomington, IN 47403
www.authorhouse.com
Phone: 1-800-839-8640

AuthorHouse™ UK Ltd.
500 Avebury Boulevard
Central Milton Keynes, MK9 2BE
www.authorhouse.co.uk
Phone: 08001974150

First published by AuthorHouse 8/10/2006

ISBN: 1-4259-3141-3 (sc)

Printed in the United States of America
Bloomington, Indiana

This book is printed on acid-free paper.

Dedication

To my wife, Betty
for her significant contribution and
who shares my respect for Stanislavski.

To my children, Claudia and Clifford
for their encouragement and inspiration.

and
To Tigger and Pepper
who often sat by my side and inspired me to work faster
so I could take them romping in their favorite woods
and fields.

CONTENTS

PART ONE   **INNER PSYCHO-TECHNIQUE WITH**
              THEATRE EXERCISES   1

   I.   Dramatic Quality   3
   II.   The Art of Living A Role   10
   III.   Dramatic Action   17
   IV.   Creative Imagination   29
   V.   Focusing of Attention   36
   VI.   Tension and Relaxation   46
   VII.   Beats and Key Points   51
   VIII.   Scenic Truth   56
   IX.   Recalling Feelings   62
   X.   Inter-Communication   67
   XI.   Inner and Outer Adjustment   73
   XII.   Mind, Will and Feeling   79
   XIII.   Through Line of Dramatic Action   84
   XIV.   Creative Mood   89
   XV.   The Super-Objective   94
   XVI.   Region of the Subconscious   99

PART TWO   **EXTERNAL PHYSICAL TECHNIQUE WITH**
              THEATRE EXERCISES   107

   I.   Physical Qualities of A Character   109
   II.   Costume For Character Dimension   117
   III.   Creating the Physical Image   123
   IV.   The Flexible Physical Instrument   130
   V.   Fluid Movement   135
   VI.   Control of the Physical Instrument   140
   VII.   Musicality of Speech   145
   VIII.   The Spoken Word and Sub-Text   150
   IX.   Emphasizing the Key Word   156
   X.   Actor-Character Duality   162
   XI.   Timing and Dynamics of Action   167

XII.	Content and Timing of Speech	172
XIII.	Personal Quality	178
XIV.	Ethics In the Theatre	184
XV.	Psycho-Physical Artistry	189
XVI.	Acting Naturally	194

PART THREE ADDITIONAL THEATRE EXERCISES 199

PART FOUR STANISLAVSKI EXERCISES OF MOSCOW ART THEATRE 229

PART FIVE THEATRE STUDY AND TEACHING SYLLABUS 259

PART SIX DIRECTING THE PLAY 271

INTRODUCTION

Tribute

On the first day of class, award-winning director, Al Pia sternly cautions his students to stay far away from professional acting and theatre. After administering a clever dose of reverse psychology, Al chuckles, admitting that "…my students never listen to me; they never seem to follow my advice!"

Indeed if you have been fortunate enough to have studied with this brilliant, loving man, chances are great that you have not only propelled your career, but achieved personal fulfillment along the way.

In the thirty plus years that Al Pia has been teaching, writing and directing, he has proudly witnessed over 150 of his students grace a Broadway stage or a Hollywood set. When referring to each student's outstanding accomplishments, Al will modestly shift all of the credit to Constantin Stanislavski for revolutionizing the art of acting. Stanislavski, however, should only be given partial credit. It is one hundred percent Al Pia who has masterfully transformed each student by bestowing them with the necessary tools to uncover their unique gifts. TONY Award Winner, David Marshall Grant says,—"I've never met any contemporaries in my profession who participated in a drama program that came near to Al Pia's. Al teaches a Stanislavski technique. He gives a sense that acting is a process, not just a result."

As in Robert Frost's poem Birches, Al makes sure that he fills each actor's cup to the brim with zeal; and more importantly "…even above the brim." Kerri Kenney-Silver, co-creator and star of Reno911! recalls how Al would pack each class with excitement, up to the last second, and even after the bell. She adds, "Al Pia's knowledge and passion for the craft of acting has been an invaluable life lesson for me." In addition to her television series, Kerri will be starring in Reno911!: Miami, a Fox/Paramount Pictures feature film to be released in 2006.

Al's positive guidance and expertise is the glue that elevates his teachings and his book, Acting The Truth from all others. He magically takes you by the hand and places you on the path towards self discovery. Once you possess the necessary knowledge and confidence, the integration of your inner life with the character's given circumstances becomes a joyful endeavor. Alisan Porter, one of Al's youngest protégés, soon to be starring in the 2006 Broadway Revival of A Chorus Line, whole heartedly states, "Mr. Pia embodies the spirit of the theatre. He brings an infinite trust and truth to his actors, which turns everything he touches to gold. His unparalleled wisdom is with me every time I step on stage."

They say that behind every successful person stands a great teacher. If you are one of the lucky ones who has been touched by this extraordinary human being, you have not only discovered truth, you have embraced spiritual beauty;—and there is no one more beautiful than Al Pia himself.

Jill Jayson, award-winning playwright and director, and founder of Center Stage Theatre Company—Westport, CT and former student of Al Pia's.

FOREWARD

This compilation of major works by Constantin Stanislavski comprises the most valued of all acting principles. They may be used by teachers of theatre students, stage directors, and by actors of any age or experience. Each titled acting principle is accompanied by ten to twenty or more exercises to aid in illustrating the working process of each principle. An additional one hundred exercises are included in part three of the handbook. The instructor or director need only select those exercises most compatible with the instruction process being employed in the classroom, rehearsal studio or stage production.

Sufficient material exists in the handbook to nurture an instructional program of theatre for a school quarter, semester, full year or even a four year curriculum. It may also serve the director of any stage play during all or part of the rehearsal period. Youth programs, too, will find the exercises functional in various ways as will adult programmers who may find the exercises to be enthralling learning experiences or useful as entertainment for brief or extended periods, even for invited audiences.

The effective employment of any Stanislavski principle has, I have observed, induced several other principles to function as well. This fact has instilled confidence in the actor, or instructor, assuring a higher level of performance in any given instance.

The acting principles of Constantin Stanislavski and these exercises for the theatre have served me well for many years as actor, director, instructor of students and acting professionals in various schools, colleges, and theatres in America and Europe. For all these years I have experimented, explored, tested and verified these valued acting principles. The time has come for me to share these ideas with my colleagues and those acting students I have not had the pleasure of meeting in my classrooms, studios or rehearsals.

Exercises in part four used by Stanislavski in his rehearsals.

Albert Pia
Connecticut - 1994

PART ONE

THE ACTOR PREPARES
CREATING THE INNER LIFE
WITH EXERCISES

CHAPTER ONE

DRAMATIC QUALITY

To arouse desire to create is difficult; to kill that desire is easy. Thus we turn to the valued principles of Constantine Stanislavski to build a firm acting foundation of creative artistry for the theatre.

Allow theatre involvement to lend beauty to your life, to enjoy great plays, major playwrights and their ideas, and learn the beauty of performance.

The actor must be subject to iron discipline, for one must commit an entire acting role to memory, page by page, then add life elements to build a human spirit and avoid mechanical acting. Acting principles, therefore, are of major importance.

The creative mood is so very fragile, thus, you must be gentle with all aspects of the creative process.

Exhibit always a good attitude to your partners, to your director, to the entire cast, technical staff and support personnel. Approach every acting class as a rehearsal leading toward a major performance. Arrive early to meet and talk with your cast, staff or class members and contribute to a creative atmosphere by relaxing, smiling, moving about, warming up, getting totally comfortable in the creative space.

In theatre exercises or performance, do not fall into a trap of feeling obligated to interest the audience. That will lead only to catastrophe! Learn to become 'private' in public, thus closing yourself off from audience by erecting a 'fourth wall' between you and the audience.

Leave life's problems outside the theatre. Bring no 'dirt' into the theatre with you. Leave all trivialities and pettiness and troubles on the door step and enter with a smile! Then try speading your smile around to all the others in the company.

When working on an acting role, do not remain too long at any one point believing that you are satisfied with the character as it is. Find something new in the life of your character with each new day of rehearsal. If yesterday's rehearsal is exactly like today's rehearsal, be fully aware that something is wrong. Too much time in rehearsals is wasted running and re-running the lines over and over, scene after scene. Rather, seek new dimensions in the life of your character in the given circumstance of the play with each successive rehearsal session and you will indeed find more significant elements of your character and circumstance with every rehearsal.

Seek your own individual way to reach a high level of comfort in your 'space' on stage. Believe in your ability to create the environment of your character's life. If you believe who you are and where you are as the character, the audience, too, will believe you.

CHAPTER ONE
ACTING EXERCISES

1.
HELLO! HELLO!

To free ourselves of tension and bring release from stress of life outside the theatre, the director calls out, "Hello, gang!" The group will shout a response, "Hello, Mr. Jones!" Seeking higher energy, the director will then call out louder, inferring he may not have heard the first response, inspiring a louder, more energetic response. A third level may be reached by trying ONE MORE TIME! It may be done at the beginning of every session.

2.
GOODBYE! GOODBYE!

At end of any given session, the director may call out loudly, "Goodbye, cast!" The ensemble may respond loudly, "Goodbye, Ms. Smith!" It helps to spiritedly punctuate the close of a productive rehearsal or class.

3.
SHOUT IT OUT!

Considerable release of tension may be achieved by gathering the cast on stage at beginning of session and shouting away the outside world with a long bellowing, sustained yell joined by shaking and stomping of feet on the floor. Fifteen to thirty seconds of time will be adequate.

4.
WATERSIDE

Sitting or lying comfortably on stage, you find yourself beside your favorite body of water. You linger peacefully beside the placid water noting that the water is as quiet and calm as you are. You have indeed brought calmness to the water and it has calmed you, an inter-play of effect on each other. Remain focused on the water, sending out your peaceful rays while receiving its soothing rays. Maintain this soothing interplay as long as desired.

5.
IMMERSION

Upon reaching peak of prior exercise, you are in a state of peaceful relaxation emitting and receiving soothing rays from the water. Then you begin to blend with the water, immersing yourself in the water, floating quietly and calmly, easily and comfortably, feeling its fluid quietness for as long as you wish.

6.
INTERMINGLE

As you reach the state of total comfort in prior exercise, you begin to feel that you are blending with the water, becoming one with the water as it becomes you. You are quiet, fluid, peaceful, placid and you feel the rhythmic pulse quality of the water for any length of time. The director will quietly lead you back to yourself looking out on to the body of water, back to here and now.

7.
ATMOSPHERE

This is you atmosphere. Move into it. Become one with it.

Then move it. Transform it into colors, changing colors at will. Then transform it into music and play melodies at will.

Now find your way to change it into other elements such as clouds--water--rain--grass--trees--etc.

Avoid repeating any movement. Keep it fresh, new vibrant. Don't stay too long at any one point repeating what is familiar. Venture out, explore new ideas.

8.
YOUR SPACE

Walk into a space which is familiar to you, such as a room or park, etc. Move into it slowly, privately to obtain an object which has value to you. Then after obtaining the object you may leave.

Remember to focus on elements about you to confirm that the place you have chosen is indeed familiar to you. Establish your privacy by closing yourself within your space and establish a "wall" between you and observers.

Allow the space to become real to you. Create levels of involvement. Know where you came from, where you are going after obtaining the object, why you want the object, what would happen if you didn't get the object, etc.

9.
CREATING YOUR PARTNER

"B" (the partner) is within a space unknown, seated or standing. Actor "A" is to enter the space and see someone he has created in his own mind, not yet revealing this to partner "B." Actor "A" begins to speak when all elements are finally known to him, who he is, who the partner "B" is, where they are, why they are meeting, where they have come from and where they are going. "B" partner must remain with an empty mind until little subtle hints are able to be grasped by the actions and words of actor "A."

Once they know who, what and where, they proceed to take the scene to a logical moment of conclusion or exit.

10.
SPEEDWAY

Entire acting group is on stage. Each begins to walk about loosening all muscles and seeking mental and physical relaxation. The pace is quickened by the director as actors find their way through the group and moving from left to right making curving patterns around the stage. As the pace increases, each actor is to get more into his own head as he avoids encountering any of the other 'objects' moving about on stage. It develops into an up-beat very spirited movement.

11.
QUICK THINKING

A short rod or stick is passed or thrown quickly from actor to actor in a circle. Tempo is to be increased until passed very, very rapidly.

12.
FOCUS

Ensemble on stage while some are in audience. Actors on stage are to first look all about, even at audience looking at them. A SELFCONSCIOUS feeling on their part will be noted. Then they are to be instructed to focus their attention on objects, as simple as looking at the floor, count the spots on the floor, or seak design of faces or animals or such created by the smudges on the floor. Or, study the ceiling composition, count the stage lights or light bulbs, count the squares of tile which make up the floor.

Their FOCUSED ATTENTION will put them at ease and all signs of self-consiousness will diminish.

13.
FOCUS ON SELF

Actors will lie on floor in quiet atmosphere with lights out. They are asked to focus their attention on their feet within their socks and to actually FEEL the socks touching all parts of their feet. They will then feel the slacks with their knees, their shoulders sensing the undershirt or blouse, feeling their hair on their head, feet in their shoes, hips felt by their slacks, etc. Allow time for each point to be fully experienced as they also SEE that part of the body and the garment or object touching the body part.

14.
DISCOVERY

Actor is to take any object on to stage. He (she) is to discover it and SEE it for the very first time; its design, weight, color, composition, its function. The actor should actually DISCOVER what it is and how it actually works, bringing no prior awareness of it to the moment.

15.
CIRCLE WITH PRIVATE OBJECT

Ensemble will sit close to each other in a circle. First actor is to reach and pick up that personal and valued object before him(her), work with it in his own private space which is also to be clearly imagined. He will pass it on ONLY AFTER HAVING BEEN TOTALLY INVOLVED WITH IT PRIVATELY. It may take ten to twenty seconds for each actor to work to desired level.

When object is passed on it changed to the personal object created in the mind of the actor receiving the object. The private space, too, will change, for they must be in their own space and NOT ON THE STAGE.

16.
RAG DOLL

On stage, the actors will be in a quiet and relaxed mood. They are to first bend forward and hang their arms down toward the floor and allowing all tensions to flow out of finger tips. Then they will stand and stretch upward, upward reaching to ceiling, through the ceiling and into sky and beyond. Then they will hang forward like a rag doll and drain again. Then they will stand and spread arms out reaching for walls on both sides, and through the walls outward, outward and to the horizon and beyond. Repeat exercise until mood and relaxation reach desired level.

CHAPTER TWO

THE ART OF LIVING A ROLE

The goal for the actor in theatre is to give your self up completely to what is happening in your 'space' on stage.

Each successful 'moment' by itself belongs to the art of living a role. To establish this moment of complete 'truth' will lead you to your subconscious intuitively. Allow yourself to be carried away by the circumstance of the play, truly living the part, no longer thinking as an actor but as the character.

Since your subconscious is inaccessible to the conscious mind, you can only consciously apply elements of our acting principles in order to lead the way toward the region of the subconscious, giving yourself completely until it takes you and immerses you in the role. The more you have of conscious creative moments in your role the greater chance you have of preparing the way for the blossoming of the valued subconscious.

Play truly at all times. This means to be right, honest, natural, coherent and logical at every moment. Also, think, feel, strive, behave, react as the character in the circumstance provided by the author. When you adapt all these elements to the spiritual and physical life of the character, that is the art of living a role.

Should you break, however, the laws of normal behavior and cease to act truthfully, then the art of living a role is lost to you. Thus, plan your acting role consciously at first, then play it truthfully.

The actor must live the part inwardly, then strive to express it in an artistic form. It is necessary, therefore, to have control of an unusually responsive, excellently prepared vocal and physical instrument. The actor is indeed the instrument and it must be kept in tune!

Living the role according to nature (rather than acting un-naturally) will absorb the actor as well as the spectator. The spectator becomes interested, leading him to understand and experience the event so as to enrich his inner life, leaving impressions which will not fade. That indeed is the 'magic' of theatre.

It is possible that you may only truly live the part for just seconds at first or perhaps minutes; longer if the spirits are with you. But, relying on your conscious application of acting principles of Constantin Stanislavski will make you connect with truth on stage and keep you in the correct creative chanel.

Your work on stage in a role must be fresh each time you do it. Your challenge is to avoid repetition, whether it be rehearsal or performance, bearing in mind these variations or adjustments may be almost indistinguishable to the observer.

Assimilate the model of the role. Know its time, country, condition, life, background, psychology, soul, way of living and thinking. Know also its customs, movements and manner then permeate it with your own feelings. Without all these elements applied, there is no art, but only mechanical acting.

CHAPTER TWO

ACTING EXERCISES

1.
PLAY BALL!

All actors are to be on stage in a quiet atmosphere. Each is to envision a ping pong ball on the floor before him (her). When confident that the ball is indeed there in his imagination, the actor is to pick it up with finger tips, sensing its complete life, its texture, lightness, size, its total existence, even listening to its sound, sensing its taste and even its smell THROUGH HIS FINGERS. They explore its life.

Roll the ping pong ball about your hands. Toss it up and catch it, working in your own space without violating anyone else's space. Bounce it on the floor, toss it to an imaginary friend, bounce it against an imaginary wall, letting it take its own life, so it penetrates space, returns to you, finds its proper space in your hands and between your fingers so it does not become crushed in a fist or tight fingers.

The director, when ready, will call for 'change' to tennis ball, and running through all the free movements with the new texture, size, different weight, etc. Then another change to baseball, to beach ball, to volley ball, basketball and finally to bowling ball or medicine ball.

2.
PLAY BALL (VARIATION)

When the director is pleased with the level of involvement, he may inform the actors that the environment will change with each ball change. The actor is to find himself in a totally different space and even with a different person every time the ball changes. Also, the time of day or the time of year may be changed by the director or by the actors, experiencing the MAGIC of each changing moment.

3.
TAKE ME OUT TO THE BALL GAME!

Group will sit comfortably on floor or chairs and are to watch a ball game being played. They are to focus on specific objects in detail. They are to be at a ball park, possibly a stadium, sitting with someone, eating and drinking as they watch details of environment.

4.
BALL GAME (VARIATION)

When desired level is achieved, the director may call for the actors to join the action on the playing field and become one of the players. He may then take the action to any desired level.

Further, the actor is to 'float' above the ball game and see it from above, and to find themselves below the action seeing it above them, etc.

At the appropriate time, the ball game ends and the actors are to envision leaving the ballpark with the crowd, going to parking lot and driving away with memory of the ball game as a pleasant experience.

5.
OUTER SPACE

In a darkened and quiet space, all are to lie on floor and free minds and bodies of tension. Feel selves become light and even weightless, to the point where you are lifted from the earth, floating slowly upward beyond this space until you are above the theatre, seeing the earth become smaller as you soar higher and higher through the clouds and beyond until you are with the stars shining brilliantly down on the earth far below you.

Drift beyond and farther until the earth has disappeared and you feel free, light, happy, peaceful. Slowly, you turn toward the distant earth and fly toward it until it becomes visible. As you approach it, you ultimately see where you wish to alight. You float downward and finally come to rest here in this space. Dwell on the experience. Slowly end it.

6.
WHAT'S COOKING?

Smell food cooking. When actors are focused on the smell, begin to discern the blend of various aroma. Pin point the scents and separate them, focusing your sense of smell on one particular favored scent. SEE it and what is making that particular scent (a particular spice or herb?). TASTE it and TOUCH it as you also LISTEN to it cooking.

7.
TWO BY TWO

Actors in pairs will perform familiar activities without any objects but using their imagination and dealing with chosen objects in great detail.

Actors will set a table for dinner; select a blanket and spread it as they make a bed presentable; use a long cross-cut saw on a log; push a car; roll up a rug and replace it with a new one; push swings; turn a long jump rope; hang a painting; mount a curtain rod; hang draperies; place a couch properly, etc. (It must be noted that all objects which are created in space are truthfully established as well as actors being honestly involved.)

8.
GO FLY A KITE!

Actor enters holding string attached to a flying kite. As he moves into this space his attention is riveted to the distant, high flying kite as it flys and dances through the sky, doing beautiful movements in space, pulling on the string, perhaps wanting to break free and float away. Actor tugs on string, letting some out, taking some in.

The actor is conscious of color, movement, distance, and its full life.

9.
LOVER COME BACK!

You see one you love come into focus in the distance. You wave to gain attention. You are seen at last. The lover approaches, reducing the distance between you. At last, your hands meet and silently you turn and walk away happily together. (The actor does this ALONE.)

10.
INNER LIFE OF YOUR CHARACTER

To prepare for the moment, the actor is to concentrate on the entire role of the character he is portraying before entering the stage. When prepared, the actor enters this space belonging to the life of the character, closing himself off from the audience. He may return quiet or begin living and speaking only when compelled to do so, taking any moment in the play and developing it. He may envision the other characters in the scene (or invite the other characters to join him).

The actor may also feel compelled to speak the subtext of any moment in the play or even an event suggested by play action.

11.
SHARING YOUR CHARACTER'S LIFE

From all the actions of the life of your character within the play, select an event that connects most directly with your own life. It may indeed be an actual experience you have had, or come as close as possible to an occurrence in your life. Build an improvisation based on the moment, playing it alone or with a selected partner.

12.
PRE-SCENE LIFE

Conceive actions which you imagine take place before any structured scene in the life of your character. Improvise the newly created moment as you conceive it.

13.
INNER THOUGHTS

The actor is to be familiar with a character's monologue selected for this exercise. On stage, the actor is to speak all conceived thoughts of his character which lead into the text of the monologue. Thoughts being spoken need not be complete sentences but perhaps just words associated with fleeting images in the character's mind, as in life.

14.
INNER THOUGHTS - EXTENDED

Using a familiar monologue (or scene), the actor is to speak all thoughts experienced by his character relative to the given circumstance of the play for fifteen to thirty seconds prior to monologue (or scene speech). Following the text of the monologue, he is to continue in the life of his character and speak his thoughts aloud for fifteen to thirty seconds.

15.
ADDING SUB-TEXT

The actor will speak the thoughts of his character aloud as in above exercises. Upon leading into the monologue or speech, he will speak brief portions, a phrase or short sentence. Then in a softer but audible voice, he will speak aloud his associated thoughts relating to the text. This will be followed by another phrase or brief sentence of the text, followed by a whispered but audible sub-text. This is to be done for the entire monologue or scene. It can indeed be done for the entire play in rehearsal as accomplished by Constantin Stanislavski.

CHAPTER THREE

DRAMATIC ACTION

Dramatic action is to be understood as inner motion or inner force, such as need, desire, purpose or intention. Thus, whatever you do in your created space on stage must propel you toward an objective or goal and must have purpose. You may, for example, stand without visible physical motion, yet, you will be in full action within if your immobility is filled with intention, such as waiting anxiously for news of a tragic happening.

Act always with a purpose in mind and avoid acting in general. Feeling, therefore, is always correct when it is the result of truthful dramatic action. Every moment of any dramatic action in your role must be justified, logical, true and coherent.

You as an actor will be called upon to create a more interesting and more profound life than that which you actually live. You must be prepared as an artist to meet that demand.

The word 'if' constitutes the basis of a major principle of acting such that it is referred to as the 'magic if.' Actors should become familiar with the 'magic if' and its many exciting functions. A role should be approached as 'if' it were indeed truly happening to you the actor. It will lead you to experiencing the feelings of the character you are portraying in the given circumstance. It is truly a creative moment of sheer 'magic,' therefore. The word 'if' excites action and imagination when the actor asks 'what if' this were actually happening to me? In this manner, 'if' become a stimulus to the creative subconscious.

Emotions of your character must be sincere and seem truthful in the given circumstance (the plot of the play provided by the author). A creative push is initiated by 'if' to the dormant imagination which then excites that which is most desired, dramatic action. You, the actor, must believe in the possibility that it could be truly your very life. 'What if' will trigger your inner life and make you sincerely believe in what is happening in the life of your character.

The actor has a continuing responsibility of bringing to life what is seemingly hidden beneath the printed words of the playwright.

The character always has a significant need for something in each beat of his dramatic action which we define as his objective. This is indeed the case at any given moment. The actor, therefore, must always strive to define that need. The inner action then moves the character forward toward the satisfaction of that need, which will be the attainment of the objective. It thus provides the character with that valued forward action, giving each moment on stage a significant purpose.

The actor has the responsibility of always knowing what the character wants and why he wants it at any given moment in the given circumstance of the play.

CHAPTER THREE

ACTING EXERCISES

INTERNAL ACTION WITH CONTRASTING EXTERNAL PHYSICAL ACTION

1.
GOLD MEDAL

Two competing gymnasts are slowly and methodically stretching and limbering their muscles of spine, arms and legs as they prepare for the final round of events in pursuit of the gold medal and acclaim. They attempt to soothe their nervous anxiety as their hearts are pounding and racing with geared up energy.

2.
I DO, I DO!

In anticipation of the approaching wedding ceremony, the bride is being dressed by her best friend. Shoes, veil and wedding gown are donned with care and the styled coiffure must not be altered. There is feverish excitement felt by both females throughout the action.

3
WILD BLUE YONDER!

The young Air Force cadet has just been commissioned an officer. He is to attend the grand ceremony to receive his Lieutenant bars and the treasured pilot wings. The tailor is measuring all parts of his body for the new officer Air Force uniform. The grueling flight training has been successful, culminating in this momentous event. He is bursting with pride, joy and anticipation. The tailor is noting in detail every measurement as he senses and shares the excitement of the young flyer.

4
DEADLY DEED

Two men crawl through rubble in an attempt to reach an unexploded bomb. They approach with great trepidation for the slightest movement may set it off and blow them away. The rubble must be moved out of their path, item by item with delicacy. They ultimately reach the deadly object and cautiously proceed to defuse the mechanism. Knowing the drastic consequences of any false move, their hearts are beating so furiously, they might believe pounding hearts may trigger the bomb itself.

5
FIRE IT UP!

Two coal stokers are shoveling the fuel into the steamer's furnace. The flame must be maintained at a high level to propel the boat across the sea. One throws his shovel full of coal through the yawning mouth of the burner as the other digs into the coal pile. They keep up a rapid, steady, rhythmic pace. Within, they feel the deadly boredom and monotony of their fruitless labor.

6.
PASSING THROUGH

Enter space from off-stage left and having had an experience which requires that you pass through this area to ACHIEVE SOMETHING off-stage right. In this space, however, you encounter a PROBLEM, which must be overcome before you are able to continue to your intended objective. The problem must not be over done just for the sake of the problem alone. The high point is beyond the exit.

7
WHAT HAPPENED?

The actor enters space concerned about what is following him (her). The attitude is one of mystery, confusion, worry, uncertainty as he makes his way across the space conceived in his mind until he leaves and is gone.

8
MAKE THAT CALL!

The space is an office or den. The actor enters and hurries to card file to seek an objective. Fingering many cards, the desired one is discovered. It is read hurriedly but thoroughly, then the actor seeks a phone book to locate the proper number. Having checked the proper address, name and the number, he goes to the telephone and dials with impatience. He encounters a busy signal or dials incorrectly. In any case, he is not getting through. He checks the time with growing concern, then examines the card and number again and proceeds to dial again. He must get through! It builds from there to end.

9
TIME BOMB

Actor approaches his object, a time bomb. He approaches cautiously and encounters obstacles in the way which must be delicately removed before the bomb can be reached. Ultimately, the bomb is reached by the actor who must sensitively remove one small item after another until the time mechanism is reached. It may go off any second. He also knows the slightest wrong or abrupt moment will mean death.

10
WHAT DO YOU WANT?

The director or any actor seated may call out a place. The appointed actor must immediately see where he (she) is, pursue an objective with urgency, and with words deal with his imagined partner(s) in what ever space is conceived at the moment.

Each actor is to go up in turn and is given three, five, or more places which he will deal with in perhaps ten to fifteen seconds each. The places called may be; auto shop, bank, park, police station, church, jail, doctor's office, hospital room, telephone booth, swimming pool, gambling casino, street corner, roof top, train station, etc.

11
INNER LIFE WITHOUT MOVEMENT

Find a moment in the life of your character in the play where there is inner intensity yet without physical movement. Perform it on stage, showing what comes before and after the motionless moment of intensity.

12
TRUTHFUL ACTION CREATES FEELING

Search the space for an object of value. Build the scenario.

Close a door. Let the purpose of closing the door have meaningful intent.

13
ACTION WITHOUT MOVEMENT

Like a cat ready to pounce on its unsuspecting prey, the actor is to go on stage and find for himself a moment when he is totally without motion, yet his inner life is pacing furiously.

Example: Actor awaits arrival of his enemy.
Character is hiding motionless. Someone is searching for him.
A lover awaits breathlessly for partner to arrive.
An attacker awaits his victim.
A character awaits the good or bad news.
Flyers are being briefed for their bombing run. Etc. etc.

14.
MOVEMENT WITH COUNTER INNER ACTION

Find situation where the external physical action is totally different than internal action.

Example: Bank robber exits bank with money in pouch and sees a policeman approaching from opposite direction. External action must be casual and relaxed as he walks toward officer. His inner life is frantically paced with fear, apprehension, danger.

Male sits opposite female at a candle lit table of restaurant. He smiles and acts pleased and loving. Inside is in turmoil for he is awaiting the correct moment to bring out the ring and propose marriage, not knowing what her response will be. He is fearful of rejection, hopeful of acceptance, jealous of rivals, insecure about his status, etc.

An assassin stands casually by the wayside of the approaching head of state, whom he is assigned to kill.

A male actor awaits with a bouquet of flowers on a street corner for his girl friend to arrive.

15
ENTERING A ROOM

Each actor in turn is to enter any room in his creative mind. The INTENT of his entrance must be made clear. Where is he coming from? Where is he entering? What does he want? Why does he want it? What is the problem being encountered as he enters? Etc.

NO MOVEMENT EXERCISES WITH HIGH INTENSITY INNER ACTION

16
ACCIDENT

A loved one was in an accident. The medics are striving to revive the victim. You wait breathlessly for the results. You are riveted and focused. The tension is painful. At last! The medics revive him.

The medics attempt to revive a loved one, victim of an accident. You wait painfully for the results. Ultimately, the medics fail.

17
HIDING

You fearfully hide from someone who is searching to find your hiding place. The ominous creature comes closer and is about to discover you. You are faced with a decision: If caught, you will die; if you run, you may escape. The tension mounts. You dash away.

You are hiding from a dangerous foe who is seeking you. The punishment would be death if captured. Tension mounts as he comes closer. Should you make a run for it or continue to hide and perhaps be discovered? The searcher comes very close. He goes by you as you remain undetected. You then quietly reverse direction and move away to escape.

18
LOVER

You await a loved one with breathless excitement not knowing if the object of your love will arrive. The anxiety is unbearable. You wait. The loved one comes into view.

Not certain if your loved one will come to meet you at this designated spot, you wait with longing. You pierce the space for a vision of your beloved. In time, you realize your lover will not arrive. You are devastated.

19.
ATTACKER

You are frozen in position out of sight of the approaching victim. The victim approaches slowly, closer, closer. You attack.

20.
ATTACKER

An unaware, innocent victim approaches you as you remain hidden from sight. You wait anxiously, motionless and tense. The prospective victim discovers you and runs off.

You wait for the person to approach from a distance as you intend to attack the victim. You remain hidden and motionless. The victim is approaching. You study the target. Something makes you change your mind. You allow your object to pass your hiding place as you remain motionless and undetected.

21.
THE ENEMY

You await the arrival of your deadly enemy. Your weapon is ready. The enemy approaches. You wait for the right moment. You kill him.

The enemy approaches your undetected hiding place. You have no weapon to defend your self. You are discovered. A shot is heard.

22.
BOMBING MISSION

You are a combat pilot being briefed for a secret and dangerous bombing mission over enemy territory. You absorb final instructions, knowing you may not return from this flight. Then GO!

The briefing by your commanding officer is in progress. It is a dangerous bombing mission in a heavy flack area of the enemy. You take in every detail of the flight, knowing it may be your last. If you survive this last bomb run, you will go back home. An announcement is made. The weather has suddenly turned bad. Mission cancelled!

23.
NEWS!

You await important news of major importance to your career. The suspense builds. GOOD NEWS!

Your career hangs in the balance. You have been called in for the decision. You wait for the news. Tension builds. Silence. Finally the moment arrives. The news is awful. Your career is over.

24.
MISSION IMPOSSIBLE!

Names are being called by a platoon leader to penetrate the enemy lines and cut their communication wires in the dark to disrupt their activity. Name after name is uttered in hushed tones...Your name is called. You are to go.

As names are being called from a list held by the platoon leader, you wait in the dark and listen intently to note if your name is to be included for this dangerous mission behind the enemy lines. The list of names has come to an end....Your name was not included.

25.
MAIL CALL!

You are away from home and have been for a long time. It may be for military service or even college. You wait for that longed-for letter from one you love as the clerk reads off the names on the letters in his possession. Finally the moment has come....You have a letter!

Having been away from home for many months, your only communication in this distant place is by mail. It is now mail call, and the clerk is loaded with letters. He calls out name after name. You wait for that letter from the one you love. Why have you not heard from your loved one? Could it be that some one else has taken your place? You listen intently for your name to be called ....It does not happen. The clerk's hands are empty of mail and there is no letter for you.

26.
HURRICANE!

A vicious hurricane has devastated the region where your loved ones live. News of the devastation is announced. Names of victims are revealed....A name of a loved one is included among the victims.

As you listen for details of the hurricane devastation, you take in all the information of the event. Then names of victims are announced. You listen intently. The list of victims has ended...No familiar names were included among the dead.

27.
FILL 'EM UP!

Two workers in a soda factory are taking Cola bottles from a fast-moving conveyor belt and quickly inserting them into six-pack cartons. They are on opposite sides of the steadily moving belt, taking each bottle on the line in alternating rhythmic movements and filling one carton after another until the case is full, moving another case in its place and continuing without let-up. At a penny a carton, their tedious labor is drudgery without reward. Their minds must be else-where to avoid losing their sanity.

28.
ROTTEN!

Two workers are positioned opposite each other in a fruit warehouse. The fruit rolls down a chute as each seeks for rotten or damaged fruit which will be picked and discarded. There is no let-up. The bored workers can only hope for a brief respite when the present crop of fruit ends and a new batch is poured into the chute on the way to the waiting boxes at the end of the chute.

29.
I GOT THE JOB!

A secretary is questioning a newly hired worker and typing the detailed information methodically on the job application form. The employee is also filling out required papers in detail. She wants not to commit a single error, for she has finally landed that remarkable career job for which she has schooled, trained and dreamed of. She can hardly contain her excitement.

30.
CANDLE GLOW

At a cozy dinner table, lit by candle light, he smiles lovingly at his partner. His movements are tender and caring and she is glowing as warmly as the candle light in the presence of her partner. Inside, he is in turmoil for he is awaiting the correct moment to bring out the ring to propose marriage not knowing, however, what her response will be. He is fearful of rejection, hopeful of acceptance, jealous of rivals for her love, insecure of his status. She is a complex, multi-faceted, emotional character, uncertain of her feelings.

31.
LAMP LIGHT

He stands on a street corner in the glow of a lamp light in a crowded city. He has a bouquet of flowers for a very special girl, whom he loves. She is expected to arrive any moment. They have been apart for a long time and have missed each other terribly. There are important people in their lives who disapprove of their relationship, thus, it is a secret meeting. He waits with great anxiety for a view of her. Soon, she is in sight. His external movements up to this point have been seemingly calm and restrained, seemingly shielding his inner emotions.

CHAPTER FOUR

CREATIVE IMAGINATION

All art is the product of imagination. The play, thus, is an invention of the author's imagination. It becomes the actor's responsibility then to use his artistic technique to turn the play into a theatrical reality, or, in other words, a newly created reality. In this artistic process, the creative imagination plays the greatest part.

Only written lines and some instructions are provided by the author in the development of a play. The actor creates all else! The role is made fuller and deeper by the actor's creative process which is led by his imagination. The actor must find ways to stimulate his imagination so as to lift all creative ideas far above a mundane or uninteresting plane. In this art of acting, there is little hope of any success unless the actor learns to open up himself to excite a truly vivid imagination.

The actor may find it rewarding to begin the creative process with the truly valuable and exciting 'magic if.' 'If' will stimulate, coax, stir the imagination. The 'magic if' becomes rather like a springboard for the actor to begin his work on his assigned role in the play.

Even a passive theme can produce an inner stimulus to dramatic action by use of a vivid and creative imagination. As an example, consider a man standing motionless on a street corner. This is truly a rather passive human element on the surface. However, add other ingredients. It is night. The man waits as he is experiencing an inner passion. He desires a young woman. He plans to attack her and even kill her if he has to. He is driven by that insane urge. In the distant shadows a woman approaches. She is unaware of his presence. As she approaches, the man waits, without motion. This is dramatic action.

In the scene described above, use the 'magic if' as a springboard to your imagination. Being cast in either the male or female role, consider what you would do 'if' you were to find yourself in that circumstance. You would act!

It is the actor's imagination which lifts him to another level of creative involvement. Without imagination, an actor remains nothing but an ineffectual pawn in the hands of a director, thus lacking any degree of creative artistry.

Your creative ability is directly related to the kind of imagination you have. If you have the kind of imagination that has initiative of its own, it can be fruitful and is developed without effort. If your imagination is less than that but can be awakened and stirred into life by an imaginative director, that may be productive for you as well. If, however, you lack creative imagination, the theatre is indeed not for you.

Exercise your imagination often to seek ever wider dimensions. Learn to free your imagination from all constraints. You will find that your creative life as well as your own personal life will grow rich.

CHAPTER FOUR
ACTING EXERCISES

1.
TIME WARP

You are exactly where you are at this moment, but simply alter the time. It is exactly twelve hours later. What conditions have entered into your life to be here at that time? Imagination will aid in developing very exciting scenarios. Take a moment to conceive of the circumstances and then improvise a scene depicting such an event.

Variations may be introduced, such as changing the season, changing the place, changing the age, etc.

2.
CHAIR TRANSFORMATION

Take an ordinary chair and alter it so it transforms to any other object. Use it in any circumstance. It may be a steeple, a boat, a person, etc.

3.
INNER VISION

Choose a time of day. You must reach your home and your bedroom from this starting point. Work in every detail of physical action as you envision your surroundings as you proceed from here to there. This may be done on stage or in the quiet of your seat or space. Details should include searching for a key, turning a door knob, climbing a stair, etc.

Establish an unbroken line of psycho-physical actions in detail.

4.
LIFE RECALLED

Re-create in your mind, specific happenings of the past; one year ago, five years ago, etc. Establish clearly, what, where, when, etc.

5.
PASSIVE THEMES

Passive elements can trigger imagination by use of "IF."

What "IF" you were an old oak tree! What "IF" you were a sculpted marble statue? What "IF" you were a park bench? As in Shakespeare's MIDSUMMER NIGHT'S DREAM, you may portray WALL. (There is a character WALL also in THE FANTASTICKS.)

Create a complete scenario, altering the passive theme with your imagination to truly activate the moment.

A tree? What if you were a tree in Birnam Wood (in MACBETH)? You would be involved in the battle at Dunsinane. Or, change the setting and lovers are carving a heart and letters into your tree bark. Or children are climbing your limbs and spying the enemy! etc.

6.
THE DOOR TO IMAGINATION

Close a door. A killer attempts to enter! A rapist! etc. Change to opposite mood. One you love has just departed. etc.

7.
OFF WE GO!

Actors lie on the floor in various, carefree positions, totally relaxed and minds drained of all human thought. At a given moment, each will slowly inflate, making an air intake sound, but without human thought. As each BALLOON is inflating, parts of the actor's body begin to move upward fluidly until it rises to full inflated height. Its lightness causes it to waver with the breeze, softly, delicately and soon begins to float upward slowly and gently freeing itself from the earth. The actor must free himself so as to attain the lightness and delicacy of the balloon in flight. Higher and higher it goes, up into the clouds and finally lost from sight.

When the proper moment is reached, the balloons will slowly begin to descend and ultimately touch down and begin to deflate lifelessly as it falls slowly to the ground in its original position.

8.
EAGLE IN FLIGHT

Few elements in nature are as stately and awe inspiring as an eagle in its flight. Actors are to relate to such a choice figure of nature. The ensemble will find a space on stage in a quiet atmosphere and very slowly begin to find a position where he becomes the image of an eagle perched high on a mountainous ridge. Soon, he flexes his body and lifts himself from its perch and soars gracefully into the sky. It continues to fly majestically seeking, perhaps, its mate, and finally comes to rest on his perch.

9.
IN NEED OF HELP

Improvisation is based on one of the actors being battered and bruised and in a hospital. Partner(s) will become individuals involved in the scene as conceived. Add who, what, when, why and take it to conclusion.

10.
CATS

Taking a cue from the Broadway musical, actors are to take on the life and actions of cats of all description and type. They will deal with their space and with each other as inspired by their imagination.

11.
HEAVY!

Actors, male and female, are to compete in a weight lifting competition. Each is to move into position to contend with the object of bar-bell and the weight designated by the director. It is to increase with each stage of the contest. Each individual is to contend with the growing difficulty of each lift.

12.
SUN RISE, SUN SET

Actors are in a crouched position on stage and instructed that they are in a pre-dawn circumstance, relaxed and mind drained of human thought. Slowly, they begin to rise. It is the east, and you are the sun rising to a new day, glowing, expanding, giving light and then setting.

13.
WALL

You find yourself a prisoner behind a wall. It is night and you are feeling your way along the wall in total darkness clinging to the ground when ever the beam of the spotlight comes your way in its timed circuit of the prison. You are seeking that break in the wall that you have secretely been working at for a long time. You crawl along, perhaps having lost your way. At last you touch it with your fingertips. Painstakingly, you remove one loose brick after another until completed. You then crawl with great effort through the narrow opening to the other side. You wait for the light to pass, rise and run off.

14.
HANDS

In pantomime, you deal with the major theme of GOOD versus EVIL. Your left hand is evil. Your right hand is good. They take on a life of their own as one moves into its conceived space performing an action and then contending with the other. The other parts of the body may or may not be used, depending upon the actor's creative ideas.

15.
THE DOUGHNUT SHOP

Several actors position themselves on platforms, which become display cases. On the 'shelves' are an assortment of doughnuts. The actors assume positions of doughnuts of every kind; nutty, chocolate, glazed, cream filled, plain, fresh, stale, broken or whole.

The doughnuts may speak and be moved (by the unseen baker and the unseen patrons). Doughnuts comment about life, each other, exhibit their attitudes about old doughnuts and fresh doughnuts, about same qualities, and about different qualities, revealing prejudices of color, sweetness, new kid on the block, nutty behavior, etc. It's LIFE!

16.
OBJECTS IN SPACE

Actors are spaced in line across the stage. Beginning at one end, an actor begins a movement at random (may be given or initiated by director) with any part of the body. With only the slightest adjustment, the random movement continues until the actor conceives that he is working with an object, which he then develops into a continuous action. He then turns to next actor who stands before him and mirrors the movement. He then makes the movement his own with only slight adjustment, deals with it and gives it to next actor who transforms it his way, etc.

Stearing wheel movement can become pounding of dough, which can become fight movement, which may turn into rope pulling, to pail lifting, etc.

17.
CIRCUS BALLOON

At a circus, a balloon is bought on a string. Actor holds it aloft. Then it gets away and floats up as he follows its flight. He takes on life of balloon in flight, floats, looks down at himself looking up. Actor then transforms to one who lost balloon and continues to focus on fading balloon until it fades from sight. He experiences great loss.

CHAPTER FIVE

FOCUSING OF ATTENTION

A major fault shared by many actors is the inability to maintain a strong power of concentration, which completely destroys any form of creative work. The common element is self consciousness caused by the presence of viewers. All humans are surely capable of maintaining marvelous levels of concentration and involvement when alone. Even when singing alone or acting out scenes in our own privacy, we feel comfortable and capable of high levels of artistry.

Our performance on stage, therefore, should be accomplished as if we were alone in our own private space. This is the pursuit of every performer following the concepts of Constantin Stanislavski. He defined this principle as 'solitude in public' brought about by the actor's concentration of attention.

The actor's attention must be focused on objects within the area of the stage setting in order to prevent any intrusion by the audience. The point of attention by the actor must always be within the created life of the character. His inner attention and outer attention will continue to be directed to objects either in the life of the character's mind or in the stage setting, which constitutes the physical environment of the character. Thus, the actor is to look at and actually see things within the circle of attention embracing all items in the life of his character.

The eye of an actor which looks at and sees an object will not only keep him in the life of the character, but it will also attract the attention of the spectator. This serves as a guiding action for the observer and shows him what to look at and what is important in the play. Conversely, an actor's blank eye, who is seeing nothing, allows the attention of the spectator to wander and lose contact with the play.

Intensive observation of an object naturally arouses a desire to do something with it, thus stirring one's inner life and inner action. To do something with the object in turn intensifies one's observation of the object, causing a firm inter-action between the actor and the object, which is a most desired level of artistry.

An actor must learn to work within his circle of attention. This is an imaginary enclosure in which the actor places himself at its center and directs his focus only on objects within that circle. This is a variable circle capable of being moved and expanded at will by the actor. It begins as a tight circle of attention enclosing the actor and the object to which he is directing his attention. When comfort is achieved, the circle may be widened to include the entire stage setting or further widened to the character's horizon or even beyond.

Should something alien to the character's life penetrate his circle, he should reduce the circle to shut out the distraction. This will strengthen the circle and keep the actor in his comfort zone. He may consider it necessary to bring his attention to a point of concentration, perhaps to the eyes of his partner or an object within his own mind. This is concentration at its strongest. When again comfortable in his space, the circle of attention may again be expanded and contracted at will.

The circle of attention helps to create public solitude, the feeling of being in your private space although in the presence of an audience. Public solitude, in turn, strengthens your concentration of attention. An actor should gain confidence in knowing how these principles work in harmony to contribute to perfecting our creative artistry.

The actor should learn to move about the stage setting and take his circle of attention with him. He is to make his own mental limit to his circle noting only that which lies within his own circle. Should he move to a telephone, for example, only the character and the phone may be within his circle. Were he to move to a table, only the character and table contents are to be within the circle.

As the character flows about the stage environment and feeling comfortable within his own space, he is capable of movement from internal attention to objects within his mind to external attention to objects all about him in his space belonging to the life of his character. This attention should involve all his senses as they connect with any element in his character's life, thus being free from audience intrusion. This free-flowing action from inner attention to external attention should be as free and natural in his character's world as it is in his own personal life off stage.

The endowment of objects with particular qualities will enhance the life of the object and the character dealing with it, arousing an emotional response of importance to any moment on stage. That simple stage prop would become, for example, quite special if it had been given to you by one you loved dearly and suggested a treasured moment you had shared in the past. Further, if that particular vase is seen by you as being truly rare antique of great quality and value, it would trigger an emotion within you. So, learn to exercise this principle with all stage properties and objects. It will serve to truly engage you with your environment within your established circle of attention.

The 'fourth wall' is another dimension of circle of attention. It is the imagined wall which separates the actor on stage from the audience. It may be a solid wall in the actor's imagination perhaps with a window in it through which he sees meadows, trees, animals, sky or hills, but no audience. It may otherwise contain a fireplace, a painting, wall paper, drapery, etc. The character may touch it and deal with the imagined wall just as if it were truly existing. It also may be a flexible element such as a beach area with the character by the water, gazing out to the boat in the distance or the sun setting on the horizon.

As you inter-act with another character in a scene, learn to value your partner's eyes as the most important object upon which to focus your attention. Not only should you seek to observe understanding in your partner's eyes of what you are conveying to him, but you also want to discern that image which you can see in his inner vision. This makes for inter-play at its highest level; mind to mind communion.

CHAPTER FIVE
ACTING EXERCISES

1.
OBJECT FOCUS

Each actor is to select an object nearby which he will study with intense awareness to ever detail. It is to be examined thoroughly for as long as director designates. Comment on every detail of the object of attention.

2.
CONTACT WITH OBJECT IN SPACE

Actor is to allow an object to enter his mind. At will, the object is to be seen close by. Then it is to be allowed to be placed at a short distance. Then the object is to appear at a distance. Place it anywhere in space. In each instance the actor is to connect with the object and relate to it so as to arouse his inner life.

3.
EXTERNAL ATTENTION

Select an object in the environment at a close distance from you. Then you are to observe an object at a greater distance from you. This is to be followed by choosing an object in your environment which is at a far distance from you. With your active imagination you are to build a story around each object as you retain it in the center of your attention until the event you have created with each comes to an end.

4.
SOLITUDE

In turn, each actor is to go on stage under full stage and house lights. The actor is to re-create an event of considerable importance in his personal life but within his mind only. Free to use the space or to remain seated, he will take the necessary time to think of the event from beginning to end, recalling time and place thoroughly enough to close himself off from the audience.

5.
RECALL

A personal object is to be chosen by the actor. Within ten to twenty seconds, the object is to be studied intently. Then the object is to be given to a partner as the actor with his eyes closed is to describe the object in detail to his partner(s). This may be repeated until details are thoroughly related. The partner will then take his turn with his own choice of object. The exercise may be done in teams or individually as desired. Objects may be a bill-fold, ring, shoe, etc.

6.
MODERATE CIRCLE OF ATTENTION

A chair is to be placed in the center of a moderately sized space such as a small stage setting. Allow about ten actors to each place a set piece or prop within the lighted designated space. An actor will be brought in from off stage, not having seen the setting which has just been arranged. He may sit in the chair for a stated amount of time, ten to thirty seconds. He will then close his eyes and list each item he has seen in the stage setting during his time of focused attention to his surroundings. Each person having placed an item in the stage setting will note whether his object has been observed. Each actor in the ensemble may take a turn at observing a constantly changing stage setting. Increase the fun; make it five seconds!

7.
SMALL CIRCLE OF ATTENTION

Ten, twelve, perhaps even more small objects are to be placed on a table illuminated by a small study lamp. An actor is to then sit for ten to twenty seconds at table to observe all the items under the light. He will then step away and with eyes closed recall the items in his inner vision and describe each object as other actors check the accuracy of recall. Alter the items on the table and allow other actors to perform the exercise without seeing the objects before the game. For added challenge, increase the number of items placed under the light, or reduce the number of seconds allowed for observation.

8.
BOUNDLESS CIRCLE

Ensemble may gather outside the theatre allowing extensive view of the environment including trees, homes, parking lot with cars, street, fire hydrant, debris, benches, walls, windows, doors, grassed areas, puddles, chimneys, clouds, etc. Each of ten actors will designate an object and direct attention of the appointed actor to the item. After an allocated amount of time, perhaps total of twenty seconds, the actor will close his eyes and recall as many objects as he sees in his inner vision. The appointed actor may be challenged to describe in detail every object designated. Other actors may then take their turn, using different objects with each person.

9.
SMALL CIRCLE WITHOUT LIGHT

Sitting at a table with full space lighting and without a study lamp, the actor is to create a mental picture of his circle as he observes all objects within the designated small space. He will be brought to the table for a period of twenty to thirty seconds of observation of the objects. He must then turn away or close his eyes and list or describe each object on the table.

10.
CARRY YOUR CIRCLE

Learn to carry your circle of attention with you wherever you go. Walk to any part of the stage. Make a mental limit to your circle of attention as you move about the stage setting. As you walk to window, include only it in your circle. Walk to piano and include only it and the stool in your circle. Perhaps there is a desk you may walk to which has a lamp and photo on it, include only those items in your circle. Move quickly, for added challenge, from one area to another as you keep your circle of attention moving with you in its center as you go from one to another stage area.

11.
CIRCLE VARIATION

Carrying a small lantern or candle in an otherwise dark stage, the actor will focus attention only on objects clearly visible within the lighted circle of attention as he moves about the stage setting. The actor may be asked to describe the items observed within his ever changing circle of attention during his movement on stage.

12.
WITHOUT SPILLING A DROP!

Fill a cup to the brim with water. Place obstacles and other objects about the stage. Each actor is to walk about the stage, even climbing over or under objects while carrying the filled cup of water. He must not spill a single drop of water as he attempts to reach his destination. There may be fun rewards for the winner(s) if desired. Or if spillage occurs, the actor may be required to relinquish the cup to another. There may be a need to refill the cup with water, etc.

13.
PERSONAL CIRCLE

Actor is to walk about the stage or the theatre focusing on his own body as his circle of attention. From tip of left elbow across his body to right elbow, including legs coming forward as he walks, he will enclose himself within that personal space and find solitude in public as he moves about among objects, other people, up and down stairs, through corridors, doors, etc.

14.
INNER ATTENTION

Review in detail each action, activity or event you can recall from the moment you awoke this morning to the present as you sit on stage in the presence of an audience. This will be the extreme challenge as you seek public solitude. The exercise may also be done by everyone in the ensemble while sitting in a group. By directing thoughts to time, place, smells, touches, sounds, etc. the actor will indeed be in his own circle of attention.

15.
YOU CAN TASTE IT!

As a group exercise, or selecting an actor to be alone on stage, each is to recall every particle of food eaten during his most recent large dinner. Drink, too, will be included. Include where, when, what, why plus taste, smell, touch, sound and images.

16.
YOUR PLACE!

Enter your home. Step by step you will pass through every room of your home, observing all, from floor to ceiling, and every window and door, each wall hanging, bed and carpet, chair and couch, fireplace and table, cabinet and closet. Add smells and sounds to your images.

17.
OBJECT ENDOWMENT

Selecting any plain object of your choice or any stage prop, you are to observe it intently. Using your vivid imagination, endow the prop with qualities which will cause an emotional reaction to it. The object, perhaps, belonged to Elvis Presley, or Abraham Lincoln, or was given by your loving grandmother, etc. The object remains unchanged but the imagined circumstance has transformed the object so your reaction to it has heightened and caused an emotional response.

18.
FOURTH WALL

Actors are to seek movement on stage and include an action that requires focusing on the down stage fourth wall. For example, each is to examine that painting which is framed and hanging on the wall, or mount a drap on that window frame, or remove a smudge on the surface of the wall, repair pealing wall paper, or open a window. Actors may move along as they view art treasures on the walls of a museum, or sit by a warm fire in the fourth wall fire place. They may also enjoy playing with the pets which are in cages along the wall of the pet shop.

19.
I SEE WHAT YOU'RE THINKING!

Actor "A" and actor "B" reveal to each other at least three objects of value which will be imagined in the exercise. Each object will have some personal connection with the life of the actor who designates the selected item. Then they will turn their backs to each other. Actor "A" will thoroughly envision his chosen object of the three he had earlier stated to his partner. He will see the image of his object with his entire mind and body and send his rays to his partner. Actor "B" concentrates on receiving the image and rays from actor "A" as he strives to envision which of the three objects is being sent into his mind. Actor "B" will voice his decision when convinced. Each will take his turn.

20.
MAKE YOUR MOVE!

Actor "A" and actor "B" will describe three movements they have in mind and may even demonstrate the movements to each other. When ready, they will turn their backs to each other. Actor "A" will decide which of the three moves he will make when prepared and send his strong rays to his partner. Actor "B" will direct his energy to sensing the move and rays of actor "A" and declare his selection of movement to his partner. Each will take his turn until they end the exercise.

21.
BEAUTY OF NATURE

Nothing in life is more beautiful than nature and should be the object of constant attention. In reality or in your imagination, see a little flower, or a petal from it, a spider web, or a frost design on a pane of glass, a leaf from a tree, or a cone from an evergreen, a blade of grass, a clam shell on the beach, a cloud in the sky, or a bird in flight, a sunset or rainbow, a sheep in the meadow or a deer in the woods. Concentrate your attention on each or all and allow your feelings to flow as you experience each image. Try to express in words what it is in these elements of nature which gives you pleasure.

22.
FOURTH WALL IMPROVISATION

Develop an improvisation with each team of actors required to deal with the fourth wall, which may be close enough to touch, or at a moderate distance away. It may even be located at or beyond the horizon.

CHAPTER SIX

TENSION AND RELAXATION

Physical tension will paralyze our actions and prevent the normal use of our senses.

Physical tension will also prevent expression of delicate shadings of feeling thus altering the spiritual life of the role.

Actors usually strain themselves in the dramatic and exciting moments in a play. Therefore, at times of great stress it is especially necessary to achieve a complete freeing of the muscles. In fact, in the high moments of a role the tendency to relax ought to become more normal than the tendency to contraction.

When assuming various positions on stage it is generally noted that tension will appear in other parts of the body tightening muscles not at all needed to maintain the given position. Actors should work at using only muscles required to maintain any position or affecting any movement, while all other muscles should be completely relaxed.

A position, or pose, or movement should always be based on some pursuit of an objective, employing an imaginative idea and enhanced by a given circumstance, thus making the physical action totally natural and without superfluous use of muscles.

A lifeless pose will become a real, lively act when it is connected to the pursuit of an objective. Any stance or pose on stage must serve an inner purpose, otherwise it will be 'stagey' and mechanical.

Only natural behavior can fully control our muscles, tense them properly or relax them.

When we use an isolated group of muscles, be they shoulder, arm, leg, back muscles, all other parts of the body must remain free and without tension. This applies even to wrist, fingers, or various joints of the hand, shoulders, neck, etc.

Attempting to identify muscles which should be tense in various positions and those which should be relaxed is not at all easy to accomplish. First of all it requires a well-trained power of attention, capable of quick adjustment and able to distinguish among various physical sensations. It is not easy, in a complicated pose, to know which muscles must contract and which should not. It is difficult to do even with simple poses and simple movements. But we should devote some time to at least learning the basics.

We could learn so much by studying the graceful movements of cats. They are so amazingly adaptable in terms of movement. They sit, pounce, leap and even play with extraordinary ease.

Try to find your centre of gravity in any pose or movement you make. We should be convinced how well the human body can be trained. Most humans are capable of attaining a high degree of agility, litheness and a sense of equiibrium, all which will enhance your personal beauty on stage and in life.

CHAPTER SIX
ACTING EXERCISES

1.
TENSION POINTS

All actors are to be on stage and asked to move about while performing a self evaluation of all parts of the body to determine where the tension points are located. They are to be identified and effort will be directed toward freeing those muscles of tension.

2.
EXTRANEOUS USE OF MUSCLES

Actors are to lie on floor and seek relaxation. Upon command by the director, each actor will move into a variety of poses; sitting, standing, half standing, half sitting, kneeling, crouching, etc. Each pose will be maintained for a period of time allowing the actor to note which muscles are being tensed in addition to those required to maintain the given position.

Actors should attempt to relax all muscles not needed to sustain the position of the body.

3.
JUSTIFY THE POSE

Actors may be alone on stage or in groups allowing space for movement. The director may instruct them to assume a particular pose and hold it while the actor notes where his tensions are and which muscles are being employed. Then, the actor is instructed to justify the position by using his creative imagination, arrive at a given circumstance and an objective.

It should be noted that the creative inner purpose will induce a more natural pose and action.

4.
ISOLATED ACTS

Actors may be on stage in any chosen position, sitting, standing, leaning, or other. The director will call for them to move only the right arm, the left foot, the head, left shoulder, etc. The actor will attempt to perform the isolated act by using only the required muscles. No other muscle must be used. If not necessary, those muscles should remain free of any tension.

5.
TENSION ON COMMAND (Variation)

Actors will lie motionless on floor. The director will command them to tense only the right foot, the left shoulder, the neck, stomach, left index finger, right knee, etc.

Tension must develop upon command only in the very spot designated. All other parts of the body must remain totally relaxed.

6.
WARM UP

The ensemble will walk about on stage, smiling at each other, greeting the others warmly, then withdrawing into their own space, shaking arms, hands, head, fingers, feet, loosening spine, moving atmosphere about them and sounding out vowel sounds and sonorous consonants as they simply free themselves from tensions of outside world.

7.
TAG

The actors will select one of them as being "IT" and run about the space trying to avoid being tagged with both hands. When the "IT" actor does indeed touch another with both hands, the touched person then becomes "IT" and chases actors about the stage to seek his victim. It continues until director halts the exercise.

8.
JUMP ROPE

Two actors take either end of an imaginary rope and begin to turn the rope cross stage as other actors take their turn running in and jumping in place for ten jumps, co-ordinating his movements with the turning of the rope. Exercise will continue until it is successfully completed.

Variation: Each actor will take his own rope and jump in place as he varies his tempo to limber all his muscles.

9.
ATMOSPHERES

Actors walk about space freeing themselves mentally and physically. They soon sense that an atmosphere of (unknown?) substance envelops them, which they begin to move first with fingers, then hands, wrists, elbows, shoulders, spine, head, chest, stomach, feet, ankles, knees, legs. Their attention is focused on moving the atmosphere with each part of the body and seeing the effect on the atmosphere which is being moved. They are not to make movement for the sake of movement.

Variation: Atmosphere may become colors, with actors forming designs in space with color; or atmosphere may be musical notes, and actors play familiar tunes in space.

10.
FULL BODY MIMIC

Actors are in a loose circle. Designated actor begins by contorting his body in a creative manner and freezing his position. Next actor will mirror the exact position in every detail, turn in his set position (or next actor take position before him). This actor will slowly alter the position while he is turning to next actor and form his own contorted design with his entire body. Following actor assumes exact position, holds it, then slowly turns to alter design of body to his new position and passes it on, etc.

CHAPTER SEVEN

BEATS AND KEY POINTS

A play is divided into commonly known scenes and acts. Familiar to many actors is the French scene, defined by a character entrance and ending with a character exit. A smaller division of importance is defined by Stanislavski as the beat or unit which is distinguished by a complete dramatic action with a discernible beginning, middle and end to the action. It may be equated to the written paragraph with its all-important topic sentence. The dramatic beat has its all-important 'key point' called 'objective' by Stanislavski.

The actor and the director will know the play thoroughly when it has been dissected into its elements down to the smallest beat. By identifying the key point or objective of each beat, each scene, each act, one is then able to conclude what the super-objective is of the entire play. This is the key point the author has in mind which made him write the play in the first place. The ideas which connect all the objectives to the super-objective will be known as the "through line of action." They will point the way to the super-objective as arrows flying to a target.

The approach may be either of two ways. The key point or objective may be identified initially. It then leads us to create the beat which surrounds it. Should the beat of action be clearly identified, then we are obligated to identify the key point being made and note this as the objective of the beat. As an illustration, a character introduces an idea to his partner. Some dialogue is exchanged, a point is made, followed by some dialogue until the idea is concluded. The beat has come to an end. A new beat is begun when the next idea is initiated. It will continue until a key point is made and the idea is concluded, ending that beat, and so onward.

The pursuit of specific objectives with purpose and intent will lend a dynamic quality to the dramatic action of the beat. This pursuit of objectives will propel the character along the path of the through line of action, also called 'the spine' of the play. It is sometimes referred to as the "unbroken line." All labels are similar in meaning, for they relate to the chanel of action which leads to the all-important super-objective of the play.

Every objective of a beat must carry in itself the seed of action. This seed is the element which moves the character forward in the pursuit of a goal, spurred on by a need, a want, an urgency. By placing a sincere value on each objective of every beat, the character's life energy is heightened, lending greater urgency and energy to each beat. The result is often a heightened level of excitement in the stage action which will capture and sustain the attention of the audience. The more exciting, the more creative the actor makes that objective, the more effective the action will be in the scenes being lived in the play.

The most creative and exciting objectives are those which are initiated by "I want..." or "I wish..." or "I need..." or "I must..."

Selecting the wrong objectives can be not only un-productive but destructive to your character and to the interpretation of the play. Objectives should be truthful, believable, should have value and depth, and be active so as to move your role ahead and provide forward action.

CHAPTER SEVEN
ACTING EXERCISES

1.
JUST A MINUTE!

A play is normally divided into Acts and Scenes which are familiar to all. The UNIT is a segment or Beat division of a scene.

As an exercise, select a one minute monologue and divide it into at least three Units or Beats. Be prepared to indicate the Key Point or Objective of each beat.

2.
THREE BEATS

Each actor is to improvise an action on stage divided into three (at least) segments as he moves across the stage from entrance to exit.

The actor must be prepared to define the key point of each segment.

In addition, the actor should be able to connect the three objectives with an ultimate goal or Super Objective.

3.
BEATS AND TEMPO-RHYTHM

As a variation, require of the actor the responsibility of assigning an external tempo for each of the three segments. The three elements of tempo-rhythm must vary in each segment.

4.
MONOLOGUE, BEATS AND TEMPO-RHYTHM

The actor should be prepared to assign a tempo for each beat of the monologue being presented.

As a further development of the monologue, the actor is to define a different life rhythm for each of the beats of the monologue.

Allow the actor to create a different physical movement for each segment of the monologue.

Finally, the actor is to present the monologue and include all of the above elements. All elements must be justified.

5.
SCENE, BEATS AND TEMPO-RHYTHM

All of the above elements will be performed by two actors in a selected scene. They are to work with each element until all are understood and able to be staged.

6.
KEY POINTS

Actors in a familiar and rehearsed scene are to perform entire scene using only the underlined objectives of each beat or unit.

7.
KEY POINTS - IMPROVISATION

A scene familiar to the actors may be improvised by using only ideas induced by the underlined objectives of each beat in the scene.

8.
TAP AND CHANGE

A metronome will be set to a tempo (or director may tap a chosen tempo). The actor must enter and feel and move in harmony with the established tempo. This will be held for a BEAT of action. The tempo will then change for BEAT TWO, at which point the actor's action and movement pick up the changed tempo with complete justification. A final change will be made in the tempo by the director. The actor will pick up the tempo and bring his scene to an end. (Actor may use speech if situation demands it.)

9.
THREE STAGES OF LIFE

Actor is to select three stages of his own life which will be presented in a planned improvisation. Phase one will be an incident in his youth. Phase two will consist of a related incident in the present. Finally, phase three will be an imagined, but related, brief incident in the future. Movement, dialogue and partner(s) may be used.

10.
THREE RHYTHMS

Actors are given this exercise to plan. Each improvisation is to consist of three different emotions in three beats of action. Actors will present scene affecting their own changes of emotion. One or both actors may work with the varied emotions in the scene.

11.
OBSTACLES

Actors are to take turns on stage. Each is to move through the space toward an objective. At given moments, the actor will encounter obstacle number one requiring time and effort to resolve, then move on and meet with problem two, and then on to problem three before he is able to achieve his objective and end the scene.

12.
KNOWING THE END

On a card or a verbal assignment by the director, each actor is given the ultimate action. It could be as simple as closing a door, or slapping face of partner, or running out. It could be as complex as acceptance of God, atoning for a sin, retribution for a wrong, or even a killing, etc.

The actors will then structure the proposed scene into several beats of varying tempo-rhythms, each beat will have its own objective. They must create all the ideas for each of the several beats.

13.
BEGINNING-MIDDLE-END

Any scene or monologue is to be staged with actor defining at least the three major important elements of dissection; beginning, middle and ending. They must avoid pit-fall of unchanging tempo-rhythm which means MONOTONY!

CHAPTER EIGHT

SCENIC TRUTH

For stage performance, we must become acquainted with two kinds of truth. First, there is actual fact of the life we live that truly exists. Then there is what is called 'scenic truth' which originates on the plane of imagination. This is what we deal with on the stage playing a role in a play.

The actor on stage is involved with a newly created reality. The given circumstances provided in the play by the playwright consist of events which could be happening and are seemingly true.

That which is important in theatre is the inner feeling of the character as played by the actor thus making him a human being and behaving as naturally as one would act 'if' the circumstances and conditions were indeed real. What is meaningful to the actor is the created reality of the inner life of a human spirit in a role and the complete belief in that reality.

As an actor, you should strive to put 'life' into all the imagined circumstances and actions until you have completely satisfied your sense of truth. In addition, you will have awakened a sense of faith in the newly created reality of your feelings.

Proceed step by step, beat by beat, building small elements of truth. Allow complete self study to continue ceaselessly, testing yourself every step taken. If there should be a false moment, a false action, then cut it immediately!

Recognize the value of working with physical objects as often as possible in a scene. This will lead to ease and comfort on stage in a role. Dealing with a physical object is in itself a truth because it is indeed real. Such valued objects may be a telephone, a book, a pen, a comb, credit card, blanket, pillow, bottle, glass, etc.

Truthful behavior on stage results in completely justified physical action. Truthful feelings and attitudes also result in fully justified physical action. The result will be thoroughly sincere faith in what you do on stage. Faith as defined by Stanislavski may be seen as confidence.

See to it that in every physical act there is a psychological element. In every psychological act you should sense its physical element. This process helps to form the 'body' of the role, leading to the creating of the human soul in the role. The bond between body and soul of a role is indivisible. The life of one gives life to the other.

Whenever you have truth and belief, you have feeling which is sincere. For example, the culminating point of Lady MacBeth's tragedy was the simple physical act of washing a spot of blood off her hand.

Find truthful physical actions for your character founded on inner conviction. Maintain an un-interrupted logical continuity of physical action on and off stage to insure the continuity of the life of the role, even if it means playing for yourself while off stage.

CHAPTER EIGHT
ACTING EXERCISES

1.
LARGE OBJECT IN SPACE

Ensemble of actors will be divided into teams of four to six actors. Each team will then decide on their own object which they will all move together, sharing full responsibility of touch, weight, resistance, pliability or solidity of object, etc. There are many choices such as car, piano, carpet, body, coffin, donkey, elephant, log, hot-air balloon, or a Macy's parade Mickey Mouse balloon, etc.

2.
MOVED BY A FORCE

Actors in teams of four to six are to decide what they are to be and which force will move them through the space. They may be leaves blown by the wind, logs floating down a river, smoke rising from a fire, kites lofted by a breeze, clouds floating in the sky, flowers blooming in the sun, shooting stars in space, rain from the sky, voice sounds propelled through space, grass waving in the breeze, spirits dancing in the night, a heart pulsating, babies being born, and so many others.

3.
CIRCLE PROP

Actors sit in a close circle. A designated actor begins by first seeing a personal and valued object before him, taking it into his hands to work with it in his own space without INDICATING. When appropriate time has been devoted to the action, the object is passed on to next actor in the circle who then transforms it to his own personal and valued object in his own created space. All others in circle must observe to see what each object is according to touch and attitude of the actor involved. Each in circle will take a turn until completed.

4.
NEW YORK, NEW YORK!

Ensemble will enter stage as they envision themselves on street of the BIG APPLE. It is their first time in the city and the tall buildings are demanding their attention. They focus at heights of buildings.

Variation: Actor are tourists atop the Trade Center or Empire State building and looking DOWN to the tiny cars and people many floors below.

5.
A JOB TO DO

Actors are given an assignment to paint a fence, paint a cabinet, set up speakers, assemble a VCR, paint a portrait, repair a table or chair. Attention is directed to imaginary brushes, tools, and details of work.

6.
AMUSEMENT PARK

Actors arrive at an amusement park and do their own thing; buy pop corn, cotton candy, hot dogs, throw at dolls, try strength on power machine, throw a basket ball for a prize, manipulate the racing rabbits, etc.

7.
BLIND

You are blind. Enter a space, touching objects until you can identify where you are. This may be established before you enter, creating all elements of who, where, why, etc.

8.
SEARCH

Each individual is required to enter the space and search for a lost item of great personal value.

The exercise may be performed by an entire group entering the space all together. They are to find a single object which is important to all.

The action must convey a truthful pursuit of the object and complete belief in its value.

9.
TWO KINDS OF TRUTH

FACT: Anything which happens to the actor in his real life.

SCENIC TRUTH: Any action originating on the plane of imagination.

Allow the actor to tell of a personal item of value which has been lost in his lifetime.

Ask the same actor to re-create the events which took place when the item had been lost. The re-creation must seemingly reflect all the truthful actions and emotional life of the original event.

Variation: Allow a second actor to recreate the exact scene as described by the first actor who had actually lost the personal item. The psychophysical action must show truth and belief.

10.
CHARACTER TRUTH

Allow the actor to take the character being portrayed in any role and with the imagination, place the character in a circumstance not actually in the play. The actor is to improvise an imagined circumstance in the life of the character.

A logical source for the imagined circumstance would be any activity or event which is mentioned in the play but does not actually take place. Example: He mentions how he remembers meeting HER at a bar. It does NOT however actually appear in the play. Improvise it.

11.
INNER MONOLOGUE

Two actors familiar with a rehearsed scene are to present three to five beats of the scene. Actor "A" will speak the lines as usual. Actor "B" will speak not only the text, but also the thoughts of the character in a modified, softer voice. The inner monologue of character "B" will be whispered simultaneously with the spoken text of character "A," who must not react to the whispered thoughts of "B." A challenging but valued exercise conceived by Constantin Stanislavski and used extensively.

At the discretion of the director, the actors will alter the procedure as character "A" speaks the text and whispers audibly the inner monologue while character "B" speaks the text as usual.

Note that the scene will ultimately be staged with each actor SILENTLY speaking his inner monologue with the audible text.

CHAPTER NINE

RECALLING FEELINGS

Those feelings drawn from our actual experience and transferred to our role are what give life to the play.

All external production is formal, cold, lifeless and pointless if it is not motivated from within.

You may allow the external plan to lead you but after that you must let it remind you of past feelings experienced and give yourself up to them as a guiding force throughout the circumstance.

Never begin with results. Let your belief in the life of the role and the given circumstance lead you sincerely to natural results.

Playing an emotion for the sake of an emotion is damaging.

Spontaneous emotions may appear and are desirable. We can only hope that these direct, powerful and vivid emotions will appear often, and help to sharpen elements in creative work.

We must be warned that some actors enjoy 'losing' themselves in a role or in segments of scenes. We must remind ourselves to always act in our own person, as an artist, but not lose ourselves completely on stage. We are capable of playing ourselves in an infinite variety of circumstances.

We have in us the seed of all human characteristics, good and evil.

Achieving the creative mood is a primary objective of all actors. Thus, even the stage setting, lighting, sound, costumes, make-up are all primarily used to stimulate the actor and give dimension to his inner life. In that manner, we can affect the audience meaningfully.

Don't think about the feeling itself, but set your mind to work on what makes it grow, what the conditions and circumstances were that brought about the experience.

The broader your emotion memory, the richer your material for inner creativeness. You must draw principally upon your own impressions, feelings and experiences. However, you also acquire material from life around you, real and imaginary, from books, art, science, journeys, museums and from communication with other human beings, at home, other parts of the population and abroad.

Although there are some who resist looking deep within themselves, it is productive and indeed helpful for most. The great actor, Morris Carnovsky, stated that emotion memory helped him to get in touch with himself. Indeed, recalling events of our early life lends comfort and faith to scenes in plays which evoke similar emotions. It's a sure way to connecting the self to the life of the character you are portraying. It does not mean that you have to deliberately recall a past event every time you play an emotional scene. The emotion may simply be familiar to you, and that is helpful to the actor.

CHAPTER NINE
ACTING EXERCISES

1.
TRIGGER TO PAST EXPERIENCE

Group of actors in a quiet atmosphere begin to move about very freely as they first empty their minds in preparation for the exercise. At a given moment, the director calls for them to freeze in space.

The position in which we find ourselves in the freeze is to trigger a thought leading to an action. The actors are asked to concentrate on what could they be doing, who are they, what action are they performing, what are they feeling, where are they, etc.

The position in the freeze normally connects with a past experience which the moment brings to his mind. The actor takes it and builds on it by going with the action.

Variations: The exercise may lead into individual improvisation induced by recalled experience.

The actors may also drain their minds again and begin free movement until freeze is called with new positions triggering new ideas.

2.
THE SETTING CONNECTS WITH A MEMORY

We may draw from actual experiences or learned even through movies, television, books, museums, etc.

Actors are to enter a railroad station individually or in acting teams of two. They may spontaneously create an improvisation based on their connection with the setting. They may also build an improvisation plan before entering.

Variation: Actors are to deal with a stage setting of a jail. They will develop a plan for an improvisation.

> Actors will enter a cathedral and create an improvisation.
> Actors are given a park and bench as setting for improvisation.
> Improvise attending a birthday (or other) party.
> Actors enter carrying back packs. Build an improvisation.
> An improvisation builds on the idea of carrying luggage.

3.
SENSE MEMORY

Improvisations may be created on each of the following sensory elements:

> Actor is to be cuddled. What is recalled? Build on it.
> Sound of crickets is heard. Improvise a past experience.
> The smell of perfume, or flowers, or other scent. Improvise an event.
> You embrace someone. Build who, what, where, when, and why.

4.
YOUR FAVORITE TOY

All actors are on stage in a quiet atmosphere, sitting or standing in a private space as they shed years and take themselves back to being age three or five or eight. The place comes to mind, and a toy or a stuffed animal or even a pet. See it, touch it, smell it, hear it as in the past. Note if OTHER elements come into their moment due to the truthful reliving of the past. It is most often a natural development.

5.
STANDING ON THE CORNER

The actor stands on a street corner in the cold. It is very cold. Only this is assigned. The actor will remain in the cold until a past event of street corner and cold trigger other elements in him(her). Add when, where, what, why and build the improvisation, adding also movement and dialogue as well as (if needed) a partner.

6.
FIRE THE IMAGINATION

Actor is sitting by a fire warming his hands. The actor remains with this action until his inner life is activated, thus adding who, what, where to an improvisation.

7.
DOCTOR, OH, DOCTOR!

Actor is a patient in a hospital (or even in his own bed at home). When the recall of a personal incident comes to the actor, other elements are added and the improvisation begins. People may enter and contribute depending upon the creative life of the actor in bed.

8.
A GIFT!

Actor is given an idea of a GIFT which is to be presented (or received). It triggers other ingredients and an improvisation is created.

9.
OFF WE GO!

Actor is at an airline office (or railroad terminal) and arranging for a ticket(s). Add who, what, where, when, why and improvise a scene using other actor(s) to aid the scene.

10.
LOST!

You enter the space and are lost. When inner life is activated, portray a moment in your life when you were lost. Add all other ingredients to build a scene.

Variation: An item of value has been lost by you. Add all elements and build an improvisation.

11.
I REMEMBER IT WELL!

For every highly emotional scene in your acting role of a major play, recall an event in your life which produced similar feelings.

CHAPTER TEN

INTER-COMMUNICATION

Communion between characters is of major importance on stage, thus placing the acting principle of inter-communication among the most valued elements in theatre. It is accepted that one is in mental communication with an object at any given moment. To give or to receive something from any object, even fleetingly, constitutes a moment of spiritual communion.

It is important to note that it is possible to look at and actually see an object and connect with the object to establish a spiritual communion with the object. However, it is a common practice among actors to 'look at' and to not actually see anything. Being reminded that the eye is the mirror of the soul, we can be made to understand how the vacant eye is the mirror of an empty mind. This appears to be a dilemma of too many actors.

It is essential that an actor's eye (his look) reflect the deep inner content of his soul.

An actor must build up great inner resources to correspond to the life of a human soul in his role and then share these spiritual resources with the other characters in the given circumstance of the play. That is known as communion. He thus becomes completely identified with the role and is thereby transformed into a believable, truthful and completely human spirit we define as the character in the play.

When an actor is distracted, however, by his personal life and gets out of character, he gives way to false and mechanical acting, destroying the communion and the continuity of the role.

Spectators become involved in the life on stage only when true communion takes place between characters through exchange of feelings, thoughts and actions. It is required that actors not only look at eyes, nose, shirts, buttons, hair or face of partner, but continually reach inside the partner to the living spirit of the partner. The same is required of an actor's communion with an object. He is to reach out to the object and connect with its inner spirit, giving and receiving a life energy from the object.

There are at least three important examples of proper inter-communication for the performing artist on stage:

1. Direct communion with an object within the stage setting.
2. Self-communion with an object of choice in the mind of your character, whether it be an image or an idea.
3. Communion with an imaginary object pertaining to the life of the character being portrayed.

Seek to develop your ability to interchange currents of life energy with your partner on stage or with any object in the play. Strive to draw in through your eyes those currents of energy from your partner or from your selected object as you, in turn, send out your currents of life energy through your eyes to your partner or to your object of choice. Send out rays. Receive rays. Experience what you transmit to your object and receive from your object. This is communion at its strongest. That is also the power of attention.

CHAPTER TEN
ACTING EXERCISES

1.
OUTER COMMUNION - ACTUAL

The actor is to walk on to the stage and look about and tell what actual object he is connecting with at any given moment.

2.
OUTER COMMUNION - CREATED

The actor enters a space as a character in a circumstance from a play. He is to look about his space and see all that is in the created space.

Allow the actor to speak his sub-text and comment on everything he actually sees in his character's space.

3.
INNER COMMUNION - ACTUAL

The actor enters the stage space and is allowed to relax as he is perhaps seated. He may then close his eyes and simply voice the thoughts coming into his own mind, random though they may be.

4.
INNER COMMUNION - CREATED

The actor enters a space as a character in a circumstance from a play. The actor as the character is required to speak out what 'character related' objects enter his mind.

The actor must overcome the tendency to see things pertaining to his own real life and reach for those objects belonging only to the life of his character and 'connecting' with them.

5.
MIRROR EXERCISE

Actors in pairs are to face each other. Actor "A" performs a gentle physical action, such as applying make-up for a role. Actor "B" is to mirror every specific physical action performed by actor "A."

After a period of time, actor "B" initiates the action and actor "A" takes his turn in reflecting movements of actor "B."

The observer should not be able to discern who is initiating the action at any given time for the exercise to be a success.

Seek a higher level of communion by commanding your partner with your mind through your eyes. Both of you may subtly initiate action.

6.
REACHING OUT

Actors lie on floor in darkness in relaxed position. Listen intently to each sound. See the sound in your inner vision. Connect with it. Leave that sound and reach out for a more remote sound. See it and connect with it. Leave that sound and reach even farther to the most remote sound possible. See it. Connect with it, then go with it into outer space and travel with it where ever it takes you. No physical movement is to happen at anytime during exercise.

7.
ALBUM MEMORIES

The actor opens an album and notices a particular item, memento or photograph. The actor is to re-live the incident it brings to mind, calling upon other actor(s) if needed.

8.
LOVE OF A FLOWER

Actor moves to a vase and connects with a flower. It was given by a special person of great value. Take the flower and deal with it in any manner as long as the flower is treated with the same feeling the person has for the very special individual it represents. The actor gives to the flower very special energy. He also receives from the flower all the powerful rays of whom it represents.

9.
OBJECT CONTACT

Actor enters a space and discovers an object. It has very special value to him, thus triggering feelings in the beholder which affect his movement and action on stage.

10.
POWER OF MUSIC

Actor will listen to certain music which affects his inner life. He will establish communion with specific instrument(s). Taking it even to a greater dimension, he will envision notes, hear notes, become notes and the sound itself. He may even float into space with the beautiful sound of music.

11.
FACE IT

Actors are to pair off and enter stage to face each other. Actor "A" will assume the features of actor "B" in detail, actually taking on the face of the partner, the body and his life as well as his very soul. At the same time, actor "B" is going through the same process taking on the face of actor "A;" his mind, inner life, body and soul.

The ultimate mind to mind communion becomes very advanced involvement.

12.
RAYS OF SILENCE

Actors in pairs (or more) are to perform a rehearsed scene in complete silence. They are to speak each word of the text within and convey the idea to the partner(s) only with the eyes, sending out the words as rays of energy. The physical actions will be performed just as they had been rehearsed as though they were speaking the words aloud. Note that extreme attention must be directed to one another as each must sense every word of the inaudible text and also when the internal speech has ended, striving to eliminate any unrequired pause.

Stanislavski used this exercise with great effectiveness.

CHAPTER ELEVEN

INNER AND OUTER ADJUSTMENT

Adjustment is identified as the inner and outer human means people use in adapting themselves to one another in a variety of relationships. It becomes the actor's responsibility to find the right adjustments in adapting himself to the circumstances in a play in the performance of the role.

When adaptation is functioning it will manifest itself in fine ensemble interplay among characters in any given scene. This will be seen as the fine adjustment or harmony among actors in roles. They are giving and receiving 'rays' among all the characters when they are all 'reaching' each other. It is the favorable opposite of "I am not getting anything from him" or "I'm not reaching her."

Work always to reach the very soul of your partner. You must sense the life of your partner and you must adapt to him or her. The quality of this communion and adaptation (they work hand in hand) is of extreme importance. This means the quality of your feeling, your words, your speech, actions, etc.

We must continually use all of our five senses and all elements of our inner and outer make-up to effectively communicate with partners and objects.

The actor's first responsibility is to adapt to the partner and not to the audience. Then he is to make use of logical, coherent actions and voice to penetrate the inner meaning of the lines and the inner life of the character as it connects with the inner life of the partner's character. This is soul to soul communion, the most desirable high level involvement.

Adjustments must be natural as well as logical and human and must be in harmony with the role of the character being portrayed within the given circumstances provided by the author.

In rehearsals, the actor should explor various adaptations in order to seek and even discover unexpected dimensions of the role. So many rehearsals are given up to simply running through the lines, which is not very productive. Actors are advised to run their lines on their own time and not take up valuable rehearsal time.

When proper adjustments have been made and inter-communication has taken place, it will be discovered that all-important subconscious becomes accessible to the performer.

To dispel the concept that your duty is to speak for the benefit of only the audience, understand that the actor's primary obligation is to work toward adapting to the partner. The successful and complete adaptation will include a strong, energetic projection with proper voice placement and diction and is directed toward the partner with energy and conviction. The audience will hear every projected word even in the last row, for they have become equally involved in the action on stage and what is being spoken by the characters. They are at this point penetrating the inner meaning of your spoken words and dramatic action.

To seek new dimensions of performance, you may explore the possibility of adapting the volume of speech in a given area of a scene. Where there had been a powerful projection, a whisper may be attempted to gain a certain unforeseen quality. Where the tempo had been slow, new levels of dramatic action may well be stimulated by quickening the pace. Dare to explore new avenues of interpretation by way of adaptation and adjustment. Such discoveries make rehearsals enjoyable, and the play performance will undoubtedly reach exciting new heights.

CHAPTER ELEVEN
ACTING EXERCISES

1.
HIDING INNER FEELINGS - Improvisations

You just received news of being rejected by your preferred college and are with someone you'd rather not know of your disappointment.

You have just been fired from a choice job upon which you had planned your future. You hide your feelings as you confront one you would rather not know of the circumstance.

Your fiance has just broken off your engagement and you meet someone you wish not to know of your heartbreak.

2.
ADJUSTING TO UNUSUAL COMMUNICATION SITUATION

Actor "A" must convey an important series of instructions to a simple minded individual.

Variations: Actor "A" must cummunicate ideas of relative complexity to a deaf mute; to a child, to a dog, etc.

3.
THE NEED TO PERSUADE

Actor "A" tries to convince actor "B" that he must leave this important meeting earlier than planned.

Student tries to talk teacher into letting him go early from class, or detention, or exam, etc.

Actor "A" is with a blind date and is now trying to get out of the commitment.

4.
CHANGE OF ATTITUDE

Find justification and proper adaptation as you change attitude three times, from severe, to kind, to anger.

Change attitudes and justify, from pleasant, to jealousy, to loving. Etc.

5.
CREATING YOUR PARTNER AND CIRCUMSTANCE

Actor "A" enters stage with a conceived idea of who his partner will be and the circumstance involving the two of them. He initiates dialogue.

Actor "B" is seated on stage, empty of mind, totally unaware of who he is, where he is, or what the situation is. He is to sense every possible idea from actor "A" who must present all elements simply and truthfully.

Scene will then develop to its logical end.

6.
RECEIVING SUDDEN NEWS

A mother receives news of death of soldier son.

Variation: Rape, suicide, mugging, illness, cure, prize, etc.

7.
OTHER SIDE OF THE COIN

Taking a scene normally played with volume and energy and present scene in secretive, whispering tone.

Select a scene of anger and energy and perform the scene with tenderness and loving mood. Or change from anger to gay laughter. Other variations may be explored to find new dimensions to character or situation.

8.
ADAPTING TO OBSTACLE

Actor "A" is in a scene with actor "B" who can not hear (or understand) what is being said by actor "A."

Vary the above situation and actor "B" is blind. Etc.

9.
ACTIVITY FROM INACTION

Actor goes on stage and remains motionless for two full minutes at least. Allow thoughts to go in any direction. After two full minutes, taking what has happened within his own mind, he will begin to act and re-act to whatever has developed.

Observers are to note physical adjustments or inner activity, no matter how subtle they may be.

10.
FREEZE CHANGE - IMPROVISATION

Actors are performing improvisation. An outside actor calls "freeze" at the moment he hears an inspiring word spoken. Action stops and he takes the place of one of the actors (actor "A") and begins new scene with actor "B" based upon the word called out. Situation must change. Scene continues with actor "C" and actor "B" until actor "D" calls "freeze," etc.

11.
TEMP0-RHYTHM ADAPTATION

Scene is performed in very slow tempo. Scene repeated in very fast tempo. Adjustments are to be noted.

12.
TIME TO DRESS

Actor gets dressed to go on a date but does NOT want to go. Alter scene.

Actor dresses for a date and is thrilled to be going out. Note tempos.

13.
TRIPLE PLAY

Actor "A" hates actor "B" but loves actor "C."
Actor "B" loves actor "A" but hates actor "C."
Actor "C" loves actor "B" but hates actor "A."

They are to choose their space where, time, when and other elements of a circumstance and build an improvisation.

CHAPTER TWELVE

MIND, WILL AND FEELING

Feel the inner life of your role and instantly your inner chords will harmonize and your whole bodily instrument will begin to function.

The mind, will and feeling are impelling movers in our psychophysical life. There is a reciprocal interaction between these three elements which, by working together, will arouse us by natural means and stir other creative elements.

The actor's mind takes the thoughts in the lines of his role and arrives at a conception of their meaning. In turn, this conception will lead to an opinion about them which will affect his will as well as feeling, for Stanislavski believes them to be inseparable.

An actor's mind is usually quite exceptional, for the task of conveying complex ideas of a master playwright to an audience is awesome indeed. The mind must be disciplined to lead the will to execute ideas, to excite the imagination, determine objectives, create a character history, arouse inner feelings which are in perfect harmony with the super objective and theme of the play, and to interpret the role in a truthful, honest and believable manner. This may well be an artistically overwhelming task.

Since these three inner motive forces form a triumvirate, inextricably bound together, we find that employing any one motive force may trigger the use of the other two. They are, however, rather elusive at times. We have indeed witnessed stage works where the mind may have been clearly at work, yet we as an audience would be only intellectually connected to the circumstance on stage because it lacked the necessary element of feeling. Thus, we remained detached and uninvolved, leaving the theatre with an intellectual awareness of ideas, but not emotionally affected by the stage event. Our lives were not enriched, nor were our souls touched. We should therefor strive to effectively employ all three inner motive forces of mind, will and feeling.

It is seen, then, that an actor's responsibility is not only to deliver lines of the playwright to be clearly understood. He is to take the character's life, his thoughts, feelings, conceptions, reasonings, attitudes, goals, make them his own and interpret the role so as to convey this honestly to the observer, who will then be touched, affected, and enriched by the experience.

There are altogether too many calculating actors and scenic productions of intellectual origin. We witness too rarely truthful, living, honest emotional creativeness.

Begin then with the use of the mind to inspire you to seek the creative objective for each beat of your dissected role. Inspired by will and feelings, they will work together in defining the beats and naming the creative objectives, then selecting the appropriate tempo-rhythm for each beat. Together they will move you to higher levels of energy, excitement, feelings and action.

The power of these inner motive forces is enhanced by their interaction. It is only when they are co-operating harmoniously that we can create freely.

CHAPTER TWELVE
ACTING EXERCISES

1.
THE WILL TO ACTION

Actor sits on stage in silence for any degree of time allowing his mind to seek out objects. When the 'right' object comes to his mind, he connects with it and develops it to a level of involvement until the inner creative state is reached. At this point, the actor allows the situation to lead into any direction and he must go with it. This will lead to feeling, accompanied by physical actions and, possibly, spoken words.

2.
FROM OUTSIDE IN

An actor goes on stage and is given a command by the director to assume any particular position.

The actor assumes the position and holds for a brief period until his inner thoughts begin to put the gesture into a justified action, at which point the actor develops the scenario on his own.

Example: Hands extended upward; reaching for a valued object.
On knees; pleading for mercy.
Crouching position; shielding himself from blows.
Fetal position; cringing with fear.
Hand extended; begging.
Hands over ears; shutting out horrible sounds. Seek variations.

3.
FEEL YOUR WAY-OUTSIDE IN

An actor goes on stage and is given any word by the director depicting a feeling.

The actor accepts the word of a feeling and seeks within himself an actual association with the emotion suggested and is to take and develop the moment truthfully until he puts the feeling into motion with a justified event.

The actor's response must NOT be mechanical. He must seek complete and truthful inner involvement, allowing the mind to influence the will which will then trigger the correct response. The reverse is also possible; the feeling, is to trigger the mind, the will, and the re-action.

4.
CHANGING OBJECTIVES

First discuss a brief scene known thoroughly by the actors. They must also specify the appropriate OBJECTIVES OF THE BEATS AND SCENE. Then, with clearly defined intent, ALTER the objectives.

The lesson will obviously illustrate how altered objectives will affect the meaning of the scene, the meaning of the play and the inner lives and behavior of the characters.

5.
CHANGING FEELINGS

Feelings of characters are known and discussed before scene. Then each actor is to intentionally alter the characters feelings and attitude and perform scene, noting the change in life of characters and the scene.

6.
BECOMING MASTER

The inner motive forces of mind, will and feeling allow the actor to become the master playing on the instrument of creation.

Knowing a scene thoroughly, the actor is to heighten the character's inner life by creating one or more obstacles of high degree. The obstacle(s) are capable of being created from within the circumstance of the scene itself. Nothing extraneous need be added. Example; a character leaves a valuable object with the partner and departs. The object falls and breaks; possibly a symbol of their failing relationship. Or, simply, a person is to exit, but door jams; certainly an easy method of illustrating the character's frustration of moment.

7.
SHARING

In performing Hamlet, Romeo, Juliet, Willy Loman, etc., the actor is to find in the life circumstances of the great characters, some particular physical or psychological connection, or a similar event experienced in real life by the actor. Discuss these points of connection. Then, illustrate by performing the scene and defining these special moments. Share with your associates those major or even minor points which you personally share with your character. It will help bridge the gap.

8.
WHAT DO YOU MEAN?

Lines are spoken by actor performing a character from a great play. The director will stop the action and point out a certain sentence. The next step is to have the actor make connection with the author's mind, move into that great mind and ask the actor to tell us just what the author may have meant by the words chosen for the sentence.

Further, from the actor's personal experience, what can be used in his life to give substance and meaning to that designated moment.

9.
CHARACTER MOTIVE FORCES - WILL

Actor is to point out exactly where in the play the character' WILL is most clearly defined. That scene will then be performed to illustrate.

10.
CHARACTER FEELINGS

Actor is to define the specific areas of his role where the character most clearly reveals his true feeling about life and circumstance. The scene will be staged by the actor(s) involved in order to confirm the observation.

CHAPTER THIRTEEN

THROUGH LINE OF DRAMATIC ACTION

A line of life flows from the past through the present and into the future which is referred to as the through line of dramatic action. This is the thread that runs through the play created by the author inspired by his artistic imagination.

The character role, portrayed by the actor, must also have a continuous being, threading from the past, through the present and into the future. The actor must penetrate the meaning of the role and the text, seek out those unbroken lines of life and triggering his inner motive forces, his mind, will and feelings, which then come into play.

The actor will then assume the responsibility of developing the life of his character which will live by the unbroken line. That is what gives life and truth as well as dramatic action to the acting role. Should that unbroken line of life be interrupted - by shallow thinking, loss of concentration, or other distraction - life and truth will cease.

The through line of dramatic action is given to us by the author in segments, defined as beats, units, scenes and acts. They are in the form of written speeches by characters as well as description of inner and outer action and emotion. This, however, is only the tip of the ice-berg. The actor must assume the responsibility of filling in all that the author has left unsaid. That is the creative aspect of the actor's work. He must define the unbroken line of life, passing from one beat and objective to another, maintaining his circle of attention and adhering to the life space and life line of the character, through each scene and each act to the very end of the play. The actor is kept in this chanel by his inner motive forces, his mind, will and feelings. This through line of life action always leads to the super objective, or the theme of the play.

By successfully implementing the through line of dramatic action, all important elements will be activated as we experience the artist in the role. The fusing of these essential elements leads the actor to the inner creative state, the very basis of our art.

To propel the actor on his artistic path, the inner motive forces of mind, will and feelings will be extremely helpful in feeling out the very soul of the role. Initially, the play must be read in its entirety several times, for it is nearly impossible for an actor to comprehend the essentials of a role instantly and create its full spirit. Since the actor's responsibility is to create a human spirit, detailed study of the play must take place requiring several readings of each act in sequence so that through line of actions and events are thoroughly understood.

In the beginning, the actor's understanding of the inner significance of a play is usually quite general. It is strongly recommended that the actor approach the play pretty much as the playwright wrote it, event by event, scene by scene, beat by beat, from beginning to end.

Stage actors have found film making often confusing and quite difficult because scenes filmed conveniently out of logical order, breaking the sequence, ignoring the through line of action - a faulty process based only on schedule, time and cost.

CHAPTER THIRTEEN
ACTING EXERCISES

1.
A DAY IN THE LIFE OF

Sitting in a quiet space, review the events of your day in continuity.

Allow yourself to see the imagined full day of a character you are portraying from a play.

Actor goes on stage and acts out the remembered personal moment and/or a moment of action from the character being portrayed.

2.
THIS IS YOUR LIFE

Actors are to select key points in their personal lives leading to the present. Further, the actor may be permitted to select minor goals in the future leading to his major goal in life.

Actors are to note that all key points and minor goals are associated with the full life.

3.
THIS IS YOUR CHARACTER'S LIFE

Actors are to review the entire life of their character, filling in with the imagination all ideas not provided by the author. Events are to begin at birth, brought to the present circumstances of the PLAY, then projected with imagination into the future. Key points of the past and minor goals of the future are to be noted which lead to major goal or super-objective.

4.
PRE-SCENE LIFE

Actors are to improvise what happens before any given scene.

Actors are to improvise any selected event in the life of the character prior to the beginning of the PLAY.

Actors are to improvise events which take place between scenes. Etc.

5.
CHARACTER MEMORY

Put into an improvised scene an event you imagine took place in the past in the life of your character. (It may be a moment or event mentioned in the PLAY but not actually appearing in any part of the PLAY.)

6.
CHARACTER DREAM

In an improvised scene, portray an event which you believe may happen in the future life of your character.

7.
DUST TO DUST

Actors lie on a quiet stage, draining mind and body to attain total relaxation and shutting out all human thought. When the feeling moves them they will slowly begin to sense life coming into their bodies and they find themselves as seeds. The seeds grow slowly to birth, to infant, to child, youth, adult, maturity then revert to childlike behavior and return to seed. Movement and feeling must suit phase of cycle.

8.
FROM PAST TO FUTURE

Each actor is to perform brief moments of childhood, from present and with imagination and purpose in life, project a scene of the future.

9.
CONNECTING WITH LIFE OF CHARACTER

Actor performing a role will create an improvisation of an imagined event in the young life of the character. Then, the actor will locate a scene in the play most closely connected with the youthful experience and stage the brief moment. As a final activity, the actor is to use the young experience as well as the action in the play and construct with his imagination a possible true event which will take place in the character's future life.

10.
INTERRUPTION

Take any activity, such as listening to your favorite music. There is a break in the tape, for example. This problem must be eliminated and then actor is to return to the mood and inner action of moment prior to interruption.

Variation: Telephone call is interrupted by smoke alarm; your brief interlude with a lover is interrupted by a neighbor, etc.

11.
VOLLEYBALL

Group on stage in a circle. A designated actor picks up the imagined volleyball and passes it to any other actor, who does the same, etc. The size and weight and texture of the imagined ball must remain the same from person to person. (Easily said, but not easily done.) They are to maintain a continuity of the life existence of the volleyball without breaking the created reality.

12.
THE FLOW OF CHARACTER DAY

Actors are to improvise events which took place during his character's day prior to any scene, and circumstances which are presumed to take place between scenes or acts of a play in production.

13.
THROUGH LINE OF ACTION - IMPROVISATION

The entire play (or any scene) is to be improvised within a brief period by using only elements relating to the objectives of each beat in every scene. This is often a fun way to brush up a play between performances.

CHAPTER FOURTEEN

CREATIVE MOOD

As a pianist plays upon his instrument to express his emotions, as a painter uses brushes and colors to create images on canvas, the actor calls upon his spiritual and physical creative instrument as the essential elements of the performing artist in the role. His discipline requires that he employ all of his psycho-physical elements.

The actor draws life from the fiction which is the play and makes it seem real in performance on stage. He feels the role, its innate truthfulness, and believes in the actual possibility of what is happening on stage. He then gives out energy, power, will, emotion and thought. These elements of the artist in the role propel him forward toward creative objectives, inspired by inner longings, intentions, ambitions, and by inner actions inherent in the life of the character. This constitutes the inner creative mood.

Stanislavski specifies that solitude in public is a truly valuable acting principle. In employing this principle, the actor learns to feel he is alone in his space, experiencing a private moment, while indeed actually in the presence of a live audience. This phenomenon is not experienced usually in ordinary life. It is an unusual and pleasant sensation for an actor to achieve this level of "aloneness" while on stage. Performers acknowledge that a theatre full of people is indeed a splendid experience. For every moment of real feeling on the stage there is a response, currents of emotion flowing back to the actors on stage, inspiring greater creative energy, resulting in a comforting, exciting, warmth and confidence.

If one creative element in the delicate composition is not functioning correctly, the whole process will suffer, based upon the fact that so many creative elements are inter-connected. We gain confidence in noting, however, that when even one creative element is functioning correctly, other inter-connected elements are more than likely functioning as well.

The moment a false note is introduced by the actor in the role, truth diminishes, belief is suspended and replaced by mechanical acting. As in a domino effect, objectives become artificial, creative imagination evaporates, audience attention dissipates and interest will vanish. At this point, there is no art in evidence.

Inner preparation for a role is absolutely essential for the actor. He should arrive early for rehearsal and with a positive attitude, allowing time to shed tensions of the outside world. Relaxation exercises are essential as are voice exercises. Focus should be directed finally on those objects connected with the life of the character being portrayed by the actor. The entire instrument-mind and body-must become fine-tuned for the role to be portrayed. Ample time should be allowed for warming up the instrument, much as a musician or athlete does.

To further the actor's preparation, he should go over the fundamental parts of the role, the key points. This emerging of the through line of life of the role will encourage development of the all-important creative mood.

CHAPTER FOURTEEN
ACTING EXERCISES

1.
SOLITUDE IN PUBLIC

The actor will take a position on stage and remains within his own space and enclosing himself within his own circle of attention. Employing his inner motive forces, he will allow himself to seek out a meaningful inner object. He will establish communion with the object and allow his imagination to develop a scenario of circumstances. When elements are in place action will take over and he begins to go with it, finding justified movement and/or speech directed toward his objects.

All action is to be contained within his circle of attention for as long as he remains involved with the inner creative mood. Action will cease when he brings the event to a logical conclusion or when the director calls "curtain."

2.
THE OBJECT OF OUR ATTENTION

Actor is to go on stage and decide to work with a prop. The object is to have a personal value to the actor within his space. He will connect with the object and work in who, where, when, leading into a circumstance of significance and take it to conclusion.

3.
WHERE AM I?

Actor is to enter a space which he finds completely familiar. He is to observe all elements within his space and take up several physical objects to work with. He must also touch three of the four walls about him, at least. This may include dealing with draperies, windows, doors, wall hangings, fire place, wall paper, etc.

The exercise may be performed solo or with partner(s) as a scene improvisation.

4.
PLACE UNKNOWN

Actor is to enter a totally unfamiliar space. He is to build a scenario illustrating why he is there. Actor must touch as many elements within the space as is considered natural in the circumstance. His focus of attention will also connect with items within the space which he will see clearly with his inner vision. A total exploration of his strange environment will allow a clear picture to form of exactly where he is with or without speech (of course used only if appropriate).

5.
DRAIN

Actors will lie on stage quietly, heels together and hands to the side. Imagining there is fluid in the body, it will drain slowly, inch by inch beginning at the toes. Eyes are closed so actor will envision each part of the body being drained upward. It is suggested that draining take place with each inhale. No part of the body already drained must move. If attention drifts from focus point, actor must return to spot last drained.

Drain may continue until director ends it. Some actors will drift to sleep before completion of exercise; a harmless yet successful state of relaxation.

6.
OBJECT ENDOWMENT

A small table or tall stool is on stage in a pool of light. On it is a little unobtrusive block of wood. Actor number one will approach the table from the darkness. Upon entering the pool of light, transformation will take place and the actor will be entering his own familiar newly created space, which he sees and feels. The object on the table becomes the focus of his attention which has also transformed into an object of value. The actor will take it into his hands as the transformed object and deal with it privately. It must be anything but a block of wood.

The actor remains in character while in the light, completes the involvement and exits the lighted area leaving the block for the next actor.

7.
THE HANDS REMEMBER

Actors are on stage in their own space. Director indicates they are in a certain environment such as a work shop, hand-craft room, repair shop, basement work bench, beach, creek, etc. Actors will work with space, with tools, with sand, clay, etc. Activity will be detailed and very specific. Hands will sense texture of clay, granules of sand, tools, etc.

8.
WINDOW SHOPPING

Actors walk along the apron and look into shop windows and observe the merchandise, prices, styles, sizes. They comment to each other and evaluate the sale of items.

9.
DRESSING

Actors determine justification for dressing elegantly. The action may include a dresser for the occasion. They view each other and see the images of elegance in the full length mirror. The attitude of joy and anticipation will be experienced as will the inner feeling one gets when truly pleased with your appearance and the anticipated event. See each item in detail, feel the item on your body, feel the cloth and design, see the skin radiate, hair styled, etc.

10.
WATER, WATER!

Actors are to imagine carrying a bucket to a creek or well and are to fill it with water. Sensing the need of the water and the weight, each will carry the bucket of water to a designated spot, careful to avoid spilling a drop, reaching the spot, pouring out the water. They are to sense the flow and the reduced weight of the bucket as they return to the water source.

11.
FIRED

Scene is to be improvised based upon actor being fired from a very important career job.

Variation: You have just wrecked the family car; you have had a driving accident and your companion has been injured.

CHAPTER FIFTEEN

THE SUPER OBJECTIVE

In a play, the entire stream of ideas, actions and feelings converge to carry out the super-objective of the writer's work. The key idea of the play, the point which inspired the author to create his great work, is the very purpose which leads one to stage the play in the first place. Should we not identify its theme or its central point, then there is no valued purpose for staging the play at all!

A sample of significant themes of great playwrights follows:

a. Lifelong Search for God. (Dostoyevski)
b. Struggling for Self Perfection. (Tolstoy)
c. Dealing With Trivialities of Life. (Chekov)
d. Belief in the American Dream. (Miller)
e. Appreciating Life As We Live It. (Wilder)
f. The Loss of Innocence in Changing America. (Williams)

It is to be noted that the greater the literary work, the greater pull of its super-objective. The theme, therefore, must be known by the performing artist in its early stage of development and should be the very soul of the actor's artistic creation.

A play is structured so that all beats, units and objectives are channeled by way of the through line of dramatic action aiming for the super-objective. They form the life giving quality of the play. Knowing the super-objective will lead to comfort, understanding, ease and confidence in the actor performing the role. It gives purpose to the character's life and all his actions in every moment of the play.

In a great play, the theme or super-objective will be more readily conceived. However, in a bad play, and there will be bad plays in the life of an actor, a theme or super-objective may be elusive or even non-existent. It may become the responsibility of the actor to point out the super-objective himself, perhaps even making it deeper, sharper, more significant than the author himself.

Difficulties exist when an actor works with less skilled performers or directors. The selection of an incorrect super-objective can truly destroy the quality of a play. It must not be left to chance. Whereas, working with a properly identified super-objective will lift the play to its deserved level giving the whole play a deeper inner significance.

It is even advised that not only should the super-objective be properly identified, but to give it a title, a name; an exciting name. For example, in Moliere's Imaginary Invalid, the major role super-objective would be, I Wish To Be Thought Ill. Once the super-objective is defined, it highlights the through line of dramatic action and galvanizes all the beats and objectives. Playing without awareness of a super-objective will lead an actor to play in a disjointed series of exercises out of tune with the ensemble.

It is essential for each actor to know the super-objective of the character being portrayed and for the ensemble to know the super-objective of the play being produced.

CHAPTER FIFTEEN
ACTING EXERCISES

1.
JOURNEY'S END

Each actor is to stage what the final objective is of the entire role to be portrayed by him; the character's goal or super-objective.

Pairs of actors in a play may create an improvisation based on the contrasting or, better, conflicting super-objectives of their characters.

2.
EYES ON THE TARGET

Actors are to define three or more main actions of their characters within the play which lead to the super-objective.

These main actions are to be acted out in two minutes scenes to heighten their awareness of these beats and objectives.

With imagination, pairs of actors may improvise brief scenes depicting these units and objectives which lead to the super-objective.

3.
CHART YOUR COURSE

Each actor is to write the key words of every objective of his character on a chart illustrating how his through line of action leads to his super-objective.

In his dissected script, each unit and objective will have been properly identified (numbered) with objectives underlined clearly (red is suggested) by each actor playing a role in the play.

Each actor will also assign a tempo (slow-medium-fast) to each dissected beat of his character as well as the rhythm (feeling, mood, energy).

Actors are to present a brief scene using only three to five beats and employing tempo-rhythm, identifying objectives, and noting how they relate to the super-objective.

4.
WITH IT OR AGAINST IT

Each actor is to define the super-objective of his character as being in harmony with the super-objective of the play, or in conflict with the play's super-objective.

Select two actors who's characters they are portraying have opposing super-objectives. They are to create an improvisation based upon these opposing goals in their lives, lasting about two minutes.

5.
SEARCH

Improvisation is based on one's long search for God.

Example: Life circumstance has been difficult. A decision is thus made to enter the ministry or a nunnery to serve God. (Sound of Music)

6.
REVENGE

An act has been committed against you or a beloved member of your family. You seek to avenge the wrong. (Hamlet)

7.
GREED

Greed is undermining our country. Build an improvisation based upon the act of greed or the result of a greedy action. (All My Sons)

8.
SELF

Self improvement is a truly driving force. Build an improvisation on the idea of the pursuit of self improvement. (The Firm)

9.
DREAM

Build a scene based upon the belief in the American Dream or the failure of the Dream. (Death Of A Salesman)

10.
LIFE

Life as it is may not be always appreciated. Create an improvisation based upon appreciating life as we live it. (Our Town)

11.
CHANGE

An improvisation is to be created on the breakdown of morals in changing America. (Streetcar Named Desire)

12.
GAMES

An improvisation is based on the games people play when they become fearful of facing reality of life. (Who's Afraid of Virginia Woolf?)

Note: Titles are included to illustrate how a significant theme is put into a play form, which are familiar to the theatre student.

However, the improvisations are to be your creation as you use these significant themes. These are forces that move you in your daily lives and affect you in everything you do. Use titles only as guidelines.

CHAPTER SIXTEEN

REGION OF THE SUBCONSCIOUS

The fundamental objective of our psycho-technique is to put us into a creative mood in which our subconscious will function naturally on stage. The elements in our approach to our art will teach us the indirect method to approaching the subconscious and just giving ourselves up to its power.

Before we are enveloped by the subconscious our feelings are seemingly true. After we are within the realm of the subconscious we have sincerity of emotions; emotions which are true, natural, logical, believable. At such times, a creative artist feels his own life in the life of the role and the life of his role seems identical with his own personal life. The two lives will merge. At that point, we are living the part. The actor will sense just what is right and true and normal, when the condition and state of mind are reached; when the actor simply feels "I am."

We use a conscious psycho-technique to prepare the approach to the region of the subconscious. To reach this state of mind, the actor is aided by achieving an inner freedom as well as physical relaxation. We are reminded of the importance of concentration of attention which allows us to focus on objects of interest, and the elements which fall naturally into place when in the appropriate creative mood. In addition, we are reminded of the importance of the super-objective and the through line of dramatic action leading to it. In short, the actor must have in mind everything that can be consciously controlled, all the elements we have valued. They will lead to the subconscious.

We are cautioned, however, not to over work any element in the acting process, for it may lead dangerously close to forced results and even mechanical acting. This, then, will lead to a chain of action which will destroy all we have been seeking in the way of the art of living the role.

There are danger signs of which an actor must be constantly aware:

a. Vagueness of the theme or super-objective of the play;
b. Unclear objectives or intentions in each beat, scene or act;
c. Uncertainty of the through line of dramatic action or spine;
d. Misunderstanding or altering of the given circumstances;
e. Adding unrelated physical or psychological actions;
f. Incorrect tempo-rhythm of psycho-physical elements;
g. Weak voice or unclear speech.

When you walk into your space as an actor, you must know who you are as a character. You must know where you come from, what you want at any moment and what are the obstacles in the way of getting it. You must also know why you want it and what you will do after you get it. Know when you are entering into a space and why you are entering. It is important also to know with whom you are dealing and know all about them as well. Nothing is to be left to chance even for a moment.

Stanislavski has an impressive image of the creative process. The father is the author. The mother is the artist pregnant with the role. The child is the role to be born.

CHAPTER SIXTEEN
ACTING EXERCISES

1.
CONNECTING WITH THE PAST

Actors are to find a comfortable space on stage in a quiet environment and within their own circle of attention. Each is to drift back into his early life until an object, such as a treasured toy, comes to mind. The space, too, will come to mind, which the actor will begin to see in detail, allowing him to touch, hear, smell, taste the environment of his past life. When the object becomes clearly defined in the actor's mind, he will begin to touch it and work with it as in the past, leading to emotional and sense recall of his earlier involvement, triggering other elements which will arise from the subconscious.

It will be interesting to note if unplanned elements are triggered and come into the actor's inner life to re-kindle feelings of the past.

2.
CONNECTING WITH A VALUED POSSESSION

Actors are to sit comfortably on stage in a quiet atmosphere. (May be done with single actor in order.) The actor is to bring to mind one of his (her) most valued personal object. With his inner motive forces at work, the actor is to begin working with the object in space and lead him into a private moment of involvement. The group of actors may be given liberty to use the space as needed. Solo actors may use space at will. All elements are to fuse and lead to the sub-conscious.

Variation: Each actor may actually bring in a valued object to work this exercise. The actor is then to transform the space into a truly existing space in his life. The action is to be taken and developed until completion, hopefully eliciting elements of the sub-conscious.

3.
IN MY SOLITUDE

Actor is to enter his space on stage and to sit quietly draining his mind of all pre-conceived ideas. From a total state of relaxation, the actor is allowed to dwell on his personal life until a particular circumstance becomes a key point. He will connect with the elements of the circumstance until he feels compelled to move and speak.

Employing mind, will and feeling, the actor is to add a problem of a severe degree to the circumstance. This should indeed heighten the moment.

4.
IMMOBILITY TO ACTION

Selecting a quiet space on stage, the actor is to stand (or sit) totally immobile. He (she) is to remain motionless. The actor is to allow a scenario to develop in which immobility is completely justified. The evolving circumstance is to maintain this motionless state as long as possible even as the inner action continues to move him WITHIN. Only when further development dictates will external physical action take place. Words may be spoken when and if needed.

5.
IMPOSED PHYSICAL ACTION TRIGGERS INNER LIFE

The director (or the actor on stage) calls out for a specific physical stance to be assumed by the actor. The actor follows the command and in detail assumes the stance which is to be held for any length of time until the actor justifies the position. At that moment, the actor will allow his inner creative state to inspire physical movement and possible dialogue.

Examples: Hands extended fully upward - Actor possibly reaching for object.

> Position on knees - Imploring of someone; God?
> Hands to ears - Shutting out some horrible sounds, etc.
> Fetal position - Terrible fear of .....?
> Hand extended forward - Begging....or.....?

There are endless possibilities all stemming from some inner element to be triggered by any position.

6.
FREE ACTION - FREEZE AND JUSTIFY

Group is on stage. All are to free their minds and asked to move with total abandon, bending spine, reaching to floor and ceiling, to far walls, twisting and turning, as they continue to empty their minds. They are to explore all possible movements without repeating any of them.

Director calls "freeze" and all movement ceases into a freeze. Each actor is to then allow his imagination to immediately justify the position he is in, even being caught in the middle of an action.

Director may then ask each to tell us what he (she) is doing, as the actor remains in that position. (There are endless possibilities as each responds to his inner life experience or pure imagination.)

7.
TOUCHING THE PAST

You sit comfortably in your space allowing yourself to relax and reflect on your life. Recall perhaps the first object you ever encountered in your young life. Let yourself move along thinking of items which were important to you as the years went by. Touch each of the items in detail, associating feelings fitting into the moment, seeing the space about you in the period, hearing sounds belonging to the moment, seeing and feeling the presence of dear members of your family, friends, pets and anything else that comes into your mind. The list of objects may be endless, as will be the list of associations which come to mind with each object. Just go with it until you reach the recent past and then the present.

8.
CONTEMPLATION

Enter a space familiar to you. Pour a drink then sit and contemplate the circumstance which comes into your mind. Let it take you to any direction. Do not force the moment, but relax and let the elements take over.

9.
HOME

Approach your home, open the door, enter and touch specific things which are familiar part of your life. Let your mood determine the action as you enter doors, climb stairs, open closets, cabinets, shed clothing, adjust items, read mail, etc. Feel your space completely and let the inner life develop and move you to acton.

10.
AGE

Take a moment to decide on a character of any age but your own. You are to create the circumstance as you develop a truthful inner life for the age of character you have imagined. Work in objects belonging to the age group depicted as well as costumes, locations and circumstance.

11.
PIN POINT

Actor sits and focuses attention on a very small item, such as a ring, locket, key, tiny photograph, a lock of hair, ear ring, wrist watch, a signature, etc. The actor must deal with the very small object in a small circle of attention.

Then, the circumstance adjusts and the actor's attention is directed to the area of the walls. It alters further and his attention pin points on an object in near distance. Then, it moves to the horizon. The development takes his attention to beyond the horizon and into space or into his head. It finally returns to the small object and the circle closes about him. All must be justified and connected.

12.
PERSONAL LOSS

The actor is to recall an event in his life when an object of considerable personal value was lost. He is to re-create the experience in a brief but detailed improvisation allowing him to be in touch with his inner feelings as he relives the event. The actor may be able to explain the feelings being experienced and even where in his body he feels the emotions. (See exercise below.)

13.
BLENDING WITH LIFE OF CHARACTER

When the actor successfully recalls the emotions in the above exercise, he is asked to select a scene from a play where the feelings of the character are similar to those of his personal experience. He is to then enter the stage and present the designated scene which will trigger similar inner life emotional responses. The actor will note the blending of truthful experiences with created truth of the stage experience of his character.

PART TWO

BUILDING A CHARACTER
PHYSICAL ASPECTS OF A ROLE
WITH EXERCISES

CHAPTER ONE

PHYSICAL QUALITIES OF A CHARACTER

Many actors find difficulty in building a character in physical terms. The process is valued for one must find a form of characterization which relates to the image conceived by the playwright so as to convey to observers its inner life. Thus, the actor is to learn to use the body, voice and manner of speaking, walking and movement of every dimension in order to truly express what is being felt within the character being created.

Stanislavski has stated that "the external characterization explains and illustrates and thereby conveys to your spectators the inner pattern of your part." By thoroughly knowing the inner life of your character, the physical qualities of a character being created will emerge without difficulty.

To encourage the physicalization of a character, the actor should strive for freedom of mind and body so as to be open for those valued adjustments which will take place, often without the actor's awareness. Actors and directors are familiar with those perfectly justified physical actions which occur when a performer is truly living the part. The eyes may continue to squint when one is struggling for a thought or a solution to a problem; or one may slouch with drooping shoulders and listless arms hanging downward when burdened with problems of life. Very often, such physical actions develop as the actor builds his character and evolve quite naturally. These are only a sample of the varied and limitless physical actions discovered by the multitude of characters being portrayed on stages in the theatre world.

There is, however, the need also to seek physical actions from the world around you as you attempt to find a way to physicalize the inner thoughts, feelings and visions of your character. You may find that deepening your voice brings you closer to the inner life of your character, or applying a beard, or a limp.

The Hunchback of Notre Dame would not have been as effective if the character were to be simply short. The twisted spine certainly fits his astounding character. The delicate limp of Laura in the Glass Menagerie exactly suited her fragile, crippled view of herself. And the deformed King Richard III is perfectly physicalized as he carries on his evil plots and murders in Shakespeare's masterpiece.

But subtleties can be equally effective for the simplest physical adjustment will help to create the external form of your character if it is reflecting the inner qualities. Stanislavski shows that dropping one eye lid makes a squint-eyed character. An actor has no difficulty imagining characters with that "squint-eyed" view of life. He reveals how a swollen lip will distort the mouth, changing the appearance quite vividly and altering the speech, an effective adjustment for specific characters.

Stanislavski goes on to illustrate the effect of turning toes inward, or outward, postures of arms and legs, shoulders, chin, and cheeks (reminding us of Brando in The Godfather). He states that external adjustments will have a bearing on feelings as well.

CHAPTER ONE
ACTING EXERCISES

1.
REGAL WALK

Physical characteristics will contribute to the spectator's understanding of the inner life of a character in circumstances created by the playwright. Assume that you are a character who is proud of your accomplishments as regal head of state. Address your imagined staff members as you walk from point to point in your quarters, noting how you carry yourself as you convey your self confidence and leadership qualities.

2.
BURDENED

Your character has aged, feels tired and burdened with the problems you are facing. Your road sales trips have become less successful, resulting in loss of commissions. Your heavy bags of sale items remain full due to lack of sales. They seem to get heavier with each hour. With such results, you will not be able to hold on to this job. Make an entrance into your home after a dismal trip, carrying your bags in each hand and allow your movements to illustrate your psychological state.

3.
SLY AND VILLAINOUS

A character possessing evil, sly, murderous tendencies is to be portrayed by you. Perhaps it is one such as the villainous and scheming Iago. Consider physical characteristics which will allow you to illustrate the distorted thinking and destructive behavior of the character.

4.
INSPIRING LEADER

Select justified physical characteristics befitting a confident and successful corporate leader as he meets with his division head to inspire greater output based on their prior achievement. He moves familiarly among them, returns to his desk to sign important memos, stands and moves about in a jovial and buoyant manner, then sends them on their way.

5.
TROUBLED PAST

The character you are to portray is guilt ridden, troubled by past experiences, fearful of possible disclosure, fragile in nature yet needful of love and acceptance. This complex character would be a challenge for any performer, yet, the Blanche role in Streetcar Named Desire is very much this kind of person and a joy to portray. Select delicate and simple but effective physical actions for this appealing acting role.

6.
FRAGILE QUALITY

Mindful of Laura Wingfield's psychological condition in The Glass Menagerie, select physical actions to depict her fragile, delicate and translucent nature.

7.
PHYSICAL ACTIONS LEAD TO INNER LIFE

Actors have encountered experiences where physical actions evoke an active inner life, exciting the imagination and elicit feelings which are found to be quiet appropriate for the character. Thus, it is suggested that the actor drop one eye lid, to become a squint-eyed person. Inspired by the imagination, the actor is to illustrate in a brief scene on stage the kind of character which emerges.

8.
SPINE DISTORTION

External physical adjustments will readily elicit impromptu dialogue and evoke feelings and an active inner life. Create a scene with a partner. Your spine, however, is severely distorted, affecting your walk and body movement as well as your psychological make-up. At no point is the topic of diologue to include the condition of your spine. See if your distorted spine will initiate a distorted and twisted view of your character's life. Certainly the imagination may lead one in this direction of character development.

9.
TOOTHSOME!

With a cloth or tissue, dry the inside of your upper lip and allow the lip to be drawn so as to expose your upper teeth. Let this free your imagination to conceive of a character with such a physical condition. Enter into a situation alone or with a partner and permit free use of dialogue.

10.
TOE THE MARK!

Develop an exaggerated way of turning your feet inward with toes directed toward each other while walking and sitting or standing. Allow a character to develop in your imagination from this physical adjustment. Add who, what, where and create an improvisation.

11.
CHEEKY!

Place wads of cotton inside each cheek to distort face and voice. Allow this physical characteristic to influence the psychological element of a character. Develop a brief improvisation with a partner.

12.
GIMPY!

Your character has a slight limp. Consider a circumstance whereby the limp is a symbol of the psychological nature of the character. Enter into an improvisation with a partner, adding who, what, where.

13.
SILENCE!

Without dialogue, each actor is to select a physical characteristic which best defines his character's inner life. The character may be an original reaction or from a play being rehearsed. The actors are to move about the stage freely performing only physical actions in character.

14.
PUNCHY

Your character seems to forcibly impose his ideas on to partners, seemingly to jab them into the minds, souls and bodies of the listener.

At the same time, you seem to tense your hands into fists and they punctuate the air as you talk and walk.

The psycho-physical element must be balanced and cliché action must be avoided.

15.
PIERCING

Being a self-assured character, you want to pierce the mind of your partner with your ideas. To stress the point, you find your self using your index finger which you point in the direction of your object (partner or idea). For emphasis, you pound away on your partner's chest with your index finger as you insist upon making your point.

16.
CRIPPLED

You have determined that your character is not a fully sound individual, facing life with serious deficiencies. In fact, you believe the character to be psychologically crippled. It is thus determined by you that the deficiency is manifested by a crippled leg, arm or spine. It may be extreme, being careful of cliché, or subtle, hardly visible to the observer. The truthful interpretation of the role will lead you to the right choice of the physical extent of characterization.

17.
BREATH OF FIRE

The dimension of your character's nature is such that you believe that the very air he breathes is foul. In fact, his inner nature is such that even the air you exhale is fouled by your inner life. You may, therefore, find that when you exhale, you infect your surroundings with contamination stemming from your inner poisons. Your mouth is widened to take in more air with which to foul your partner(s) or your space.

18.
UNSEEING

A study of your character reveals you do not see things fully or clearly as other characters. It may be that your character lacks the vision or intellect to comprehend fully. Eye glasses may become the physical expression of your condition, or diminished vision without glasses, or even a blindness in one eye. Try that characterization with which you feel most comfortable after exploring all possibilities.

19.
NOSEY

Things which other people do interest your character. Even their personal and private matters become important to you and you may want to move into their lives, becoming, so to speak, nosey. Your nose becomes your focal point as you seem to see, touch, feel your way, and smell your way through life situations. The movements are, of course, subtle and in perfect harmony with your character's inner life.

20.
HEAR, HEAR!

Listening is the main element in the life of your character. You have determined that the character you are portraying places great value on things heard; sounds, words, plots, discussions, private matters, speeches, instructions, etc. You send out rays with your ears, making them super-sensitive to sounds. Your ears become sensitive receivers of rays eminating from the sound source. As you sit or walk through space or stand opposite your partner, your ears gravitate toward your object causing your head to turn slightly as one ear and then the other seeks out the source of sound.

21.
EARTHY

The psychological make-up of your character is such that you feel you are in touch with the earth. You are either low-bred, or earthy in other aspects of life. You are drawn downward toward the earth. You find it is easy for you to slouch, bend, or stoop as you encounter the circumstances of your character life, rarely, if ever, standing up-right.

22.
ASTRAL

Your character seems to have lofty ideas, with high aspirations, perhaps exhalted. It will be easy for you to walk upright, elevating yourself while seated or standing, drawing your energy from the stars above. All movements will be light, airy, flowing and lofty. Even your speech will become breathy, airy, light and free.

23.
HUNGRY!

Food seems to be important to your character, or the devouring of elements of your character's environment. Your stomach may become your center of energy as you go through your play situation wanting to satisfy that hunger. You stand or walk with your stomach, perhaps, sending out rays of energy or receiving rays from objects of importance. And it may seem that the stomach protrudes to a degree and leads the way as you penetrate your space hungering in its fashion.

24.
TWISTED?

The inner life of your character appears to be off center and possibly a bit twisted in his perspective of life. It seems to affect your mouth, which becomes slightly twisted while talking or in repose, in perfect harmony with the degree of psychological dis-orientation.

CHAPTER TWO

COSTUME FOR CHARACTER DEVELOPMENT

Stanislavski reminds us that each of us is capable of playing a thousand variations of our self. With the portrayal of any character, one must not lose the sense of being still himself. The actor becomes to a limited degree his own observer at the same time that the greater part of him becomes the character. Thus the character is derived from the actor's own nature. He divides himself, as it were, into two personalities. One continues as the actor, the other develops as the created character. The duality must not, of course, impede the creative work.

Finding physical characteristics to more clearly reflect the newly created inner life of the character not only includes body movements, gestures, distortions, voice quality, etc, but also dressing the character appropriately. The costume designer is as much an artist as others who have responsibility of bringing to life the author's creation.

A character being created by the actor is to be envisioned in a costume which illustrates the inner life. The actor may not always have access to the valued presence and advice of a costume designer. It becomes essential for the actor to understand the color of his character, the costume of the period, the psychological make-up of the character, the status of the character in the given circumstance, and the conditions which exist. Even the fabric of the costume will be determined by all the circumstances of the character's life.

Just looking at a costume will excite the imagination of an actor. The viewing of an old morning coat, its faded color covered with spots and dust mixed with ashes might evoke an image of an old man looking like a ghost. Looking at the coat, one would tend to imagine a particular hat, gloves, old shoes and even wig and make-up. Images of a sinister character seem to evolve.

Is Willy Loman dressed nattily, or could he be wearing a suit which is somewhat too large, a bit frayed and tired-looking? If the costume is to depict his physical and psychological condition, the actor will see that the job is too big for him, and he is too old and tired to carry on the job. The shine is gone from his shoes, and his hat is rumpled if we picture his condition properly. His props, too, illustrate his condition, thus his salesman bags are much too heavy and also frayed.

A costume can arouse the subconscious life of an actor portraying a character. Upon donning a top hat, black bow tie and tails plus a cane, one gains the impression of a sophisticated gentleman. Apply a flower to his lapel, and the imagination soars.

On the other hand, Blanche in Streetcar Name Desire can easily be seen in the delicate, soft and light colored fabric perhaps in pastel shades, styled like the southern belle image she strives to maintain.

The costume often is seen to affect the walk as well as the speech as it blends into the psycho-physical make-up of the character. The costume lends another dimension to the truthful creation of a character as it is presented to a viewing audience.

CHAPTER TWO
ACTING EXERCISES

1.
MASQUERADE!

Each actor is to enter the stage with a costume completely depicting the nature of the character, its inner life, condition, circumstance, time period, etc.

2.
WHAT DO YOU SEE?

An assortment of costumes will be placed on stage. A designated person will exhibit one costume at a time, allowing actors to describe the kind of person seen wearing such a costume. Seeing the costume only suspended on a hanger, the imagination must freely envision the time period, place, setting, character, circumstance, etc. Even the stage setting and personal props may emerge in the minds of the observers. To carry it further, actors may choose to don a particular exhibited costume and create an improvisation for the ensemble.

3.
YOUR CHOICE

Partners are selected for scene improvisations. They are sent to the costume room to choose a costume for each of them. The costume will trigger their imagination. By deciding who, what, where, when, they will don costumes, acquire personal props, appropriate set pieces for their improvisations presented to the ensemble.

4.
DESIGNING THE COSTUME

Selecting a well known play, the ensemble will contribute ideas leading to the design of each costume worn by each character in the familiar play.

They are to include color for each character. The fabric must also be appropriate, as well as patterns, style, time period, etc.

5.
DRESSING THE CHARACTER

The actor is to make a full study of the character to be portrayed in the play being rehearsed for stage production. When thoroughly familiar with the character's circumstance and inner life, the actor is to conceive of an appropriate costume, accessories, make-up, hair style, personal props, etc. This will be done with permission of the director and costume co-ordinator, of course. As a learning exercise, the actor will advance his awareness of all artistic dimensions of the production. In the process, the actor will learn that lighting design and color as well as stage setting colors will contribute to the character's final fabric and color choices. All must be in harmony with the director's concept and interpretation of the playwright's creation.

6.
THE FABRIC OF CHARACTER

Each actor is to procure and display a piece of fabric which will best illustrate the psychological nature of the character in mind or to be performed on stage. Color and pattern designs will also be considered. It is probable that a delicate character would wear delicate fabric, while a colorful character would wear bright colors normally, etc.

7.
COMPLETE THE PICTURE

While wearing typical casual rehearsal clothing, actors are to perform a scene on stage from a classic American or European play. The ensemble as spectators, upon viewing the scene in its entirety, will be asked to describe the costume of each character, the accessories, hair styles, personal props, make-up, set pieces, stage setting, colors, fabric, additional physical adjustments, voice adjustments, etc.

8.
POT LUCK!

The director will distribute costume items to each actor in the ensemble; a royal garment to one actor, a cape to another, a top hat to another, a gown to an actress, a torn coat to another, a uniform to a person, ragged pants to another actor, an old hat, a fedora, a slit skirt, a shawl, etc. Each actor will then conceive from the one item given, a full character in a circumstance imagined by the actor. It will then be left to the director to have each actor reveal the full nature of the character, its inner life, background, additional costume items, props, setting, etc, and stage each of the scenes for the ensemble.

9.
ACCESSORIES

A collection of accessories will have been made by the director or stage manager prior to the session. It will then be presented to the ensemble, each of whom will comment on the items. Their imagination will lead them to envision the character wearing such an accessory, the nature of the circumstance, the costume that might be worn by the character along with the accessory, etc. They may consist of ear rings, eye glasses, bracelets, wrist watches, bill folds, brief cases, canes, umbrellas, necklaces, rings, credit cards, etc. The actors will then take any item in the collection, and with an active imagination develop an improvisation by adding who, what, where, when, etc.

10.
SEEING THE CHARACTER AND SETTING

Actors are to present a scene for a normal scene-study assignment. Since scenes are often staged in casual clothing, time will be provided for each actor to define the character, its inner life, the circumstance and problem of the scene, the costume envisioned, the accessories to join the costume, colors, fabric, style, time period, set pieces, stage design, lighting, etc. Following this description, the scene will be presented to the ensemble. Observations upon completion of the scene will include items earlier described as well as scene content.

11.
CHARACTER DIMENSIONS

To your established character, add a cane, a vest with watch fob and chain, a monocle, lorgnette, fan or parasol. Use such items to add interesting dimensions to your role. They will also affect one's inner life as well to further the interesting character development.

CHAPTER THREE

CREATING THE PHYSICAL IMAGE

To create a true physical image of a character, the actor should study features and characteristics of human types by way of keen observation. He should then learn to uses his own emotions, sensations, instincts even when "inside" another human spirit. This obviously demands a highly refined technique and a great sense of artistry so the character being portrayed will emerge from the actor. The actor must avoid any degree of overacting as he strives for the physical image of a character.

Actors of quality, performing artists, must create an image on stage by using characterizations which enable them to become truly incarnate, to take the human form of the role being portrayed. This may be accomplished by avoiding a purely external imitation of a character. As in any art form, it is advisable for actors to be reminded that copies are not works of art. Search for the elements of character within yourself.

Learn to use your body, your voice, a manner of speaking, walking and moving to enable you to create a form of characterization which reflects the image conceived by the playwright. Without achieving this form, you will not do justice to the writer's creation, nor will you be able to convey to an audience the character's inner, living spirit.

Without an external form, neither your inner characterization nor the spirit of your image will reach your audience. Your truthful characterization defines and reveals the inner pattern of your role to the spectator.

By devoting sincere effort in discovering the full dimension of your character, you will identify the appropriate inner values of the role you are to portray. This knowledge of the inner life of your character will help you to create a physical image more correctly than by other approaches to the role.

Most actors admit to the difficulty of discovering a physical image of a character being portrayed. Most often, they become confused due to the many possible images which cross their minds, or due to seeing many portrayals on stage of classic characters. However, one of the most helpful approaches is from within. The physical materialization of a character to be created emerges pretty much on its own once the right inner values of your character have been established.

While playing the character, there will still be a foundation based upon not losing the sense of being yourself. The character becomes a part of you, being derived from your own nature; sort of a duality.

The actor should learn to trust himself. The character you build will have you as the foundation. Characterization accompanied by your real transposition is indeed a sort of re-incarnation of yourself. Thus, all actors who are artists, the creators of images, should seek characterizations they feel they can give a bodily form to which can come from themselves. It is the most productive, most honest, and safest approach for the performing artist.

CHAPTER THREE
ACTING EXERCISES

1.
FLOATING HANDS

Ensemble on stage in a quiet space. Standing in your own space, you will begin to move your hands and fingers before you in a soft and gentle manner. The atmosphere before you is fluid as perhaps water would be. You feel the water before you and you sense it needs to be calmed by you. You move your hands and fingers thus to calm the waters about you. The water has expanded until you note you are entirely surrounded by a huge body of water extending to the horizon. You have the capability of bringing calmness to the water by simply softening your hand movements about you. The soothing, rippling effect extends outward from your hands and you feel you control the water out to the horizon and you are bringing a placid calmness to the entire atmosphere of water about you.

2.
RIPPLES

As you reach a level in the prior exercise when you feel you have a gentle control of the water and you have brought it to a state of placid peace, you begin to move your fingers so that little ripples are made in the calm surface of the water. The ripples extend gently outward from your center of energy slowly out to the horizon. You watch the ripples as they move away from you in ever widening circles, farther and farther, rhythmically dancing on the surface toward the horizon. You create ripple after ripple, enjoying the effect of your movement on the quiet water.

3.
WAVES

Having created ripples on the placid surface of the water about you in prior exercise, you highten the movement of your hand in the water. Now the ripples are transforming into waves. They flow with energy outward from you to the horizon. Continue making waves until the director brings you slowly downward to ripples again and then to end.

4.
TEMPESTS!

You are immersed in a large body of water as in prior exercise. You have stirred the waters with strong hand movements into waves flowing outward toward the horizon. With hands and body movements, your energy and tempo will increase until you are vigorously moving the atmosphere of water with your hands and body to the point where the waves are becoming very active and even mountainous. As you expel your breath, you are causing high winds to agitate the mountainous waves into a tempest.

125

Nature, which you now control, is unleashed and all powerful. When reaching your peak, you decrease your energy and slowly bring a calmness to the atmosphere. Your movements again become soothing and gentle and then to a halt.

5.
WATER AND SPACE

Being immersed in a large body of water, you float peacefully in the water feeling its soothing quality. You then become one with the water as it becomes you. You feel its fluid, rhythmic quality. Above you is sky. Soon, you blend with sky and become all of water and space.

6.
HAND PROPS AS CHARACTER EXTENSIONS

Each actor either selects a prop or is given one. Before going on stage, the hand prop is to be studied until it triggers in his mind a type of character who might use such an object. With imagination at work, the actor conceives of a circumstance and a character and creates a scene where the prop plays an important part.

This exercise may be performed solo or with partners.

7.
COSTUMES AND CHARACTER TYPES

Each performer is to search for any costume which might trigger his imagination. The costume is then to be worn as the actor conceives of a character type who might wear such a costume. The circumstance is created and an improvisation is staged briefly to illustrate the connection between a character, what he wears and his inner life.

8.
STAGE SET-PIECE AND CHARACTER TYPE

A stage setting is suggested by the director or by actors who are to perform an improvisation. Explicit details may be included at the discretion of the director. The actors are then to conceive of types of characters who would be associated with such an environment. Who, what, where, when and why are established and the improvisation takes place.

Stage set may vary from a homeless tramp locale, to bench in a park, to street corner, to roof top, living room, bed room or castle, etc.

9.
PAST OR FUTURE

Actors are given a choice of improvising a scene involving characters five, ten or more years younger. They are also given the option of selecting characters ten, twenty or fifty years older.

A circumstance is imagined and an improvisation is performed.

10.
PHYSICAL ELEMENT DEFINES CHARACTER

The director suggests by a description on a card a physical characteristic. The actor builds a character and situation based on these few words. Example: Gimpy left leg; or Blind in one eye (or both); Nervous tick in the neck; Hunched back; Useless left arm; Walks with both toes pointing inward; Can not bend either leg; Walks with chin jutting forward; Elbows flap like wings when walking; Shoulders far forward when standing or walking, etc.

Actors will stage an improvisation based on inner life suggested by such physical characteristics.

11.
JUSTIFICATION

Actor is given a physical action to execute and build a brief scene letting the physical action be the dominant action as it triggers the inner life and is totally justified from within. Some examples follow: Pound fist on table. (The gang leader is trying to put down a possible riot by demanding their attention.) Knock on door. (You see smoke.) Crawl on floor. (The combat soldier is approaching a sniper.) Climbing. (Rescuer is trying to reach a person about to jump, etc.) Add; search, hide, fall, stop suddenly, float, swim, jump, stumble. Actor is to work in who, where, when, why, and build scene.

12.
AIDS

Your character has been tested HIV positive. Deal with yourself and characters as needed in a space created by you.

13.
BAG LADY

Your character is dressed as a street type of New York, carrying a bag and searching each trash can for objects of value for her survival.

14.
HOMELESS

Man is seated and appeals to people passing for help. He is dressed in worn clothing and has a blanket. Build on these physical elements.

15.
TOGETHER

Bag Lady and Homeless man chance to encounter. Build a scene on these characters, revealing a totally different dimension of these human characters living this unfortunate circumstance.

16.
FIGHTER MUSICIAN

A battered fighter with much ring experience holds on to his valuable possession, a violin. He can not play it, for his hand has been broken in his recent match which he lost to the champion.

17.
ATMOSPHERE IN GROUP SCENES

When rehearsing group scenes or even brief walk-on or cross-overs, have each actor write a created history of his character, such as age, relationship to main characters, objectives, early life experiences, likes and dislikes, physical characteristics, personality traits, etc. Allow them to create and then to verbalize inner monologues during certain rehearsals. This may be accomplished in small groups, individually, or in full groups. New levels of energy will be discovered which will enhance any group scene by permitting them to go well beyond their performance level of activity. Allow them during such sessions to argue, exchange ideas, laugh, shout and even fight. Not only will they have fun discovering the full life of their characters, but when performance takes place, their silent activity will excite the atmosphere of each scene they are in. It will heighten their character awareness, deepen their involvement and lend dimension to the play. (A favorite Stanislavski exercise.)

CHAPTER FOUR

THE FLEXIBLE PHYSICAL INSTRUMENT

Most people do not know how to make use of their physical apparatus as it is. They neither know how to develop their body nor keep it in good working order. Thus, physical shortcomings become very apparent on stage for the actor is working literally under a magnifying lens.

Actors need strong bodies which are developed in good proportion. A fine process for developing and maintaining a good physical instrument is to employ gymnastics, dance as well as varied exercises. When defects are found in the body, they must be corrected. Strive to develop a strong and healthy body. Live correctly to keep body and mind in excellent condition. Exercise regularly to make the body mobile, flexible, expressive and sensitive.

The actor should be aware that proper nutritious food is essential in developing a healthy body, thus, make it a practice to avoid the common "junk" foods. Good food along with exercise and proper rest and an appropriately healthy life style are essential for the fine-tuned physical instrument required of successful actors.

Avoid theatrical tricks and clichés as well as peculiar acting habits and bodily mannerisms. No matter how good or bad they are or seem to be, they are only surface substitutes for real artistic feelings and emotions.

The sensitive actor and artist is a being who is endowed with ability to see and experience things which are obscure to the average person. With his active and creative mind and expressive body, he is able to convey impressive ideas to the spectator. Since the actor's body and voice are the only physical instruments upon which he can play, he should protect them against all hostile elements.

The actor's body can be of value to him only when motivated by an unceasing flow of artistic impulses. Only then can it be more refined, flexible, expressive, sensitive and responsive to the subtleties which constitute the creative artist's inner life. The actor's body must be molded and re-created from inside. A sensitive body and a rich, colorful psychology are mutually complementary to each other.

Constantly enlarge the circle of your interest as an artist. Try to assume the psychology of persons of other eras by reading plays, historical novels and histories. Penetrate their thinking without imposing your modern views. Reject the idea that all people are the same.

Penetrate the psychology of different nations as well as the people around you toward whom you feel unsympathetic. While observing them, notice their movements, gestures, expressions and mannerisms. Since every human being is unique, notice what the differences are between you and every other individual, no matter how subtle. These differences are what make character differences on stage.

The actor must consider his body as an instrument for expressing creative ideas and must strive for attainment of complete harmony between body and psychology.

CHAPTER FOUR
ACTING EXERCISES

1.
THE FLUID BODY

The group is given instruction on performing simple gymnastics and to include stretching warm-ups, free movement, dance, somersaults, etc.

2.
DANCE AS A FORM OF EXPRESSION

The dance leader is to conduct exercises to music background and to include ballet positions and movement to jazz, to interpretative dance.

3.
NATURE AS GUIDE

Actors are on stage in a group and are asked to copy nature in physical movement. Using their own individual space, each is to follow the directions of a leader who guides them to use full body movement to fly like an eagle, float as a cloud, swim as a fish, move as a blade of grass in the breeze, flow as water, bloom as a flower, grow from seed to plant, walk like a duck or turkey, move as a bird, grow into a tree, move as a flame or smoke from a fire, etc.

To reach higher levels, the actor is encouraged to seek an inner life inspired by the object of nature.

4.
MACHINE IN MOVEMENT

Number one actor enters the stage and begins a movement which is to be continued throughout the exercise. A second actor will then join and add a counter movement to the first so they harmoniously work together. A third actor joins and adds another movement which blends into the existing movement. Each actor joins, one at a time, sensing the rhythmic movement of the "machine" being created and contributing to the whole movement. If the director asks for a sound, then actor number one begins a 'machine' sound and each will add a fitting sound to the machine movement. This continues until director calls a halt.

5.
MOVING ATMOSPHERE

On stage, the entire group is asked to believe that the body is surrounded by an atmosphere of density which can be moved by any part of the body.

When prepared, each actor is to begin moving the atmosphere first with fingers, then wrists, elbows, arms, shoulder(s), head, chest, back, hips, knees, ankles, toes, head, chin, stomach, etc.

The movement has a purpose in that each part of the body must move the atmosphere causing ripples in space. This is to avoid movement for the sake of movement alone. The goal is to seek total freedom to nearly the point of abandon.

6.
DO-BE-DOO! GIBBERISH

A scene is to be performed or an improvisation is to be created using only a simple gibberish sound so only emotional life is expressed with physical actions.

7.
HUMAN SCULPTURE

Ensemble is on stage, relaxed and free of human thought. Slowly they begin to move in broad, wide, sweeping actions, freeing themselves so legs and spine bend causing the body to work from depths of floor to heights of ceiling or sky. They become a substance in the creative hands of a spiritual artist as the actors twist and turn and gyrate from floor to sky, bending and stretching inward and outward. (This may be done with a tapping beat or even with music, but must not be dance.) They move slowly outward from a center point and then are drawn inward toward the center by the artistic force moving them.

As they close in toward center, the sculpture will begin to form. The first actor 'substance' which comes in contact with any part of another actor 'substance' must freeze in the position when contact was made. Others will begin to touch and freeze as their free movement attracts them toward center. The sculpture begins to take shape as each actor freezes when contact is made until the very last actor 'substance' connects itself to the sculpted piece. The freeze position is held briefly and then dissolves. They may do others.

8.
CENTER OF ENERGY

Cards are drawn by actors who find one word written; any part of the body from toe to head, from hands to knees, to elbows. That part of body will be the center of energy for the character you are to create. Develop an action, or improvisation, with dominant energy centered in that part of the body. If it is nose, the character penetrates the atmosphere with his nose, being perhaps nosey. If it is eyes, the character seems to perceive very clearly. If it is groin, the character may be a sensual character. If it is elbows, the character may flutter about like a chicken or turkey, etc. Build situations suited for the characters.

9.
MOVED BY FORCE

Forces of nature play upon your character which you develop into a scene with a partner. It is sweltering; it is very cold; you are stuck in the mud; lost in a rain forest; water is flooding the house; a fire is gutting your building; a blizzard renders you helpless, etc.

10.
FUN FORCES

With imagination, actors become pasta boiling, beans sprouting, corn popping, bread toasting, salad being tossed, bacon frying, eggs being scrambled, flowers blossoming, snowman melting, banana peeling, etc. Just have fun!

11.
FREEZE

Actors move in very free, big gestures as they free minds as well. At any point director calls for them to freeze! The position will trigger the imagination as each actor in turn tells what he is doing; praying, reaching, in a race, imploring, hiding, fearing, begging, etc. They will continue as often as director wishes.

CHAPTER FIVE

FLUID MOVEMENT

Exercise regularly in order to make the body flexible, pliable and fluid on stage rather than stiff and limited in movement. Only then can the actor's body become truly expressive and sensitive.

In any instance, the performing artist is to avoid any movement on stage which lacks inner content or purpose. Artificial poses of any sort should be avoided.

It has been determined that most human beings, and certainly this includes most actors as well, walk incorrectly. Most actors therefore must actually learn to walk correctly on stage. This is not to suggest tht the actor use a theatrical or stagey walk, but to walk easily, naturally, smoothly and lightly by simply keeping the body elevated and walking fluidly without "bouncing."

By those who have been seen to move well, their walking manner seems to fall into one of three commonly used patterns:

    a. The heel touches the floor first, which is most common, but the body is seemingly "lifted" in the area of upper torso in order to lighten the walk.

    b. The sole is planted on floor first a fraction before the heel touches down. The movement itself helps to "lift" the body to move lightly and fluidly.

c. Seen perhaps more with dancers, the toe touches floor first, followed quickly by the sole and then the heel.

Continued practice of walking patterns is suggested which will allow a subtlety to develop so that an observer will not notice which of the three patterns of walking is being used. Only a fluid lightness in the walk will be noted. Early exercises will reveal much awkwardness. Eventually, actors will note improvement and smoothness in their walk, much as athletes and military personnel as well as dancers move.

A common manner of achieving fluid movement is to imagine an element such as mercury flowing into any part of the body which is to move. The "mercury" then is allowed to flow gently into the next designated part of the body which is going to move. Exercising this process and perfecting it will result in graceful, fluid, appealing movement.

As a variation of the above movement exercise, let your attention focus and move in constant company with the current of energy associated with the "mercury," thus creating an endless, unbroken line of movement always essential to our art. Art originates in the very moment when that unbroken line of movement is established. And when energy travels along this unbroken line, that is the motion which creates fluency, the plasticity (as Stanislavski calls it) of body movement necessary to our art. Thus, the inner flow of energy-thought, feeling, content-forms the very foundation of movement.

This inner feeling of an energy passing through the body is often referred to as the sense of movement.

CHAPTER FIVE
ACTING EXERCISES

1.
FLUID MOVEMENT

Entire group may take place on stage. Each is to imagine that mercury is being poured into the finger tip. It is then allowed to course throughout the body, gradually letting it flow from finger tip, to hand, to wrist, through fore arm to elbow, etc.

The attention of the actor must be focused on the exact spot where the drop of mercury is located and moving at any given moment. The flow is to be un-interrupted, and the attention is to move in constant company with the current of energy. Thus, an endless, unbroken line of flow and energy will be maintained, as is often called for in this art.

2.
THE SENSE OF MOVEMENT

Actors are allowed to work in a group on stage and begin random movement to free selves of tension. Then, with inner motive forces inspired, the actor begins to move freely to express any feeling emerging from his inner life. The actor is encouraged to use every part of his body in communion with his inner thoughts and feelings as he expresses his mood freely with movement. (Music may be added softly to background.)

3.
EXPRESSIVE WALK

Actors are to walk easily and lightly on stage by sensing that the body is 'lifted' and suspended from above. Thus, the arms and legs will move, but the head will not appear to 'bounce.' This is similar to the military march movement. The heel begins the step. This is the most common walk. (In life, however, humans appear to 'bounce' when they walk.)

A second manner of walking smoothly is to plant first the sole of the foot, then followed by the heel. The body must be 'lifted' to permit this movement to take place, thus it is popular with dancers and actors. (Athletes know the value of this movement.) The walk becomes fluid and smooth. (Ballroom dancers know the value of this gliding movement.)

A third manner of walking is to allow the toe to touch the floor first, followed by the sole, and then the heel.

The director is to allow all actors to enter the stage and work with each of the three types of walking until it happens easily and naturally.

4.
WALKING ELEGANTLY IN CHARACTER

Actors are to be paired and assigned to improvise scenes involving character who will walk gracefully, imploying one of the three walking examples previously illustrated.

5.
MUSIC TO MOVE YOU

Without dancing, actors are on stage while music of an appropriate nature is playing in the background. Actors will simply move to the music as they express feelings generated by the music. They are to use every part of the body to express ideas.

6.
YOUR DAY

You are to conceive the entire day in the form of movement, condensing your day into two minutes of such movement. Do not plan or structure the movement. Be free to express any feeling you experienced during the day until the present moment and into your projected end of day.

7.
NATURE AND YOU

Select any part of nature which appeals to you most. It may be plant, animal, sea life, or any part of land, water or weather. Put your idea into brief movement freely and without structure.

8.
LIFE THEMES

Select a major life theme and design a brief moment of movement to present on stage. Some sample themes are; the American Dream, love makes the world go 'round, man's inhumanity, international conflict, loss of morality, pursuit of happiness, honesty, greed, illusion, harsh reality, jealousy, fight for peace, striving for success, etc.

9.
BEAST OR FOWL

Select an animal or bird which you may find interesting. Take on its life, its movement, its characteristics. Then find a brief scene in which the character you play may have a hint of the characteristics you discovered in the animal or bird.

10.
MUSICAL INSTRUMENT

Actor draws a card with a word denoting a musical instrument. Actor may actually find an appropriate musical passage featuring the instrument, or it may be played in the actors mind. He will not dance, but create movement inspired by the sound and feeling of the instrument.

11.
SYMPHONY OF MOVEMENT

Ensemble is on stage. A symphonic piece is to be played. The actors will have selected a particular instrument, or it may be assigned by the director. Thus, each actor is a different instrument. He is to move to the sound of the instrument as the symphony is being played. All will therefore move in harmony to the music selection.

CHAPTER SIX

CONTROL OF THE PHYSICAL INSTRUMENT

Every actor must be completely in control of his physical instrument. When creating a character, he must rid himself of all superfluous actions, movements, gestures of any kind. Excessive movements, expressions, gestures will only blur the design of the role being created by the performing artist. He is to employ physical action only to the extent it conveys the inner spirit of the role being portrayed.

Don't "tear a passion to tatters," says Hamlet to the Players, which is pure over-acting and must be avoided in performance. Yes, Stanislavski did encourage some over-acting in rehearsal in an attempt to rid actors of timidity or to seek new, unexplored levels of energy. But only for experimentation and never in performance.

Let the audience cry for the actor who sincerely experiences an inner torment. Such restraint becomes very effective. The very reduction of use of gestures, and being selective of their use, will be compensated by heightened inner intensity, expressive eyes revealing the inner soul of the character and a vibrant voice. Superficial gestures, expressions, movements will interfere with restraint and control and the true and natural state of the character in its given circumstance. Thus, the gestures which are selected for being right for the life of the character gain significance and strength in their use and remain totally relevant.

Restraint and control of the physical instrument by the actor will allow the character to build slowly, surely, naturally and truthfully. Art begins with slightest of touches; the most delicate and simple of actions.

Successful actors have shaped the beginnings of a character with subtlety in early scenes of a play. They then proceed in subsequent scenes to add delicately to the role, bit by bit, until all elements have gradually developed and are in place. This is possible only when an actor approaches the building of his character with control and restraint.

The actor should approach his moment on stage with calmness, ridding himself of every sentiment alien or obstructive to his role. He is not to peak to the highest levels of his emotions, but leave some in reserve. Allow the audience to be more affected, seemingly, than the actor. His energies should be more directed to within as he creates the truthful inner life of the character. Some great actors have said it simply, "Do less on the outside and more within."

There is great value in learning to underplay on stage. Overplaying any part of a role will interfere with restraint and control and the true natural state of an actor. With restraint and control, the actions of a character being portrayed gain immeasurably in significance, beauty and effect.

CHAPTER SIX
ACTING EXERCISES

1.
PANTOMIME DRESS-UP

Without the use of actual costumes, actors are to enter their created space with a circumstance in mind as well as a character. They must select each 'costume' article from a 'rack' and are to begin putting on each article of costume and dress as the character about to enter a projected scene on stage. Do not 'overplay' any movement.

Variation - Actors are to seemingly come off stage from a scene and disrobe article by article and replace costume items on the 'rack.'

There must be attention to detail without overdoing any gesture for the sake of 'telling' what article the actor is putting on to his character.

2.
PICNIC TIME!

Group on stage has arrived at a lake side picnic area. Each is to unpack his items and picnic lunch. Items are properly set up on blanket or table and they proceed to have their lunch in detail while enjoying the environment.

Details are of utmost importance without exaggeration. Taste, chewing, swallowing, feeling of thirst and hunger satisfaction, smelling, touch, hearing, must all come into their minds in a natural, truthful manner.

3.
TUG-OF-WAR

On stage, the group will be divided into two teams. The imaginary rope lies on the floor. The team will work in harmony as they, on command, reach for the rope and begin to pull (with each other) in competition with the opposing team.

Balance, movement in co-ordination and team work are essential.

4.
SAND CASTLES

The beach becomes the setting as each person uses sand, stones and shells to build a sand castle. Water, pail and scoop will become useful props.

5.
CYCLE OF LIFE

Group will lie on stage in a quiet mood of relaxation as they drain mind and body of human life. When ready, each person will begin the life cycle; first as a seed gestating, then birth, to crawling, to rising, growing through life phases to maturity and old age, then back to seed.

Subtle actions are encouraged without exaggeration as they proceed through each stage. Sound may not be necessary, although it may add a new dimension to the exercise.

6.
YOU AS PAINTER

The actor is to create color designs with body movements. They are to be large, sweeping, brightly colored designs in space, but with sensitivity and without exaggeration.

7.
CHARACTER GESTURES

Select a moment from the play you are doing where your character gestures are defined and unique. Sensing them as psychological gestures, explain and then illustrate what psychological elements initiate these gestures used by your character.

8.
ACTOR GESTURES

Actor is to evaluate his own gestures, possibly having a psychological implication, and select those which he finds are appropriate for the character. Illustrate your personal gestures in a brief moment on stage, then let the character demonstrate the use of the gestures in any given scene from the play you are staging.

9.
CHARACTER EMOTION

Without use of words, envision the emotional scale of the role you are portraying. You may move about the stage, but emphasis will be on sounds you emit as you experience moments in your character's life. Humming may be considered, but also sighs, groans, squeals, whistles, etc.

10.
FULL LIFE

The actor is to condense the entire life of the character in two minutes of movement without words. Movement will depict the life energy and idea of the character, not entrances and exits, or setting the table or pouring a drink. These are to be interpretative movements of concepts, feelings, conflicts, pleasures, celebration, etc.

11.
REACHING NEW DIMENSIONS

Some actors tend to be rather timid as they build the emotional life of a character. Stanislavski often encouraged overplaying in some rehearsals for such actors in order to take them to higher levels. Once having experienced the higher level (or overplaying) the actor could then be brought down to the required performance emotional life.

Select a volatile circumstance in a scene from a play in rehearsal. Heighten the event so that each character in the scene reaches an extreme level of emotional and physical action. Anger may become rage. Loudness may become a roar. Joy may become hysteria. Tenderness may become passion. New dimensions will be discovered in actors which may become productive.

CHAPTER SEVEN

MUSICALITY OF SPEECH

Your voice is your fortune! This observation is shared by many and especially in the world of theatre for the voice is the most important single
element an actor uses on stage. Every person in the audience must hear and
understand every word of the script projected from the stage and without
effort. That is an actor's primary obligation, to convey the spoken word
clearly to the last row of the theatre. That also means every part of every
word, such as each vowel, consonant and syllable.

Speech in the theatre is not unlike music. The playwright's text is seen as
a melody, or even a symphony or opera. The voice should be seen as the
delicate instrument it is. It should be trained with care in order to provide
the actor with clear pronunciation, sharp diction, vivid articulation and
strong projection. A fine actor's voice is like an instrument in a symphony,
such as a cello, oboe, violin, flute or brass.

The actor should feel responsible for piercing the very soul of each word
used in the role being portrayed. He is responsible not only for the sound
of the word but its image. He must allow the audience to see with their
inner vision the images he has developed out of his own creative imagination.

It is essential that the actor become familiar with common errors of speech,
such as telescoped beginnings, dropped endings, omitted letters or syllables, distorted sounds, lost words, etc. In addition, the actor must actually learn to hear properly, himself as well as others. Speech errors are so

common, most people are totally unaware of the errors begin committed in anyone's speech.

Members of the audience will lose interest when words are unclear. They lose their involvement in the events of the play on stage and become restless, look about, clear their throats, cough and check the time on their wrist watches. These elements are deadly to any stage play in progress. Thus, it is imperative that actors work at speaking correctly, even beautifully. It is known that a fine voice is indeed a beautiful thing to hear.

Vowels are the most resonant and sonorous of spoken sounds. Learn to deliver each sound openly and roundly. The vowels are A - E - I - O - and U. Their sounds are so appealing they are used very frequently in poetry and music.

The most pleasing consonants are M - N - L - R - V - Z - soft G and TH. They are appealing to the ear and are also used often in poetry and music. The less appealing, but necessary, stop consonants are B - D - and hard G - and W. The difficult plosives are P - T - K - and B.

Actors must learn to place their voice properly and support the spoken word with the diaphragm and not place it strainingly in the throat. Actually, even breathing correctly is a problem for some actors. Your voice is your fortune! Work at improving it.

CHAPTER SEVEN
ACTING EXERCISES

1.
SLOWLY DOES IT

Select a brief monologue to be spoken from the stage. As a mechanical exercise, speak each word very slowly. Enunciate the beginning, middle and end of each word, giving full value to each consonant and each vowel.

Most notable speech errors are distortion of sound, omission of letters and slurring of sounds.

2.
TONE THE INSTRUMENT

Exercise to free the tongue, palate, cheeks and jaw. Stretch and open the jaw slowly to a yawn position, moving the tongue about quickly and freely. With pure open tones, sound out fully each of the vowel sounds; A - E - I - O - U. Extend the sound of each, for the beauty of speech lies mainly in the vowel sounds. Repeat as often as time will allow. Exaggerate the muscle usage of jaw and lips, opening as much as possible.

The most pleasant sounding consonants are; M - N - L - R - V - Z - N - G and TH. Sound each fully and extend the tone, projecting strongly, noting that these consonants are almost as musical in quality as the vowels. Employ jaw, tongue, lips and cheeks with exaggerated usage to the point of distortion for the sake of exercising the instrument. Repeat as often as possible.

Allow time to work with and recognize the stop consonants; B - D - the hard G and W. Then the difficult plosives; P - T - K and B.

The remaining letters are lesser obstacles to speech clarity and sound.

3.
FACE IT

Lie on the floor and make sounds from the front of the face, as a sick person may sigh or groan.

With lips closed, let the sound almost tickle the lips, aiming the sound toward the nose as well. Become familiar with this part of the facial mask as being most helpful for resonant speech.

Slowly sound out all the vowels and sonorous consonants in this manner with a relaxed and well projected effort.

4.
DOUBLE TIME

When very slow speech becomes easy and natural, quicken the tempo of the words, over and over again. Then continue to increase the tempo until words are spoken in double time, yes, even faster, for the sake of exercise. Some plays will often call for very fast, but articulate, speech patter, and words must be sounded completely and clearly.

5.
CHANGING PATTERNS

Take sentences and speak them often, changing pauses and accent words to alter the meaning. As a variation, alter the volume.

6.
DIAPHRAGM SUPPORT

Place your hand firmly against your diaphragm. Speak the words of your monologue slowly as you place your speech so that the sounds are supported by your diaphragm, the muscle below the center of your rib cage.

7.
QUICK TIME

From the main stage, actor is to speak the lines of his role very rapidly, perhaps twice the speed called for. Emphasis will be on clarity of projection as the director places himself in the very last row expecting to hear every vowel and consonant of every word.

8.
RELEASE OF TENSION

Actors will lie on floor and speak all lines of the role. It will be noted that the position itself naturally releases tension and the voice finds its way to appropriate placement. Speech will be more resonant and mellow. Actors are to make an evaluation of the total speech mechanism in this position and attempt to achieve same quality while standing and speaking.

9.
VOWEL SOUNDS

While lying on floor, take deep breaths and sound out all vowels and sustaining each for about ten seconds or more; A, E, I, O, U.

10.
BREATHING AND CONSONANTS

While on the floor in a relaxed lying position, sound out all the sonorous consonants with one full breath, trying to extend the sound of each from eight to ten seconds each; M, N, L, R, V, Z, N, G, TH.

11.
TROUBLE! TROUBLE!

There are words which are nothing but trouble! Make a list of such words in each group of actors and work on them constantly to reduce the problem or even eliminate the trouble. The "H" is often omitted in all words such as where, when, what resulting in sounds such as ware, wen, wot, etc. Trouble words are often those ending in "T" such as that, which will sound like that! Others are caught, fat, fight, kite, and so many others where the speaker will omit the final consonant. Middle consonants are often distorted, such as little, which sounds like liddle; twenty, which becomes twenny; fated becomes faded, and fatal most often sounds like fadel, which may mean something in another country.

Laziness in speech has become so common that incorrect speech has become the norm for so many. Stage actors may become the only Saviour of the English language in America. Laziness has led to omissions in such expressions as last season, which is most often heard as lass season. East side is heard as eass side, while wess side takes the place of west side. Reconize is heard more often than recog-nize and goverment has replaced government, or so it seems.

CHAPTER EIGHT

THE SPOKEN WORD AND SUB-TEXT

Most people speak poorly but are unaware because they are accustomed to it. Their defects, therefore, are not known by themselves. Thus, actors must be made aware of their speech deficiencies to break poor speech habits. They have the responsibility of speaking words of the author which take on a heightened level of concern and interest, for on stage, words spoken are more acutely perceived.

In one's daily life, a person speaks of things seen, felt and experienced. On stage, however, the actor deals only with the imagination. Rehearsals and repetition tend to evaporate content of spoken text leading often to mechanical acting.

As we live our daily experiences, we generally listen because of interest and need. On stage actors often pretend to listen or else force themselves to listen which induces over-acting and cliché on the part of the actor.

Recitation of lines is not acting. Such recited lines lack life, truth or any kind of feeling. Therefore, the performing artist must truly listen to the partner and speak to the partner, not recite lines lifelessly. The spoken words must have sub-text, ideas, images, feelings which lie beneath each spoken word of the text.

Sub-text is the inwardly felt expression of a human being in a role which flows uninterruptedly beneath the words of the text, giving the words life, energy, inner patterns, circumstances, objects, meaning, feeling, etc. Actors should become so at ease and comfortable with the sub-text that, just as in life, the sub-text initiates the words of the play. The words will lead, then, to the super objective of the play.

Our feelings must reach down into the sub-textual stream to find the through-line of dramatic action, the spine of the play, which guides us to the all-important super objective.

The printed play form is not a finished piece of work until the actor brings it to life on the stage. That is his creative contribution to the art of theatre. The spoken word by the actor will arouse feelings, desires, thoughts, inner images, reflections of past, present and future.

Using the image of an ice-berg, the words of the play come from the author and may represent the tip of the ice-berg. The sub-text represents the very life of the play and it comes from the creative aspect of the actor at work in his art. This element represents the major part of the ice-berg which lies beneath the surface.

To hear is to see what is spoken of. So, speak each word to convey an image to your partner. Speak, therefore, to your partner's eye for him to see what you are saying. This requires that you know the author's given circumstance thoroughly in order to convey the appropriate ideas. The actor thus invents a whole motion picture of inner images, a running sub-text to be played out for the partner.

While speaking to your partner on stage, take the time to look into his eyes to note any re-action to what you are saying. Then pause, even wait if necessary to see the effect of your words on your partner. Isn't this done in life?

As in life, your partner must absorb your words, your ideas, your sub-text. You must infect your partner with your life. Actually insinuate yourself into his soul, and be infected in so doing! Your job as an artist is to instill your inner vision in others.

Know the play thoroughly and the author's given circumstances. And know your character fully, meaning his past, present and projected future.

Thus, you may be successful in truly making the words of the author your own.

On stage, your inner vision should be akin to the visions the character would have in the circumstance were you actually to live that life. This puts vitality, truth and life in your role. This is creating the inner life of the role, which is the goal of every successful actor. One needs a truly disciplined power of attention to bring about this level of artistry.

When pausing, and pauses can be very effective, fill such pauses with life action. They are called psychological pauses or pause accents. They become an eloquent silence indeed. Be mentally active during such pauses. Otherwise the through line of dramatic action is broken and the character actually may die for that period.

Proper speech, intonation, clarity, sub-text, psychological pauses, attitude, manner, feeling, all affect the actor and the partners in the given circumstance of a play. They give life to a play.

At this point the actor should be reminded that loudness of voice is not power. Rather, it is only shouting. The actor should use loudness rarely and judiciously. Proper projection of the voice is an art.

CHAPTER EIGHT
ACTING EXERCISES

1.
VISUAL IMAGES

Actors may sit or lie on stage in a quiet atmosphere. They are to run their lines in their mind slowly and without sound. With each word slowly passing through his mind, the actor is to clearly envision a picture that relates to the life of the character associated with each word.

The actor should be able to run entire speeches in his mind, with accompanying pictures like an endless movie, scene by scene.

In groups or individually, actors may then be allowed to speak their lines audibly with as much volume as desired, still seeing clear pictures in the mind with each spoken word.

When comfortable with the spoken word and associated image, the actor may then quicken the tempo of the spoken lines until performance speed is achieved, still creating the inner vision with each word.

2.
ALTERED MEANING

Take words in phrases and sentences and play with their meaning by altering stress words, inserting or extending pauses in different places and accenting different syllables and words. Note how meanings can change slightly or drastically.

3.
ALTERED VOLUME

Actors are to speak their lines first in their normal volume level. They will then perform the same speeches in a soft whisper throughout the brief scene. Note the changes in meaning, in feeling, in the mood of the scene.

Vary the scene and character further by going to the other extreme and increase the volume to a roaring shout. It is to be noted that the exercise will open new avenues of meaning and feeling that should not be dismissed completely as meer exercise. Interesting discoveries may take place.

4.
EXPANDING SUB-TEXT

Actors are to speak single words or very short phrases followed by very lengthy pauses as he dwells on an entire scenario evoked by the word or phrase. The pause should be continually filled with the sub-text to any length of time. Picture upon picture must be created with real feelings emerging from emotion recall or the sub-conscious.

5.
WORD PICTURES

The director may call out a single word to a group of actors on stage. Their eyes may be closed or open as they put pictures to each word called out by the director. He may ask certain actors to tell us what is being seen and felt by the word. Words may be randomly selected or connected.

6.
THE WORD OF IMPORTANCE

Having full knowledge of the role and completely dissecting the role of the play, select segments of your role. Speak only the most important words of each objective.

7.
MIND TO MIND CONTACT

Partners in a scene present a segment on stage. Actor "A" will speak short segments of lines as partner actor "B" probes the sub text of actor "A." Actors are to take turns performing the exercise as "B" will speak and "A" will probe his partners mind to analyse the sub text.

8.
REVEAL SUB TEXT

This very advanced exercise will prove fruitful. Brief segments of scene are presented. Actor "A" speaks first. Actor "B" listens to "A." Then director stops the scene and has the LISTENER define the speaker's sub text, and explaining the reason for his analysis. "A" will then confirm or disprove the analysis of sub text made by "B."

This exercise, challenging as it may be, is to be continued until the director decides to end it, but highlighting the importance of mind to mind communion.

9.
SPEAKER'S SUB TEXT

Partners present rehearsed scene. At any point, the director calls a halt to the action and asks the speaker to expose the sub text underlying the last words spoken. The speaker will stay in character, freezing the action, explain all his inner thoughts to the satisfaction of the director. The scene will continue until the director again calls for the action to freeze and sub-text to be exposed by the speaker.

Variation: This exercise is to be done with monologues as well.

10.
SOUND OF SILENCE

In a scene having been rehearsed, actor "A" will speak his lines. Actor "B" will respond in depth, but in total SILENCE. He will convey his attitude and inner life in silence and subtle physical action.

They will then exchange as "B" speaks and "A" responds in silence.

11.
CHOICE WORDS

Using a well rehearsed scene, actors will have underlined all the very important words in each speech. They will then stage the scene using only audible underlined words with pauses for words spoken within the speaker's mind. The silent pauses will be intensified as eyes become very expressive as they convey the silent words to partners and only the key words are audible.

CHAPTER NINE

EMPHASIZING THE KEY WORD

The accented or emphasized word is like a pointing finger which singles out the key word and high point of the speech and sub-text. The actor should emphasize only a few select words which must be noted as the key words being spoken. Emphasizing too many words will tend to confuse the ideas and simply work against the speech. Clarity of speech will be determined by the three important elements of intonation, psychological pause, and emphasis of key words.

The stage actor should literally attempt to make a painting with the key word so it is clearly seen by all who hear the word spoken clearly. Stanislavski further states that each word should conjure up an image in the mind of the speaker on stage. And it is hoped that the partner will see each image being spoken. This intense interplay reflects the highest level of inter-communication on stage, a most desired level of artistry.

It is harmful to listen to yourself speak while acting a role. Yet, this is exactly what many faulted actors tend to do. Rather, direct your attention to your partner while speaking in order to see what affect your words have had on your partner. Always attempt to affect others by what you say.

It is difficult to escape the fact that many valued elements are so interconnected. We note that the inner life initiates the sub-text which gives life to each spoken word and by concentration of attention is directed along the through line of dramatic action leading to the super-objective. These elements become the foundation of our art.

Projection of the spoken word is indeed essential on stage. This is not to be confused with volume which leads to shouting. Rather it is important for the actor to be aware of the quality of the spoken word and the proper emphasis of the key word.

Stanislavski noted that there are two forms of proper emphasis of key words:

a. Masculine emphasis is a definite, strong, sometimes harsh stress of words sometimes like the blow of a hammer.

b. Feminine stress does not come to an abrupt end but the word is extended, drawn out or may even be slowed in tempo to serve its purpose.

Both forms of emphasis should be used to proper advantage. Note, however, that the terms have nothing to do with male and female. Masculine and feminine simply are terms to define the manner of speech by Stanislavski.

Emphasis may be combined with intonation as well as psychological pause for effective speech when emerging from an appropriate inner life. Even without stressing a word, it may be emphasized by putting a pause before it, after it, or before and after it. The psychological pause itself may even be the accent point such as; "Don't......ever.....do that!" At other times a key point may be made by simply altering the tempo-rhythm of the phrase being stressed. But remember while speaking, try to tell your partner what you see in the retina of your inner eye.

CHAPTER NINE
ACTING EXERCISES

1.
SEEING WHAT YOU MEAN

Select a phrase or short sentence from your character's speech. Study it to determine which single word is indeed the most important word in the sentence (or phrase). Take the time also to dwell on the sub-text of the short speech. When ready, speak out only the one chosen word to reflect the feeling and entire sub-text of the entire speech.

The object is to convey the entire meaning, feeling and life of the entire moment by the use of that single word.

2.
DISSECTING THE ROLE

Actors are to go through their entire role and dissect it into acts, scenes, and beats. In addition, they must underline the objective of each beat. Then, they are to take each sentence (or phrase) and note the KEY WORD, which may be circled, underlined in red, or other identifying manner.

3.
INFECT YOUR PARTNER

Actors are to position themselves comfortably opposite each other on stage. They may sit or lie on stage, for they will speak very slowly a few words of their role at any given moment. The object will be that actor "A" will speak a few words, then voice his intent, telling what he wants and what he expects from his partner.

The partner is then allowed to speak what is within his mind as he is listening to partner actor "A" saying those words.

Actor "A" will then continue until his speech is completed, at which point actor "B" will speak a few words, express his sub-text, telling what he feels and wants from partner actor "A," etc.

4.
MASCULINE AND FEMININE STRESS

Taking turns to exercise this stress element, actor "A" will speak his words using masculine stress; which is definite, strong, harsh, firm.

Actor "B" will counter by use of feminine stress; softer, extended words, slower and more drawn-out.

Whether partners are males or females will not matter in this exercise.

5.
MASTERING THE PAUSE

Take any given speech. Intentionally add pauses where ever possible in order to alter the speech in every possible way to seek new dimensions not previously conceived.

6.
MASCULINE STRESS

Present monologue using the force of masculine stress; strong, harsh, emotional and energetic.

7.
FEMININE STRESS

Monologue is to be presented using feminine stress; extending words, sustaining vowels, slower speech, select pauses and delicate emphasis.

These are terms and in no way mean that males speak one way and females stress another, for sex has nothing to do with the classification.

8.
SEE WHAT YOU HEAR

Actors are to take short segments of a rehearsed scene or a scene that they are quite familiar with. Short lines are spoken and partner must SEE what is being said. The director allows the listener to tell what he SEES, while still in character. The speaker may also tell what he SEES as he speaks. Thus, the director is illustrating that speaker and listener must put pictures to words spoken and heard.

9.
THE SENSE OF IT

The director selects words of the script they are working with or simply words at random to illustrate the exercise. The actor designated will respond to the word explaining what is seen, what is heard, what is tasted, touched and smelled.

The depth of involvement will be very encouraging when the actor indeed is able to use all his senses each moment while in character. The role will be truly solid.

10.
VARY THE STRESS

Actors will select short lines to illustrate the exercise. The line will be spoken three or more times. The actor will stress a different word each time the line is spoken, and altering the placement of pauses as well.

It is to be determined to what extent the meaning of the line has been altered with each delivery, thus, illustrating the importance of stressing the correct words, the degree and nature of the stress, the proper use of pauses, etc.

11.
KEY WORDS

The most important word of each sentence will be underlined in a brief familiar scene. Actors are to then perform the scene using only the words each has underlined. The words must be filled with the life and energy each has developed in the fully rehearsed scene. This will be accomplished by silently speaking and feeling every other word in each sentence. The inner life and eyes will be extremely active.

CHAPTER TEN

ACTOR-CHARACTER DUALITY

In performing an acting role, we must be aware of two perspectives. One is related to the character in the circumstance provided by the playwright. The other is related to the actor playing the role. As an example, we may consider Hamlet as a character who has no idea of perspective, for he knows nothing of his future. On the other hand, the actor playing the role must keep his role in perspective, for he is totally aware of all the circumstances of the past, present and future of Hamlet the character.

Part of the actor is absorbed by sub-text, through line of dramatic action, and the super-objective, all of which make up the actor's creative state. The other part of the actor operates on his psycho-technique. By way of perspective, he measures himself, balancing this acting technique with the newly created life of the role.

The actor must be constantly aware of the two parallel lines of perspective. One is the perspective of the role of the character conceived by the author. The other is the perspective of the actor, his life on stage, his psycho-technique.

Dissecting the play and the role will aid in gaining perspective. The actor will know the play thoroughly when it is dissected into beats and their objectives, determining the through line of dramatic action, the sub-text, the objectives of each scene and act, and finally the super-objective of the entire play.

It can be seen that without perspective one would approach a play as one would read an unfamiliar book.

The actor who is thoroughly familiar with the entire play sees that the end of the play hinges on to the beginning and he knows the past, the present and the future. While in scene one, for example, the actor knows what will happen in scene two or scene five. While in act two, he knows what will take place in act three, etc. So, the actor gauges himself, much as a long distance runner does over the course of the run, or as a fighter does who faces fifteen rounds of encounter with his opponent.

We must see the important link between perspective and through line of dramatic action. They are closely related elements of our art.

An actor lives, weeps, laughs on the stage, but as he weeps and laughs he observes his own tears and his joy. It is this double existence, this balance between life and acting that makes for art. These are ideas Stanislavski gained by observing the great actors of his time. This division, or duality, does no harm to inspiration, for one actually encourages the other.

There should be no acting, no movement, gesture, thought, word or feeling without its appropriate perspective and purpose. We must understand the relation of the various parts to the whole.

CHAPTER TEN

ACTING EXERCISES

1.
CONNECTING "A" TO "Z"

Each actor in a role is to select an objective of importance from scene one of his role in the play.

The actor then selects a key line in his final scene. He must then explain the connection between the two thoughts, speeches, or objectives.

Variation: The actor associating the line from scene one with the line from his final scene will improvise a scene tying both ideas together.

2.
IMPROVISATION "A" TO "Z"

Words having a connection with other words are to be put on a card. Several cards may be made up in this manner. Examples: Hello! Goodbye! What are you doing here? Get out! Also, where are you going? and Let me go with you! Consider, I can't bear you! I don't want to see you!

The improvisation demands that either actor speaks the first thought and the other thought must be the final line of the improvisation, spoken by either person.

The actors must see and affect the continuity between the two lines, firmly holding on to 'First Line - Last Line' concept.

3.
KNOWING THE OPENING

Improvisation is based on two actors entering a scene knowing only the circumstance in the beginning. This may be planned before the start of the improvisation.

The ending of the improvisation is not to be known in advance. The actors are to build on the opening circumstance and take it to a surprise ending.

4.
THIS IS THE END

Improvisation is based knowing in advance exactly how the scene is to end. A last line may be assigned; a final action may be decided; a relationship may be concluded, etc.

Actors may enter stage not knowing where, or what, or when, or who. They must begin totally unstructured. A beginning takes place, then each is to build on each other with only the end in sight as they improvise a foundation to the scene.

5.
FIRST AND LAST

Two actors enter stage. One is given an opening line, while the other actor is responsible for the final line to be spoken. All else is created by the actors in the improvisation.

6.
MAJOR CONCERNS

Cards are given to actors with a major concern of our current lives entered on each card; rape, abuse, child molestation, AIDS, divorce, infidelity, dope, illegal immigration, terrorism, unemployment, recession, high cost of living, loss of career job, taxes, high cost of medical care, distrust of politicians, etc.

They are to build an improvisation on one of these, and other significant issues of our lives.

7.
MAJOR THEME

Select and agree upon the major theme of the play in progress. An improvisation is to be staged, condensing the high point of the play in a matter of two minutes.

8.
HIGH LIGHTS

Determine three to five or more key points in the life of the character you are portraying. Improvisation is to be structured from these main points, all being put into one scene.

For some characters, this may prove to be complex. In this case, base the improvisation on one or two key points of the character's life.

9.
DISSECTION

Take a music sheet and lay out the entire role of your character on the scales, using tempo rhythem of each beat as notes of the scale. With medium placed on middle of the scale, very slow will be at lowest point of scale and very fast at top of music scale.

Write in the dynamics (life energy and emotion) beneath the scale as they appear in music compositions. Value of notes will vary with the length of each beat.

10.
COLOR OF THE ROLE

Using color, design the entire role, based on the emotional life and action of the play in any given scene, from cool colors to colors of passion. The tone and harmony of the role will be illustrated.

Variation: Use instruments to illustrate the quality of each beat as sensed in musical terms. Designate an animal or fowl depicting the nature of each character in the play. These elements will work their way into the physical characterization of the role.

CHAPTER ELEVEN

TIMING AND DYNAMICS OF ACTION

Tempo is the speed or slowness of dramatic action of any dissected beat or scene. Rhythm as used by Stanislavski is considered to relate to the life energy or dynamics of a scene and will include inner and outer movement and sound in any segment of the play.

Each dissected beat of action should constantly change and contrast with beats preceding and following in terms of its tempo-rhythm. Otherwise we will experience a sameness leading to total monotony.

The actor seeks out his own character life energy and then will blend into the established tempo-rhythm of the beats incorporating the entire ensemble. The director of the play has the responsibility of establishing the appropriate tempo-rhythm of the ensemble and the entire play. His function is similar to that of a conductor of a symphony orchestra who has control of his ensemble of instrumentalists.

Tempo-rhythm has the power to affect the inner mood of actors as well as audience. When all elements are working properly, the tempo-rhythm will feel totally correct, very natural and harmonious in any scene of the play. It is essential, therefore, that the appropriate tempo-rhythm be suited to the given circumstance of the play to achieve the desired effect. Thus, the given circumstance must be known to create the appropriate inner creative mood, which will then influence the tempo-rhythm of every beat, scene and act of the entire play.

All elements blend into a perfect whole for where there is life there is action, wherever there is action there is inner and outer movement, and where there is movement there is tempo. Finally, where there is tempo, there is rhythm.

Conflicting tempo-rhythms may be extremely helpful in performing the role, just as in our daily lives. On stage, these conflicting tempo-rhythms become very exciting. As an example, we may consider a character who appears to have a passive exterior. Within, he may be experiencing absolute turmoil. It may be a person sitting quietly in a waiting room of a hospital. At any moment, the doctor will appear with the results of a crucial test or surgery performed on a loved one. The contrasting tempo-rhythms being experienced could be highly volatile.

Different characters in a play will also have contrasting and even conflicting tempo-rhythms in any given scene. These elements will contribute to conflict, essential in the performance of any play.

The right tempo-rhythm is of major importance to an actor. It should seem that tempo-rhythm is a two edged sword. It can be harmful as it is helpful. If used correctly, it helps to induce the right feelings in a natural way. But, if used incorrectly, the wrong feelings and actions will be aroused, both for the actor as well as the audience. They are in control of muscles and emotions as well as creative moods. They can put everyone to sleep in the audience and on the stage. But, when correctly initiated they can raise everyone to the highest pitch of excitement.

CHAPTER ELEVEN
ACTING EXERCISES

1.
PERSONAL TEMPO

Each person is seated comfortably, concentrating on his own life at the moment. With his (her) fingertips a tempo will be tapped which will match the inner and outer action of his life as he senses it.

Each actor is then to consider tapping out the tempo of "going home." The voyage home is to be dissected into segments, with each of the beats of the journey home taking a different tempo; walking, hurrying across the street, into car, driving, avoiding a collision, stop light, drive way, garage, to front door, lost key, seeking an open door or window, entering, message on phone receiver, excitement, apprehension, phone call, resolution, undressing, to bed, etc.

Each actor is to set up his own problems which requires altering tempo.

2.
TEMPO OF LIFE

Actors are to tap out various major experiences they encounter during the course of their lives; Dressing for the senior prom; Preparing for a sports competition; Registering for courses; Applying for a job; Going on a date; Visiting a college, etc.

3.
RHYTHM OF LIFE AFFECTING TEMPO

Without external movement, each is to tap out the emotional life energy being experienced within, such as: Think of a lover; Jealousy of a competitor; Auditioning for a Broadway play; Humorous incident; Playing with a pet; Taking a trip with a friend; Hatred of something or someone, etc.

4.
TEMPO AND RHYTHM COMBINED

Actor performs a medium tempo of movement (cleaning room or setting up dining table) and thinks of an emotionally up-beat circumstance: An important person is about to arrive; A marriage is about to break up; An important phone call of that job is expected; That college application is being considered; Will the money stolen be discovered? Etc.

The inner emotional state will be completely different than the physical action being performed.

5.
EXTERNAL IN-ACTION CONTRASTED WITH INTERNAL INTENSITY

Person very slowly enters wary of possible discovery and capture. Person stands motionless, having heard a sound of someone following who may attack.

Person sits as he awaits the results of doctor's decision.

Captors are to enter soon and one of you waiting is to be sentenced to die.

6.
SEE ROLE IN MOVEMENT

Knowing the role thoroughly, the actor is to conceive the entire life of the character in movement. The director will decide on segments of the play and have the actors in ensemble create a brief scene in pure movement and without words.

Each actor may do one to two minutes of his role in interpretative movement depicting the action and inner life of the character. New dimensions of character awareness will evolve.

7.
COMPOSING THE MOVEMENT IMAGE

On a sheet of music, the actor is to place notes, representing beats, on the lines and spaces. The life energy dynamics and tempo will determine their place on the scale. Slow and low toned life energy will be at the bottom of the scale, moving upward as life energy heightens. Whole notes for long beats, quarter notes for brief beats. Dissect entire role in this manner to gain a thorough understanding of the tempo-rhythm of movement of the role.

8.
CONTRASTING TEMPO-RHYTHM

Improvisation of a scene being prepared for staging will be done with beats contrasting three to five different tempos in movement.

9.
LIFE ENERGY CONTRASTS

Determine the emotional contrasts in the life of the character in any working scene. Perform the scene, illustrating the beat rhythm changes of the inner life energy of the character being portrayed.

10.
SCENE DISSECTION

Stage a scene of two to three minutes length dissected into beats and illustrating contrasts in both tempo and rhythm of life energy. Major emphasis will be on movement changes.

11.
MAGICAL TRAY

Using very slow tempo-rhythm, pantomime loading a tray and justify the very slow movement. Consider clearing a table of valuable objects, etc.

Pantomime the setting up of a dining table from objects on a tray using very slow tempo-rhythm. Then enjoy the fun of having actors find things to do as the demand is made to increase the tempo-rhythm until it becomes very fast as a waiter rushing to distribute drinks in a crowded and fast moving railroad dining car on a bumpy track, etc.

12.
CRAZY SEARCH

Create a search in your clothing for a very important piece of paper or other object. Begin with very very slow tempo-rhythm and increase each beat to very slow, slow, medium, to medium fast to ultimately very very fast. The eventual panic becomes amusing to watch.

CHAPTER TWELVE

CONTENT AND TIMING OF SPEECH

The voice sounds of syllables and words provide a means of conveying the tempo-rhythm of the inner meaning of any play. In the process of speech the line of words proceeds in time, and that time is broken up by the sounds of letters, syllables, words. This division of time makes rhythmic parts and groups.

The nature of certain sounds, syllables and words requires a clipped pronunciation such as eighth and sixteenth notes in music. Other word sounds must be produced in a weighty, longer form such as whole or half notes. Along with this, some sounds, syllables and words receive a stronger or a weaker rhythmic stress or accentuation.

These spoken sounds, in turn, are interlaced with psychological pauses and rests for breathing of variable lengths. All these are phonetic possibilities out of which to fashion an endless variety of the tempo-rhythms of speech. In making use of them an actor will develop a dimensional speech style providing a range of word usage from the exalted emotions of tragedy to the gay mood of comedy.

A measured, resonant, well blended speech possesses many qualities similar to those of music and singing. Letters, syllables, words are the musical notes of speech. There is good reason to describe beautiful speech as musical.

Many actors who are careless of speech, inattentive to words, pronounce them with such thoughtless slipshod speed, without putting any endings on them, that they speak with completely mutilated, half spoken phrases. Shifting and uncertain rhythms are also destructive to speech on stage. In proper and beautiful speech there should not be any of these manifestations, except where a change of temp-rhythm is required for the characterization of a role.

Many actors lack proper training in two important elements of speech; on the one side there is smoothness, slowness, resonance, fluency, and on the other, rapidity, lightness, clarity, crispness in the pronunciation of words.

Rarely do we hear good rapid speech on stage, well sustained as to tempo, clear cut in rhythm, enunciated so as to be intelligible. Most actors cannot do real patter, for they babble, spatter and spew out words. Real patter has to be learned and it begins with the mastery of very slow, exaggeratedly precise speech. By long and frequent repetition our speech apparatus becomes so trained that it learns how to execute the same words at the quickest possible rate of speed. This demands constant practice because dramatic speech at times requires such speed.

In speaking, learn to give the proper length to sounds, syllables and words. Use a clean cut rhythm in combing their tonal particles; form your phrases into measures of speech, regulate the rhythmic relationship among whole phrases. Learn to love correct and clear accentuation, associated with remembered emotions and to the creation of a character image.

Speech consists not only of sounds but also of pauses. Both of these must be equally impregnated with tempo-rhythm, whether in his actions or when he is inactive, when he speaks or is silent. Actors should know how to be rhythmic not only in speech but also in silence. He must reckon the words together with the pauses and not take them as separate entities. Actors are often afraid of pauses because they sense the lack of sub-text. We are reminded that sub-text illumines both the pause and the word from within.

One can easily judge the all-important part tempo-rhythm plays in an actor's work. Together with the through line of dramatic action and the

---

sub-text it runs like a thread through all movements, words, pauses, the emotional experience of a role and its physical interpretation.

Correctly established tempo-rhythm can intuitively trigger feelings of the actor and can arouse in him a true sense of living his role. Thus, it is essential for the actor as well as the director to establish an appropriate tempo-rhythm for the movement of the play in production.

Even a great play and fine actors may be devastated by improper tempo-rhythm established by a director. It is little different than a symphony orchestra destroying a fine piece of music because of the conductor initiating improper tempo-rhythm.

Proper tempo-rhythm is achieved when there is a complete union of text and sub-text.

Proper rhythm is achieved when it is bonded completely with inner life and inner feeling.

To illustrate his point, Stanislavski would often tap out the tempo-rhythm of characters of scenic action with a baton, or by clapping his hands, or with the use of a metronome. He would quicken or slow the beat to gain what ever effect he was seeking. It has proven to be a highly effective process for rehearsals.

CHAPTER TWELVE
ACTING EXERCISES

1.
ENUNCIATION

Each actor is to select a monologe and speak each word precisely, taking time to articulate each consonant and each syllable and to round out every vowel sound. The word must have a beginning, middle and end and be spoken without distortion, slurring or omission (most common errors).

When complete success is achieved, the same monologue will be presented with tempo-rhythm increasing in rapidity until spoken twice the normal rate of required tempo-rhythm. Clarity of enunciation is required at every level of the exercise, even to the point of exaggerated preciseness of articulation for the sake of mastering the mechanical process of speech.

Finally, each monologue is to be acted sincerely. Articulation and clarity of speech will be combined with inner feeling, emotional content and clarity of inner vision and complete sub-text.

2.
VARIATION OF SPEECH PATTERN

The monologue is to be dissected by each actor. Each beat will be assigned a tempo, varying from medium to slow to fast, to very slow, to very fast, etc. Actor should tap out the tempo of each beat in rehearsal.

Dynamics will be also noted for each beat. The life force may be loving and caring, or hateful and resentful, or jealous rage and fear, or forgiving and understanding, etc. In rehearsal, tap out the inner life.

Tempo may harmonize with the rhythm or be in total conflict. The inner rhythm may be totally opposite the outer tempo, or blend in a synchronized manner.

Each monologue is to be presented on stage, having been dissected into three to five beats (including objectives). Attention is to be directed to the varying tempo-rhythm of each beat, noting external and internal changes affected by inner creative mood and action.

3.
ADVANCED DISSECTION

With beat tempo-rhythm fully clarified, each actor is to take a single beat and break down each sentence for tempo-rhythm preciseness.

The tempo of a sentence within the assigned beat tempo-rhythm may also have its varied changes. One sentence may be more urgent in nature than another sentence, thus, having a more urgently tempoed delivery than the calmer sentence which follows.

A phrase, within a sentence, may need special stress of volume, due to heightened emotion, or a pause accent, or slowly drawn out to make a key point. These changes will be noted by the actor.

The monologue is to be presented noting these detailed changes.

4.
INTERNAL EXTERNAL CONTRAST

Stage a scene or devise an improvisation where the actor illustrates how the EXTERNAL tempo is on the slow scale, while the INTERNAL subtext is rapid.

5.
SPEECH CONTRAST

The staged scene will illustrate vivid contrasts in speech tempo with each of three to five beats.

6.
GUESS WHO? GAME PLAYING

Cast is gathered and scenes are well known as are the characters. The director will tap out a tempo all cast members can hear. And the cast is to determine which character is being depicted. Take it a bit beyond and consider WHICH SCENE is being tapped.

The director may carry this on to include the identification of every character in any given scene by tapping its tempo rhythm. A challenging and worthwhile level of work.

7.
TAP TAP THE SUB TEXT

Director may work with one cast member at a time, or with a small cast all together. Designate the scene to be worked on. The director will tap out the tempo of one of the actors in the scene. That actor will then tap out his sub text at the same time the director is tapping the text. Indeed, they could reach the same tempo. However, in many cases, the sub text will be tapped slower or faster than that being tapped by the director.

8.
ALL TOGETHER

Using a small cast scene, the director will tap his own designated tempo of that scene, changing with each new beat.

Each cast member will tap his own tempo of the character in the scene, thus, having all actors in the scene tapping along with the director.

Character tempos will vary among themselves since they are all different people, but the sum total will be in harmony with the directors assigned tempos of the scene.

9.
SEEKING NEW DIMENSIONS

Stage rehearsed scene in very slow tempo. Then very fast. New dimensions?

10.
FOLLOW THE CONDUCTOR

Stage a scene. Director taps tempo rhythm, making changes with each new beat. Cast makes immediate adjustment with total justification.

CHAPTER THIRTEEN

PERSONAL QUALITY

Each individual has a unique quality which is capable of enthralling any given audience.

Any discomfort revealed by the actor on stage will alter that uniqueness and turn it into a totally negative feature and turning off the audience.

Ease, confidence, lack of tension lead to comfort on stage.

Self consciousness, is probably the most destructive force exhibited on stage by an actor. Since the actor is under a magnifying glass on stage, the slightest degree of discomfort becomes magnified to the audience.

The actor, therefore, must work extensively to perfect his psycho-technique to ward off any degree of discomfort on stage.

Self admiration and exhibitionism tend also to impair this quality on stage.

This quality is indefinable and does differ by degree with each individual. But it is known that natural, relaxed attitude on stage will enhance one's qualities for the viewing audience.

An actor must gain sufficient courage to trust in the value of being truly your unique self in everything you do and building on that alone.

Avoid the impossible task of trying to be some one else or copying another actor. Your individual charm is your value. Venturing away from your self to seek qualities foreign to you will work against you.

If an actor has shortcomings of any nature, he should tone down whatever the negative aspect might be. First, of course, the person should under-stand, or sense what the shortcoming might be, and then, when he has reached the realization, learn to cope with his particular problem. It is not easy. It requires intelligent self evaluation, close observation, great patience and hard work aimed at altering natural traits to turn them into neutral elements or positive qualities.

As for attaining that indefinable something which attracts an audience, that is illusive indeed. One's natural qualities are generally very appealing, and it has nothing to do with outward appearance. Many performing stars have characteristics that may be considered unattractive, but by being purely them selves, have gained the heights of popular acceptance.

Shakespeare often provides us with thoughts of value. In Polonius' speech to Laertes, from HAMLET, he says, "This above all; to thine own self be true, and it must follow, as the night the day, thou canst not then be false to any man." Worthy advice for us all. We must be true to our selves at all times.

You have a higher self, the same higher self which is the individuality that makes artists of us. It is the degree of inner activity of the higher self, producing those purified feelings you are capable of, that is the final deter-minant of quality in the creations of all artists.

CHAPTER THIRTEEN
ACTING EXERCISES

1.
SOLITUDE

In a small circle of attention, the actor will work with a personal stage property of value, such as a pair of eye glasses, a bill fold with credit cards, a personal letter of importance, a wedding ring, a memento from a dear friend, etc. A scenario is to be developed so as to include what it is, who may be associated with the object, why it is of value, when the event it recalls took place, etc.

The personal relationship with the prop will trigger emotion memory, and true feelings will be evoked fully occupying the inner life of the actor. All that lies outside the circle of attention will disappear, leaving the actor comfortable and natural in his space.

2.
YOUR FAVORITE WALK

The actor, as a solo or in a group on stage, will create in his mind a very special place to walk; a beach, forest, park, street, mountain, field of flowers, etc. The actor may be in the company of an imagined friend or pet, or completely alone. Every element of the space must be created in his inner vision. The actor will see, touch, taste, smell and hear every detail of the space being experienced as he walks.

3.
MUSICAL INTERLUDE

Finding a comfortable spot on stage, the actor will relax and listen to his favorite music being played in his mind. Every note will be distinctly experienced and every part of the melody. He may also identify particular instruments being played or words being sung.

4.
REFLECTIONS OF MOONLIGHT

It's suggested that the actor walk in the moonlight and come to a point where he approaches the water. He (she) notes the reflection of the moonlight on the water, causing gentle movements of light.

The actor will connect with the light reflection on the water and sensing its movement begins to move as well until the actor becomes the moving light on the water and gently moves to its rhythmic pattern.

5.
LIGHTBEAM IN THE NIGHT

A beam of light is seen by the actor. He finds his way into the beam becoming one with the light. The actor then floats upward along the beam and into the night and beyond, losing all connection with earth.

6.
INVOLVEMENT WITH SMALL OBJECTS

Work with candy bar, a ring, a particle of dust, a photo, a letter, or any one of countless small objects, keeping attention focused.

7.
LIFE EXPERIENCE

With a partner, stage an improvisation of an experience you may have in common, or as close as you can manage to keep it personal.

8.
SOMETHING SPECIAL

Solo improvisation. The actor is preparing for a date with a very special friend (lover?).

9.
SOMETHING AWFUL

You are preparing, perhaps dressing, for an engagement which you consider to be extremely distasteful. It is a blind date? Could it be with an employer who is about to fire you? Or must you perform an act to gain money, a job, to survive? It's awful.

10.
DISAGREEMENT

With partner, you reach a point of disagreement which builds as far as you wish to develop it; to argument, to fight, to killing, etc.

11.
PERSUASION

Try to convince your instructor to improve your grade.

You try to obtain a grade change.

You talk your way out of a paper which was due.

You want to make up a "no make up" exam.

You are failing the course by five points.

Stage an improvisation of a true persuasion challenge of importance which happened to you.

The important element required is for you to be purely yourself on stage to attain that mysterious charm or quality that works.

12.
THE MOBILE FACE

An actor must have a face that reflects one's inner life and inner beauty. Each actor is to enter the stage and experience three varied inner experiences without words. They may select sorrow, love, hatred, joy, happiness, contentment, fury. Encourage the use of a broad smile, for the glowing smile is a premium feature.

13.
A TREASURED VOICE

Actors should have well trained, strong, pleasant voices with expressive timbre and perfect diction. Each performer is to present a monologue to illustrate these qualities.

14.
WALKING ELEGANTLY

Most people walk incorrectly, bouncing with each step. Each actor is to walk as if suspended from above, touching heel or ball of foot lightly with each step. Avoid bouncing. Walk as dancers or military marchers, who walk with upper bodies "elevated" yet body relaxed and loose. The rough walk can be reversed for gamblers in GUYS AND DOLLS, etc.

CHAPTER FOURTEEN

ETHICS IN THE THEATRE

Ethics in the theatre is an important element contributing to a creative state. Combined with discipline and the sense of joint enterprise, ethics will inspire artistic animation and an attitude of readiness to work together. The actor needs order, discipline, a code of ethics for the general circumstances of his work and for his artistic and creative purposes. The first condition towards bringing about this creative state of mind is to follow the principle conceived by Stanislavski: "Love art in yourself and not yourself in art."

Theatre has the capacity to ennoble the performing artist and make him a better person. If not, the actor should select another field of endeavor and flee the theatre.

The fine elements of theatre will further the growth in you of a passion for what is fine, elevating and for great thoughts and feelings. They will help you to commune with the great geniuses such as Shakespeare, Ibsen, Moliere, Chekov, O'Neill, Miller, Albee and Williams, etc. Their creations and traditions live in us. And when their ideas become your ideas then you become a greater person.

The joy of performing in this art comes with accomplishment, which will renew the spirit. Joy will also come with new discoveries of the ideas of the great playwrights.

Temptations are great and may affect one's personal vanity. This is a danger which is ever present. Receiving ovations, praise, reading glowing criticisms are difficult to withstand. But if the actor lives only on that and similar stimuli he is bound to become trivial and may well be destroyed by it.

Never come into the theatre with so called mud on your feet. Leave the dirt and dust of triviality outside. Check your little worries, gossips, squabbles, pettiness at the door. These are all destructive elements that ruin your life and draw your attention away from your creative art of theatre.

Treat theatre as an altar, a cathedral, a shrine. That is the manner in which a true artist should feel all the time he is in the theatre. Be a standard bearer of what is fine in life. Conduct yourself worthily outside the theatre as well as within its walls. An actor should learn to live by rigid discipline. If incapable of feeling this way, an actor will never be a true artist.

In the theatre, one should work for all, and all should work for one. The theatrical involvement should become a mutual responsibility. This suggests that ensemble acting is valued over the star system for every role is a major role. Included also in the ensemble is the backstage worker, each of whom is to be respected and treated accordingly.

No member of the ensemble must take advantage of the work of others by way of unpreparedness during rehearsals and during productions. Each must be prepared at all times.

CHAPTER FOURTEEN
ACTING EXERCISES

1.
ATTITUDE OF READINESS

It is essential to free our minds and bodies of all tension brought into the theater from the outside world. The drain exercise is recommended.

Group of actors will lie comfortably on the floor in a darkened and quiet atmosphere. Heels are together and hands relaxed on the floor along side the body.

It is imagined that the body is filled with a liquid, such as mercury, which will drain slowly upward away from the toes. The mind is to focus at the point of the body being drained. Inch by inch, the fluid drains out with each inhaling of the breath. No movement at all is to take place in the portion of the body having been drained. It should be sensed that all tension has drained out and that part of the body has 'melted' away.

If at any time the mind drifts from the point of focus, return to that point and continue. Should movement take place where body has been drained, begin again. The relaxed state may induce sleep or a semi-conscious state, which is pleasant and in no way harmful.

2.
EXPANDING OF SELF

Standing in a quiet atmosphere the mind is drained of extraneous matter and concentration of the self is begun. When in control of the "I AM" image, begin to sense yourself growing in size. Feel at the same moment a growth in strength, power, control over your environment. Continue expansion until the earth itself is at your feet.

Variation: During any part of expansion, feel growth of power in your mind and assume command of all forces. Move the power to the chest and rule over your subjects of your environment. Move the center of energy to your hand as you elevate it to command troops, armies or subdue the enemy, level mountains, recede flooding waters, part the oceans, etc.

3.
TRUSTING EACH OTHER

Actors stand in small circle, shoulder to shoulder, one foot back for strong support, hands held up palms outward at chest level. One actor is to stand rigidly in center with arms folded tightly across chest and as he maintains a solidly stiffened body. Actors in circle will gently halt his fall and return him easily to just beyond center point so he will fall in another direction. It is important to note that no fewer than THREE actors are to halt his fall each time, so as to eliminate ANY POSSIBILITY of him falling to the floor, which is DANGEROUS.

4.
CHANGING ATMOSPHERES

Actors are to walk through mist, then snow, rain, shrubbery, fog, etc.

5.
WARM UPS

Ensemble is to move about on stage in relaxed manner. Then they will encounter obstacles which require that they move over and under and around and crawl and climb to reach 'safe' objective. Encounter each obstacle with sincerity in belief. What happened? Where are you going? Why are you trying to get there? etc.

6.
CHANGING ENVIRONMENTS

Ensemble will move as individuals facing their own problems. The environment changes (by director) from shrubbery, to jungle, to desert, to water, blizzard, quick sand, etc. Each is to immediately seek justification by adding who, what, where, when, why, etc.

7.
WORKING TOGETHER

Actors are to roll a huge carpet, lift it and carry it off. Then the actors are to carry in a new carpet, lay it down, unroll it, arrange it properly and for a purpose. You are all working together as a team dealing with all of the elements in harmony.

8.
BODY LANGUAGE

Actors stand at a distance facing each other. One is to convey a message to the other using only the body, no words, without exaggeration.

9.
MOVED BY FORCES

The group is on stage as an ensemble. They are to get into an elevator and climb to designated height. They ride on a carousel, each enjoying his own animal figure. They ride on a boat in an approaching storm. They ride a train, an aircraft, a balloon, etc. All must sense the same movement of force. They may encounter a strong wind or snowstorm, or fall into a surging river, etc.

10.
BEING CLOSE AND TOGETHER

All actors lie on floor facing designated direction and quite close. Starting at one end, each moves up against the actor before him (her). They will place their free arm over the waist and rib cage of the person in front, being close enough to feel the breathing of the person. They are to relax and encouraged to blend their bodies as close as possible. Lying on their side, upper arm is over partner's waist, the lower arm may cushion the head of partner in front or self. Each is to sense the breathing rhythm of the person in front and try to breathe in harmony with that person. Ultimately, the director will note that the entire ensemble is indeed breathing in the same slow rhythm. They are together, relaxed, united as an ensemble.

CHAPTER FIFTEEN

PSYCHO-PHYSICAL ARTISTRY

The creative process starts with the imaginative invention of the author, followed by the creative artistry of the director and actor and scenic designer as well as the technical staff.

Significant elements of the creative process include the magic-IF and given circumstances, which lead us to define the theme of the play, called super-objective by Stanislavski. We are then capable of seeing the form of the play permitting its dissection into beats and objectives following a through line of dramatic action.

The actor then applies discipline to maintain his concentration of attention on an object, to define one objective after another as he moves from beat to beat leading the actor along the un-broken line toward his super-objective.

To bring life to the objective as well as to the objects of his attention, the actor needs a sense of truth, of faith in what he is doing so as to get rid of all artificiality, clichés, and negative elements not belonging in the life of his character. He needs also desire and intention, which lead to involved dramatic action in which he must believe completely.

The actor then establishes communion with his various objects such as his partner or setting or other inner and outer focus points. Communion will initiate inner and outer adaptation, both physical and psychological adjustments to his life.

All of the consciously applied elements of this system will then trigger the actor's inner feelings which will then initiate appropriate tempo-rhythm. The resulting true feelings will release emotion memory to give free expression to repeated feelings and to give sincerity to his emotions. The outcome will be natural behavior in a circumstance we understand, which is logical, coherent and retains a sense of continuity.

When all elements are combined, it is described as the creative state and employing successfully the double aspect of inner psycho-technique with external physical-technique. This is the Stanislavski system in summary; the process of reaching the subconscious via the conscious.

By employing this system, the play becomes a natural and human event similar to any experience which could happen in our own lives.

The very cornerstone of our art form is the organic creativeness of our own nature expressed by Stanislavski as applying conscious technique to reach the subconscious by creation of artistic truth. This does not however mean that we study the subconscious, but only the paths leading up to it. Our conscious technique of employing acting principles is directed on the one side towards putting our subconscious to work and on the other to learning how not to interfere with it once it is in action.

CHAPTER FIFTEEN
ACTING EXERCISES

1.
OBJECT EXERCISE WITH ENDOWMENT

A non-discript object, such as a small block of wood, is placed on a small table on stage in a beam of light. Actors are seated in the dark outside of the circle of light.

At any given time, an actor will approach the table having endowed the object with qualities of value to him personally. He may touch it, take it, deal with it in any way the life of the object induces in him. It may be cuddled, kissed, squeezed, worn, embraced, smiled at, cried over, etc. It changes texture, size, weight, what ever the actor sees in his mind. It must never be the block of wood. The space, too, must change to the actors conceived environment. The object is then replaced at the end as silence is maintaind and all wait for another actor to approach the object which then changes according to his concept, etc.

Each actor goes up until all have taken their turn with the object.

2.
FURTHER ENDOWMENT

Each actor is to bring in a prop to build the following exercise. A simple cloth is brought in, a pistol, a rifle, a banner, a knife, pilot wings, a pen, etc.

The actor will take stage with the simple prop. He will have endowed the object with very special qualities and deal with it accordingly.

Example: The cloth becomes the bloodied cloth in which Christ was enshrouded when removed from the cross. The pistol was used by Booth to shoot Lincoln. The rifle was used to kill John Kennedy. Pilot wings were worn by dead hero father. The pen was used by the president to sign a law. Etc.

3.
BECOMING WHAT YOU SEE

Actors working solo or in group on stage will concentrate and focus their attention on certain objects in their mind. They will connect with the object and when the proper creative state is reached will indeed become the object and take on its life. Actor may take on life of a balloon in flight, a tree in the forest, a flag waving in the breeze, the statue of David, an eagle in flight, a cloud floating in space, a table, a glowing lamp, a roaring fire, etc.

4.
ACTION INDUCED FROM EMPTINESS

Actor sits on stage without preconceived plan. Mind is to become blank. He remains inactive until he is motivated to move and conceive of action which puts life into him in a circumstance. He may use objects, speech, whatever the creative state requires.

5.
INNER INTENTION

In an improvisation of a relaxed nature, (such as dinner, walk in park, standing at street corner, riding in a car) deal with your partner knowing you are going to propose marriage, or similar situation. The object is to do one thing, while the intention is not yet revealed, but certainly is felt within.

6.
MOTIVE FORCES WILL MOVE YOU

Actor "A" positions actor "B" on stage in a freeze in any unusual position (bending, stretching, lying, crouching, arms twisted, head between legs, etc.). Actor "B" remains in that position until he is compelled to action by the MIND working with WILL and evoking some FEELING emenating from that position. The scene develops briefly with partner "A" or other actor.

7.
IMAGINATION AT WORK

We are all a part of nature. Actor is to take on any element in nature; animal, bird, river, mountain, tree, cloud, wind, flower, or what ever is created by the imagination. It is to develop simply into a movement with a sense of inner life to reach a point of artistry.

8.
HEAVY, HEAVIER

Actors are to lift weights, which become progressively heavier. Units are added to heighten the challenge. Ultimately, it is too much and the competition comes to an end.

9.
REMEMBER IT WELL

Actors are to work with an object which takes them back to an earlier period in their lives. They are to experience the object completely and deal with time and place, touching, tasting, smelling, hearing, and seeing in detail. The object then leads the actor into an action which belongs to an occurrence. It is to be carried out alone or with a volunteer in a brief improvisation. Re-create the prior occurrence.

10.
SWAYING TO ACTION

Ensemble will be on stage in relaxed and quiet mood. They begin to sway gently, easily, each in his own space. The swaying movement is to continue. Each actor may then sense a need to slow or quicken the swaying rhythm. Out of this will come a feeling, an inner vision, and a need leading to action. The actor will allow this to build and move him into any creative idea, just letting it happen.

11.
CHARACTER BIOGRAPHY

Every actor in a play is to create his character biography which should include: Who am I? How old am I? What is my profession? Who are members of my family? What is my circumstance? Where do I live? What is my relationship to other characters in the play? and other elements of importance.

CHAPTER SIXTEEN

ACTING NATURALLY

Although our acting technique is called the Stanislavski System, it was firmly stated by Constantin Stanislavski that he did not discover or invent anything that was new. He has constantly reminded us that his psycho-physical technique is based purely on natural behavior.

This psycho-physical technique of acting is the art of living the role and not mechanical acting or cliché. The Stanislavski system must be studied in each of its parts and then merged into a whole in order to understand it fully and apply it properly. In the process, actors are transformed by way of their art into real, believable human beings on stage. Both in spirit and in body this method of acting is a part of our organic nature. It is based on the laws of nature. Since we are born with an innate capacity for creativeness, we should therefore express it in accordance with a natural system.

What, then, drives us to exhibit false acting on stage? It appears that actors stray from natural behavior on stage by the condition of having to create something in public view. It impels an actor to exhibitionism and insincere representation.

The approach we have chosen-the art of living a role-rebels with all the strength it can muster against those other acting "principles." Stanislavski asserts the contrary principle that the main factor in any form of creativeness is the life of a human spirit, that of the actor and his role, their joint feelings and subconscious creation.

Any other approach to acting the role will be artificial, contrived results of non-existent experience, devoid of feeling and truth.

The demands of our psycho-physical technique are simple, normal, and therefore they are difficult to satisfy. All we ask is that an actor on the stage live in accordance with natural laws.

Our interest is not surface impressions or visual and audible effects. What we hold in highest regard are impressions made on the emotions, which leave a lasting mark on the audience and transform actors into real, living beings with whom we become familiar.

The basis of this acting system is to develop a means by which to struggle against the tendency to distort natural and human behavior on stage and to direct the work of our inner natures to the right path which is carved out by devoted work and proper practices and habits.

Stanislavski has found that the more talent the actor has the more he cares about his technique, especially with regard to his inner qualities. He noted that a true creative state while on the stage, and all the elements that go to compose it, were the natural endowment of the great actors. They worked unremittingly on their technique. We, of perhaps more meager endowments, must work even harder to perfect our art.

CHAPTER SIXTEEN
ACTING EXERCISES

1.
THE WORDS ARE YOURS

Actors are to pair off and create an improvisation dealing with their characters in a play. A scene will be selected by the actors. The content and substance of the scene will be dealt with, but only their very own words can be used. They may speak sub-text, but no words from the actual text may be used.

2.
DIMENSIONS OF YOUR CHARACTER

Many events are mentioned by characters in a play, but do not actually take place in the play as seen by the audience. They are memories or dreams of characters.

Actors are to select any moment so mentioned in the play by his character. It is to be improvised by the actor playing the role. He may use any partner of his choice in bringing to life only that which is recalled by the character or dreamed of as a possible future happening.

3.
RECOLLECTIONS

Each actor is to take himself back to an event of childhood. The event recalled is to be improvised, setting up the familiar space with objects of his childhood, such as toy, pet, gift, etc.

4.
THROUGH LINE OF ACTION

Identify in your role, three to five or more key points which define the spine of the role, or the through line of action which leads to the super-objective of the character being portrayed.

5.
SPEECH ARTICULATION

Actor is to take any speech and speak the words very slowly in order to articulate every consonant and syllable and sound out every vowel so that the beginning, middle and end of every word becomes clearly defined and understood.

6.
COMFORT

Taking a brief segment from a play in progress, the actor will select that moment which makes him most comfortable in every respect, as actor, as character. It will be presented on stage. Then a discussion will be encouraged to explore the value of "comfort" on stage.

7.
MARIONETTE

Actors drain mind and relax; body lying collapsed on floor. They are to feel strings pulling them up and given life from above. They will perform simple actions taking on the life action of a marionette.

8.
TRAPPED

Actor is trapped within a confined area. He is in solitary confinement in a concrete cell block. It is dark, thus he is unable to see anything. He feels with his hands, the enclosure. He moves his hands along each of the walls, floor and ceiling, hoping to find one little opening, for air, perhaps, or a crack he can probe and open enough to seek escape.

9.
TRUST

A table is placed securely against a wall. A volunteer actor will stand on edge of table. The ensemble of actors will line up opposite each other, close to and extending out from the table. One actor will lie on the floor facing upward and toward the table. He is to extend his hands up as possible cushion for the actor on table. When ready, the actors facing each other will overlap their hands, palms upward, with intention of fully supporting the falling actor.

All is now ready, so the actor on the table will turn, his back to the actors who will catch him, feet on very edge of table, together, hands stiffly to side. He closes his eyes, stiffens his body so it is NOT TO BEND when he falls. EVERY ACTOR below is to catch him! Finally, he allows himself to fall RIGIDLY into waiting arms below.

UTMOST CARE MUST BE TAKEN TO INSURE THAT ALL AC-TORS MUST CATCH THE PERSON FALLING. BREAKING THEIR TRUST IS NOT TO HAPPEN - PLUS DANGER!

10.
MYSTERY TRUST

Actors in close circle, shoulder to shoulder. One actor in center drains his mind but holds body rigidly, with heel and toes together and arms folded across chest and eyes closed. Actors in circle will place one finger tip lightly on the body of the actor in center. All finger tips are in line around the body at upper chest and shoulder level. Pressure of finger tips must not change and all must be quiet.

The director will quietly designate one person in the circle as key. All will concentrate but make no gestures or sound nor will they alter the pressure on the body.

The actor in center will simply drain his mind. Ultimately he will feel a tendency to lean his rigid body (or fall) in a direction which he can not control. Lo and behold! It will generally be in the quadrant of the actor designated by the director. Try it over and over with different actors in center. Often, he will fall to the actual person designated. He will be supported and not allowed to fall. His eyes will open when he commits himself to the direction of fall.

PART THREE

ADDITIONAL EXERCISES

ADDITIONAL EXERCISES

1.
WARM-UP TIME OPEN UP!

Ensemble on stage. Make wide, broad, simple movements using all available space and involving your whole body, easily and without strain. Open completely by spreading arms, hands and legs. Maintain your open position, then imagine you are expanding, becoming larger and larger. Then return to neutral position for a period of time after which the exercise is repeated. Sense that you are opening, freeing and awakening your body and mind.

2.
SHRINKING SPACE

From a neutral position, cross arms, hands on shoulders, kneel on one or both knees and bend your head. Imagine becoming smaller and smaller, curl your body and contract as you close yourself. Sense that you are disappearing within your self as you free your mind of all thought, and the space around you is shrinking. You become smaller and smaller. Hold for a short, restful time and then return to neutral.

3.
THRUST

Stand in a relaxed position. When ready, thrust your body forward on one leg, stretching one or both arms. Withdraw your body and then thrust to the side, first right, then left, using as much space as you can. Make all thrusting movements as bold and free as humanly possible. Repeat.

4.
POWER HOUSE!

Sense the power within your self. Your body is capable of mastering the space about you. With huge movements, imagine you are digging earth and tossing it aside; heave huge objects in different directions; lift mighty objects high over head; pound huge stakes with a sledge hammer; drag a large and heavy object across the space; push a stubborn object to another position; toss logs onto a pile; pull a dead tree out of the ground; all done in moderate tempo. Sense that you can overpower any resistance.

5.
CHEST AS CENTER OF ENERGY

Gain a feeling that all energy is centered in your chest. All parts of your body radiate outward from your energy center and are connected to this center within your chest, even your arms and legs (rather than shoulder and hips). Perform simple movements, lifting and lowering arms, stretching, walking, sitting, etc. Feel that all movements are instigated by that power source in your chest. Then perform simple actions as moving objects, putting on coat, hat, removing them, etc. Continue to feel that all you do is powered from your energy center in your chest.

6.
SENDING OUT

Before performing each movement you are planning, take time to think of your power center in your chest, let it flow from your chest and let the power <u>precede</u> the movement itself. Send the impulse out first then let the impulse move you to perform the action. Try it before you sit, or rise, or step forward, or backward. Let your body <u>follow</u> the center. The result will be smooth, graceful and pleasant movements.

7.
RADIATE YOUR PRESENCE

Perform movements of previous exercises. When a particular movement ceases, allow the power to flow and radiate for a while <u>beyond</u> your body into the space around you. Allow yourself to experience the freedom, the power as well as a sense of accomplishment. It becomes a psycho-physical achievement at your command, affecting your presence on stage, eliminating self consciousness and building confidence. You will gain the sensation that your body and your mind are approaching an "ideal" type of humanness. Do it often until it feels natural, without special attention.

8.
MOLDING SPACE

Try molding the space surrounding you by imagining the air around you as an element or substance which resists you. Leave forms in the atmosphere which are made by the movements of your body. Think of each movement as having a beginning and an end. Begin a movement which creates a form. Then finish the movement and the form is there in space. Try various simple movements and perform them over and over until the idea of molding the space into forms comes easier and easier. Try different parts of the body, molding air around you using only shoulder, arm, elbow, back, knee, forehead, fingers, hand, foot, etc. Then perform simple natural movements of everyday business.

9.
CONTACTING OBJECTS

Allowing your power to emanate from your energy source within your chest, try to pour your strength into objects upon which you focus your attention. Make contact with mind or body, but fill the selected object with your power. Try this with different objects, connecting first with mind and then with fingers, hands or body. Notice how you will get to deal with objects with ease, skill and command.

10.
CONTACT WITH PARTNERS

With your power flowing from your energy source within your chest, make contact with your partner on stage. Fill your partner with your power sending out your strength, assuring a true and firm connection on stage.

11.
FLOATING MOVEMENTS

Perform wide, open and free movements with different parts of your body using all the space around you. Imagine the space around you as a surface of water which supports you. All your movements are to be imagined as lightly skimming over the water and giving you the sensation that you are floating each movement you make. Merge one movement into another, gracefully, gently and beautifully.

12.
FLYING THROUGH SPACE

With big and free movements, seek the sensation of lightness in every part of your body. Imagine the air around you as an element which induces your flying movement. Let each movement flow into another movement using first broad, big movements, then natural, simple everyday movements. Even when you reach a static position outwardly, continue to feel like you are soaring aloft inwardly. Imagine your whole body flying through space.

13.
SENDING RAYS

As you perform any movement, send out rays of energy from your body into the space around you in the direction of the movement you make and <u>after</u> the movement is made. For example, as you sit, after completing the action of sitting, radiate that you are sitting (enjoying your relaxation). Try standing and radiating you are standing (glory in your heightened vantage point). After climbing movement, send out rays into space (exhilarate the joy of freedom, for example). Send out rays even before a movement. For example, you are seated. Before you actually rise from your seat, send out rays that you will be rising. Or, before moving your right arm to command, send out rays that you will be raising your arm to command. Send out those rays of energy before you make the movement and while you are static and after the movement has been completed. Try it with all parts of the body.

14.
MOVEMENT WHILE STILL

Lie down and relax with eyes closed and body motionless. Being familiar with molding, flying, floating and radiating, reproduce each of them in your imagination. See and feel all your movements as you mold, fly, float and radiate in various situations.

15.
MOVEMENT WITH BEAUTY

Create all prior movement exercises with the feeling of beauty which rises within you, until your entire body is permeated with it and you begin to feel an aesthetic satisfaction. True beauty has its roots inside all human beings, whereas, false beauty is only on the outside.

16.
ATMOSPHERES

Imagine feelings spreading around you filling the air as you command. Transform slowly feelings which you initiate, going from one to another but only after truly allowing yourself to experience the feeling and its affect on the atmosphere about you before you create another. Try first the feeling of coziness. Let it permeate your mind and body and then the atmosphere around you with all the elements which come about naturally. Then, transform to solitude. Go with it until the total atmosphere is affected, but without rushing it. Then, awe, followed by love, then joy, fear, sorrow, exhilaration, pain, calmness, etc. Allow yourself to feel your mind and body permeated with the atmosphere chosen.

17.
ATMOSPHERE AND MOVEMENT

Having affected your atmosphere all around you, allow the atmosphere to inspire movements of your body in harmony with the atmosphere created. An atmosphere of caution will allow certain movements of your body, whereas an atmosphere of ecstasy will initiate other movements in harmony. Explore various possibilities until movements come easily.

18.
OBJECTS AND ATMOSPHERE

Having created appropriate atmosphere, deal with various objects which fit into the picture. Allow objects and movement to be influenced by and in harmony with the atmosphere created and which permeates you and the space around you.

19.
PHYSICAL ACTIONS WITH ATMOSPHERE

Complicate your movements after creating special atmospheres. Open a door, search, put on clothing, put on equipment, seek through a file, move furniture, steal a treasured art piece, study a photo, smell a flower, etc. Allow your movements to become influenced by the atmosphere.

20.
SPEECH AND ATMOSPHERE

Try first some simple dialogue inspired by the atmosphere which is permeating the space around you. For example, "Please sit down." Speak first without movement, then try it with gestures influenced by the atmosphere created. It could be a loving request, but it could also be a command. Create other simple dialogue with gestures, repeating words but changing atmospheres from calm to passion to fear, hatred, etc.

21.
QUALITY OF MOVEMENT

Perform simple actions, such as lifting an arm, moving a chair, setting a table, putting on a coat, etc. Then color the action with a quality. For example, the quality of fear will affect the simple movement if you know what is causing the fear. Once the mind is activated by the imagination, it affects the feeling which influences the movement. The gesture, then, is no longer a mere physical action for it has acquired a psychological nuance; fear of attack, of rape, of capture, of death. That fear permeates the mind and body and the action causing a psycho-physical sensation. Explore with qualities of warmth, coldness, love, tenderness, astonishment, curiosity, etc.

22.
PLAY CATEGORY AND QUALITY

The playwright's creation originates with a quality. A tragedy has its quality, which is obviously different than the quality of a comedy, farce or drama. Perform actions with a comedic quality. Then try the same action with the quality of tragedy. Continue to explore as you perform actions with quality of drama, and then explore the quality of farce. Notice that the quality of one category will not work at all in another. The very fast tempo-rhythm and lightness of a farce certainly will not be appropriate for a powerful and heavy tragedy. Prove this by finding simple actions with various qualities in different situations.

23.
QUALITY AND TEMPO-RHYTHM

Select simple movements with objects, props and actions with dialogue. Perform it very slowly and heavily. It will generally become associated with drama or tragedy. Try the same situation, but perform it very rapidly and lightly. One will associate it with the qualities of comedy or farce. Explore this further, using different tempo-rhythms each time it is performed. Use actions which take no more than one minute for the sake of illustration. It tends to be very revealing. (When the performance of a comedy takes the quality of a drama, the production is in serious trouble.)

24.
TEMPO-RHYTHM CONTRAST

Assign an improvisation where tempo-rhythms contrast between actors, and also with the actor (inner and outer t/r). Example, one actor moves quickly, other slowly, meanwhile, their inner lives also contrast.

25.
PSYCHOLOGICAL GESTURE

It is always fun when the actor finds a gesture that perfectly suits the character being portrayed. The nosey character seems to penetrate the space around him with his nose when he moves. The blustery bantam character fidgets about seemingly with elbows flapping at his side like chicken wings. The fighter seems to center his energy in his fists as he punches the air for emphasis. The self conscious character fumbles with clothing, touches buttons, straightens folds or tie. The proud character appears to penetrate space with chest, whereas the stubborn person moves through space with jutting chin. Etc. Avoid any cliché as you seek a gesture that fits the psychology of your character. Who is it who walks slumped forward? Which character walks as if he has a club foot? We are reminded of the character with one eye closed; the twisted mouth; pigeon toes; the limp arm; spastic head; stutter and stammer, etc. Create brief improvisations with such rich characters, but avoid clichés!

26.
WARM-UP!

To seek relaxation, ensemble may be on stage or in their seats as the director calls out for them to shake fingers, loosely shake out hands until they feel they will fly away. Stretch all parts of the body upward and outward, shake arms loosely and freely. Repeat until you feel all parts of the body will dissolve or fly apart. If you don't feel that way, then you didn't give yourself completely to the exercise. Repeat!

27.
SOUND OFF!

Call out a greeting to all in the group. They should all respond loudly and openly and freely. Keep it going. Build up volume and energy. End.

28.
NEW DIMENSIONS

Perform a known, rehearsed scene. Then find improvisations of any physical elements within the scene. It could be physical and psychological gestures, and it could also be movement and physical actions. You may also seek adjustments in emotional elements based on changes in your interpretation of the psycho-physical life of your character.

29.
HEIGHTENED INTENTIONS

Stage a scene of your choice. Then heighten the urgency of intentions (or inner actions) to seek higher levels of energy and dynamics. Experiment further by altering intentions of various beats, noting the changes which take place in the action and life of each adjustment. (The purpose of rehearsals is to explore, not to "run lines.")

30.
THEMES TO LIGHT THE WAY

Build improvisation based on common themes you face in your world today. For example; to make a better life, to achieve success, fear of physical abuse, pursuit of love, prejudice can destroy, hatred is destructive, difficulties of single parenthood, abortion, sexual abuse, greed, our troubled economy, losing faith in friends, jealousy, etc.

31.
FEMALE STRENGTH

Select scene of strong women; Lady Macbeth, Queen Gertrude, Linda Loman, etc.

32.
MALE MODELS OF STRENGTH

Male actors to stage scenes with strong characters; King Lear, Falstaff, James Tyrone, Richard III, Stanley Kowalski, etc. Take on their power.

33.
BIGGER THAN LIFE

Select a monologue or scene where you challenge yourself to believe you are twice the size you normally are. Take on voice, physical aspects, inner life, and circumstance.

34.
YOUR ROOTS

American way of life will often tend to thwart your strength and creative verve. Seek and identify your ethnic roots. Build an improvisation and use only such ethnic qualities to develop character and situation.

35.
TIMIDITY

Stand on stage and talk to an audience. Talk to them about any topic of your choice. You will note that you must combat timidity. Learn of its effect on you and how to deal with it. Group is to discuss it openly and lovingly as each person gets up before audience.

36.
NOW LISTEN HERE!

You will berate an audience for doing something wrong. You are furious with the entire audience and you criticize them soundly, finding as much fault with them as you can create. You will do this with loud voice and big physical gestures. Add three additional physical gestures and seek a higher level of volume before you exit. Note any change in your attitude. This is to be discussed after each actor takes his turn.

37.
BURSTING WITH INTENTION

You establish a strong intention before you go on stage. When ready, burst into the scene. If the door is locked, break through the door. If an object is in the way, kick it out of the way. Throw a chair through a window. Beat on a closed door. Tear pages from a book. Pry open the metal bars of your cell. Etc. The physical actions are to be assigned or are of your creation. You must know what has taken place and what your intention is that incites this violent action.

38.
SHAPE IT!

You are to create an object in space of large size. You may sculpt the statue of David, or create a snow man. You may consider forming the Statue of Liberty, build walls of an out-house, or build a wall, etc. When done, surprise everyone by demanding they become the object they created, taking on the life and stature of the object. Note their response and see how creative and inventive they can become.

39.
HOW BIG?

Work on improvisation with normal props. The actors must not know that they will repeat the scene, but with props expanded five hundred times!

40.
WHERE AM I?

Begin with an empty space on stage. Actor number one enters and places an object or set piece in the space and establishes its complete physical life without exaggeration. The next actor enters, works with the object created by first actor with natural actions, then places another object in the space, which blends with the prior set piece and works with the new object or set piece. Third actor enters, works with all existing objects and set pieces and adds his own set piece to the growing stage design, works with it and exits. Each actor enters to build stage set.

41.
I'M FLYING!

Each actor is to enter and work with an object that moves in space. It may be a kite, a paper air plane, a bow with an arrow, bowling ball, a fishing line, a baseball, balloon, etc. Upon putting the object into motion, the actor assumes the life of the object in movement and with creative imagination performs the movement, taking on its life and action.

42.
MIRROR, MIRROR!

Actor is to sit or stand before a mirror and apply make-up and put on costume, all with imagination. Make-up is to be applied in detail as if using real make-up for a character. Each item of costume is to be conceived in the imagination and dealt with in detail as it is put on to the growing character. When character is fully established, made-up and costumed, the actor is to perform some actions in a created situation before ending the exercise.

43.
THE REAL ME

Actors are to sit in a circle, comfortably, relaxed and in a loving and positive mood. Each actor takes time to reveal his own sincere impression of his mind, his body and his spirit.

44.
AS I SEE YOU

Comfortably seated in a circle, with a most giving and loving mood, each actor is to reveal his impression of each actor's mind, attitude, actions, humor, good points, and lovingly exposing even some negative points, strengths and weaknesses. This can be done fully in a close knit group of actors. It may be tried first by voicing only the positive qualities of each actor.

45.
ELEVATION TRUST

One volunteer actor stands in center of a tight circle of actors. Actor in center maintains a stiff body, with arms folded and eyes closed. He falls freely into the waiting arms of <u>several</u> actors in the circle who will then lift the actor up over their shoulders, with <u>every single</u> actor supporting him fully and safely. The actor is elevated to highest point, then lowered, then raised in a wave-life movement and passed on in treadmill fashion as actors in front of the group move to the other end to receive the body. Actor elevated must drain mind while maintaining his body in a rigid position. Actors supporting him must remain silent and conscious of their responsibility to support the actor in total safety.

46.
TWIST AND TURN TRUST

To further prior exercise, when trust is fully established and ensemble feels capable, they may, while body is supported by all, move the body in every way, elevating, twisting and turning the body, reversing the movement, heightening the rise and fall of body, increasing the wave movement, and even turning the body upside down, tossing him upward and catching his fall, then lowering him to the floor gently. Play it SAFE!

47.
MUSEUM

Actors are to enter an imaginary museum, transforming the empty space into a real experience of visiting a museum of note. Putting the fourth wall principle into effect, actors as visitors will look upon all art work and sculpture which will be on exhibit. All walls will be used, including down stage fourth wall. They must focus on objects in space, allowing proper distance, and activate their inner vision.

48.
PET SHOP

Actors are to enter a pet shop, where they will see and encounter live pets in a hand-on situation. They are to see, touch, hear and smell the objects encountered. Attitudes will be varied, exhibiting love, apprehension, timidity, fear, revulsion, etc.

49.
NOT WHAT YOU EXPECTED

Actors view a beautiful person. Every aspect of beauty is to be seen in detail. Inner vision and emotion will become activated, perhaps coached by the director. Then, the director will advise them that the beautiful person is performing an ugly act of revulsion. Transformation of inner vision and attitude will take place. The director will not hint earlier that this ugly act is to take place. It must be a discovery.

50.
DISCOVERY

The group of actors view a thoroughly ugly character in complete detail, looks, mode of dress, behavior, attitude, etc. When ready, the director will announce that the ugly character is performing a beautiful action. It will initiate a transformation when the discovery is made by the viewer.

51.
MOVING IN

Actor are to enter the space, seeing it in detail as they mount wall hangings, put up drapes, move furniture into place, open window, look out to the surrounding area dealing with distance and elevation, store objects, unpack boxes, etc. They will deal with flexible fourth-wall and imagery, discovery, objects in space, inner vision, etc.

52.
FUN FOR ALL AGES!

Free your mind and revert briefly to your childhood years. Without props, play hop scotch, jacks, marbles, checkers, bowling, shuffle board, jump rope, tag, dodge ball, etc. Use exercise to loosen up, to relax, to bring about cast unity, develop positive and co-operative attitudes.

53.
PASS IT ON!

Actors are in a loose circle. Designated actors begin a full body mirror action with big movements until actor "A" freezes the position. Actor "B" will hold the position briefly then turn, in the frozen position toward actor "C," During the slow turn, he makes adjustments in his "grotesque" position and passes his image to actor "D" who will mirror the image. Hold the position briefly, turn slowly and pass on the newly created "outlandish" image to actor "E," etc. It may end when it finally gets to actor "A" or, indeed, it may go around again as new body movements and images are explored.

54.
FACE IT!

Actors are in a circle as in prior exercise. Actor "A" distorts his face as much as possible and is mirrored by actor "B," who then alters the contorted face mask and creates his own horror mask to pass on to "C," etc.

55.
SHAPING FORMS

Using music or a beating drum, ensemble moves about the stage creating beautiful forms in the atmosphere, shaping one appealing form after another. Stay with your form as long as you wish, working with it in your own way before moving on to another creation. Music quality and tempo may be varied, as may also be with the drum beat, noting the effect the changes will have on the movement and forms being created.

Albert Pia

56.
SEASON AND TIME CHANGES

Actors are to walk through space. Director will announce time of day and actors will justify their created action, life and movement for that time. The director will then announce it is night, followed by immediate transformation and justification by the actor. A different day may also be announced, or a total change of season from winter to summer to fall. With each change in time, day or season, the actor will transform his life and seek immediate justification.

57.
MORE PSYCHOLOGICAL GESTURES

As the actors find positions on stage, the director will call out a series of positions or movements. Actors must immediately add who, what, where, when and Why as they perform the action and seek justification. Some suggestions would be; hail a cab, pick up a coin, smell a flower, wave your arm, call a halt, on your mark, open an envelope, dial a phone, answer the door, buy a ticket, answer the phone, etc. Some humorous announcements by the director would add new dimensions of fun to the game.

58.
FLEXIBLE CIRCLES OF ATTENTION

With attention focused on the smallest possible object, such as a comma or dot, expand circle to nearest wall, beyond window, to horizon and beyond, then withdraw your circle of attention to your back yard, your wall of your den, to that desk, a photograph, a ring from a friend, to lettered inscription on inside of ring, etc., etc. The director may suggest as many objects of attention as can be created, going quickly from near focus point, to far, to near, etc.

216

59.
SPACE FLIGHT

This relaxation exercise is done while lying on the floor in a darkened space and with eyes closed. Briefly drain mind and body, then begin slowly to feel that you are elevating, up through the ceiling and beyond, upward into clouds, seeing the earth below you getting smaller as you continue rising, rising into the distant sky and out into space, passing through daylight into darkness, playing tag with stars and suns and galaxies. When reaching your distant goal, you may slowly return to earth floating gracefully to your desired landing spot, to this spot, safely returned to here and now. Actors should maintain a pleasant feeling of joy and lightness throughout the exercise.

60.
TENPINS!

Ten actors will line up in a "V" position at an appropriate distance from the "bowling balls," who are designated actors. When ready, the actors who are bowling balls will somersault or roll along to the ten pins knocking them slowly on to the "alley" for a score. Take turns being "pins" or "bowling balls," continuing to a completed score if desired.

61.
BUS STOP

The space becomes a bus terminal. Actors will enter as characters of any age but their own actual age. Each is to add who, what, when, why and carry on an improvisation, giving and taking ideas from each other and carrying it to a conclusion.

62.
LOOK, NO HANDS!

Teams of three to five will be designated. Allow each team to go off to its own rehearsal area. After five minutes of searching for ideas, they will have decided and rehearsed moving large objects across the space, but without use of hands. They will all be called to the stage and the director will announce the order of presentation. The fun is not knowing what each team will create. Ideas will vary widely, from a coffin on shoulders, to body bashing against a closed door, to supporting a collapsing ceiling with shoulders, etc. A car could be pushed with no hands, and a wall may be bolstered by the body. There are many creative possibilities.

63.
WHISPERING

The situation created by single or paired actors will allow no speech above a whisper. They are to add who, what, why, when.

64.
ROAR OF THE CROWD

Conceive of improvisations based on dealing with crowd roars. Whether it be a riot, revolution, ball game, war, earthquake will be the creative idea of the teams who will add where, when, etc.

65.
COLD

Improvisation will be created by actors dealing with the image of cold.

66.
IT'S HOT!

Improvisation will be created using the idea of dealing with heat in any conceivable manner. It could be temperature or attitude or pressures of a job, or imminent arrest, etc.

67.
HUNGER

Using the idea of hunger in any form, actors will improvise a scene. It could be hunger for love or respect or belonging. And, of course, it could be starving in a prison camp, modern day homelessness, etc.

68.
SCENT OF LIFE

Build a scene based on the sense of smell. Is it the smell of smoke coming from a fire in the night? Is it the smell of gas leaking? Or is it that lovely scent of the flowers you received from a loved one? Could it be the scent of a plot to overthrow a leader? Or do you smell a "rat" in the group? Is there a spy in your midst?

69.
AWAKENED

The idea for an improvisation will be based on being awakened. You may be awakened in the night or awakened to an idea which has suddenly come to your conscious mind. Has a nightmare awakened you, or did a sound of an intruder penetrate your sleep? Have you awakened to the idea that your best friend has attempted to steal your lover? Etc.

70.
GOOD NEWS!

Select for your brief improvisation an idea based upon receiving any kind of good news. Add who, what, where, etc.

71.
TOUCHING YOU

Walk about the stage and touch as if the first time any and all objects which make up the space; the floor, the lighting instruments, seats, the fabric of seats, floor boards, draperies, walls, ropes, pipes, etc. Discover each element of every object coming to your attention as if you come from another planet and have never seen anything like it. Penetrate each object with your gaze. Look at it, and allow it, the object, to look at you. Listen to its presence. Touch it in detail, and then let IT touch YOU. Seek levels of dimension as you connect with each object.

72.
MIND TO MIND

Two actors stand back to back. Actor "A" is to radiate his idea of a simple movement to actor "B" and in due time makes the movement slowly. When sensing it is happening in his mind, actor "B" will have received the rays of actor "A" and will make what he believes to be the movement made by actor "A." It can work! However, in the beginning, you may limit the movements to perhaps three possible movements known by each.

73.
IT'S IN THE BOX

Fill a box with a number of imaginary objects, dealing with each in terms of value, texture, weight, size, etc. When all objects have been placed in the box, lift it, being conscious of the weight of accumulated objects, and then carry it to another spot. There, you will unpack the box in reverse order, taking out each object which was placed by you, again dealing with the specific elements of one valued object after another.

74.
IT'S POURING

You are to pour different levels of wine or soda, milk or water into various glasses. Lift and move glasses and bottles about, noting the different weights of each glass and bottle as you fill some and empty others. If other actors are in the exercise, note that the weight varies as each drinks the liquid, pours, or spills. The subtle differences are to be stressed by the director.

75.
COCKTAIL PARTY

Actors are guests at a cocktail party. Each is to deal with snacks and drinks in detail. Take the time to concentrate on tasting, biting, chewing, sipping, swallowing, including the sense of having had a drink or having eaten something you enjoy (or dislike).

76.
THE ATTIC

You enter an attic which is meaningful to you. It is a home, present or distant past, which contains valued objects of family: Old trunks with clothing, wedding dresses, photographs, toys, letters. Cob webs are every where hanging from the low roof. The smell of time past is every where. Add what, when, why, etc.

77.
A WAY OUT

You enter a space, encounter strange objects and obstacles. Try to open a jammed window, crawl through it, on to a ledge, high above the ground, move along the ledge with caution, and try to find your way out of captivity. Use a minimum amount of space.

78.
BED TIME

You are an older brother or sister or parent and you are to undress your young sister, brother or child and get him (her) ready for bed. Each item demands your attention. Then, dress the child in pajamas, send her off to bed, but call her back for an embrace. Then take her to her bed, put her under covers, making certain her favorite stuffed animals are with her and in place. Kiss the child goodnight, turn off light.

79.
BUNGLING OAF

You enter and trip, walk and bump into person, turn away and bump into a wall, reverse direction and fall off the curb, rise to cross the street and have difficulty avoiding cars, trip over or into a man hole, etc. FUN! Enjoy this antic exercise, for mimes have made fortunes with it.

80.
HALLOWEEN MONSTER BECKY WECKY

You are dressed grotesquely as a monster. Candles are beside you and you sit at a table filled with goodies for the incoming children. When they arrive, you cackle and howl as you greet them and toy with them before giving them their deserved candies, then send them on their way.

81.
BURDEN OF LIFE

You enter the space with the quality of tragedy, carrying a burden you can only manage with difficulty. You have been defeated by life. As you approach objects in your space, they become grotesque obstacles which you must encounter. Cliffs rise above you, chasms yawn below you. You conceive of a development in pantomime and then an ending.

82.
CAGED!

Creating the idea of life in pantomime, you enter the space growing into exuberant youth. You develop the circumstance and become caged and trapped. You struggle with great effort to free yourself. You devise the ending as either becoming released or failing.

83.
APE MAN

You visit a zoo. Before you is a caged ape. You study it thoroughly, mirror its movements, taking on its body, mind and life. Ultimately, you become the ape, are caged, looking out at curious people in the zoo.

84.
THE ROPE

A single actor may perform this exercise, or a group of actors may work in harmony. A rope lies on the floor before you across the stage. It is picked up by you and you begin to pull against the opposition. First you lean toward the opposition to grasp as much as possible so that you can pull the opposite in your direction. You pull and tug. Move your hand over hand to take more of the rope and continue to pull. You end up defeating your opposition or losing to it.

85.
TANGLED

Your environment is water. You wade into it and walk along the bottom of the sea. You encounter fish, sea weed and octopus, dealing with each in turn as you continue to move in a buoyant manner due to water atmosphere.

86.
STAYING CONNECTED

Select a movement with an object which you propel, such as a ball hit by your bat or golf club. Once the object you propel is on its way, you follow its path with your body, conveying its movement in space. The ball is curving beyond the foul pole, or the golf ball is slicing into the woods. The kite is dancing in space, or the bowling ball is curving into the gutter or hitting a strike. Your fishing line is caught in the rocks or is in the mouth of a fish, etc. Let your body take on the flight characteristic of the ball, javelin, kite, etc.

87.
SUNNY SIDE UP!

You are to cook eggs on a stove in a frying pan. Deal with all objects, from egg carton, to heat of stove, to cracking egg shells, melting butter, placing eggs in pan to suit your need. They may be scrambled, turned over or cooked sunny side up. Deal also with toast, butter, utensils, etc. This is a challenge for the most experienced of actors to deal with accurately in view of the great number of details. Thus, you may simplify the exercise to suit your need.

88.
OBJECT DETAIL

Assign actors to polish and place delicate glass animals, or polish finger nails, apply detailed make-up, fold a bed sheet or blanket, sew a garment, trim paper figures, wrap or unwrap small gifts, open envelopes to deal with letters, etc. Attention to detail is the point of exercise.

89.
NO PLACE LIKE HOME!

Return to your own room after a long absence. See, touch, connect with every personal set piece and object in your room. There are trophies, photographs, treasured objects all about. Your old toys, stuffed animals are in place. There is a dog collar belonging to your departed pet, etc. Add when, why to develop the quality of the scene.

90.
BLIND

You assume a condition of blindness, adding who, what, when, why, etc. Enter a space that is either familiar to you (as in prior exercise) or contend with strange, new objects. But, you must establish exactly where you are by detailed contact with all objects in your space.

91.
OUCH!

You are in severe pain. You seek justification for this condition. Then you are to perform certain normal everyday actions, but dealing constantly with the ever-present pain.

92.
LOADED!

You are in a city trying to catch a subway car to the terminal. The problem is, you are loaded with packages and cartons containing recent purchases. You enter, buy a token, wrestling with coins and bills, attempt to enter through turnstile, combating the crowd, entering the doors of the subway car, jamming into people, trying to find a seat, exiting, etc.

93.
LATE!

You sneak into your home after a night out. It is late; very late. No sound can be made for fear you will waken someone and be in real trouble. Add when, why, etc. Heighten the seriousness of the problem.

94.
CITY SIDEWALKS

The acting ensemble will become the individuals in a big city walking along Broadway. Enter as characters; changing each time you enter. Conceive as many different characters as possible.

95.
SHOCKING!

All actors are in a circle on stage and holding hands. The director is to designate the actor who will initiate the "electrical charge" which he will send to his right or left by the simple quick squeeze of the hand. The person receiving the "shock" will send it on by squeezing the hand of the actor next to him. It must travel with lightning swiftness around the circle. After a few circuits, some one may reverse the current. The timing and dexterity required may cause much hilarity. Especially as you quicken the speed.

96.
THE MASTERS

Select photographs of great works of art by master painters. Study them and allow teams of actors to choose their painting. Each team will then assume the characters and poses within the painting. Hold the position for a time. When ready, dissolve the painting pose and carry on with the life of the character you have chosen. Build an improvisation based upon the period and circumstance conceived by your knowledge of the times and the period and circumstance conceived by your knowledge of the times and of the painting as well as the characters. Results can be very rewarding.

97.
KNOCK, KNOCK!

Actor "A" is on stage, without character or thought. Actor "B" is off the stage and is about to enter. He knows who he is and what he wants. Thus, he approaches the door and knocks. He will try to send his rays by way of his knock as to the nature of his situation. Actor "B" will open the door and must not anticipate a thing, but receive the rays from actor "A" by way of movement, attitude, and selected brief speeches. Actor "B" will answer only what is required until he begins to sense just who he is and who "A" is and what the purpose is of the entrance. The scene builds, moment by moment. Actor "A" may likely already know who "B" is. But, that is left to their creative idea.

98.
COMMON MOVEMENTS

First actor is to create a broad movement (or be put into movement by the director). The actor continues the movement until his sense memory is awakened and he sees himself performing an action, such as driving a car or chopping wood. Actor "B" takes on that movement and performs it with slight adjustment until his sense memory is triggered and he finds himself performing a truthful movement, such as pulling reins of a horse or boxing a fight partner, etc. The assumed movement must not be pre-selected or anticipated, nor should it be an abrupt and obvious change from the preceding movement. It must grew out of the earlier movement and come from the subconscious. It need not happen immediately. Do not rush into a forced movement. Let it happen, no matter how long.

99.
IT'S A CHOKE!

Actor enters choking, or build a scene based on choking. Use any variation.

100.
BAD NEWS!

Develop an improvisation based on receiving bad news. Add who, what, why, where to lend dimension to situation and characters.

PART FOUR

STANISLAVSKI EXERCISES

STANISLAVSKI EXERCISES

Highlighting theatre exercises used by Constantin Stanislavski for his selected actors at the Moscow Art Theatre. Recommended for advanced actors and directors.

1.
THE WORLD ABOUT YOU.

As a performing artist, you need to be perceptive of life objects in your environment. Find a comfortable seat with a partner which allows you a wide scope of activity about you. It may be a busy village street, a park or plaza. Taking turns, tell your partner all that is seen which is considered important and interesting to you. It may be anything which catches your attention, animate or inanimate. It may be a taxi or carriage, child or curious pet, flower or rays of sunlight, pathway or stone wall, beggar or train whistle, bird, executive, bag lady, homeless vagrant, leaves, the rustling of leaves, crying child, chirping bird and so on.

Taking the exercise to another step, you may create a scenario for any or all objects or events observed. Try to determine the relationship of the two people walking along the path; why is the little boy crying? You may imagine what position the person has who is carrying a briefcase. If an attorney, what case might be the present assignment? What may have led to the bag lady's present condition? Exercise your imagination to the fullest.

2.
PEOPLE WATCHING

Building on the prior exercise, observe people in depth and with your imagination build a character with each individual observed. Study the persons in detail; the manner of movement, attitude, age, clothing style, personal grooming, physical mannerisms and so on. Try to determine the life condition of the person, education background, vocation, personal interests, married or single, business person, athlete, teacher, banker, messenger, electrician, etc. If conversing, try to imagine the subject of their discussion, their relationship, and their flow of life activity this day.

3.
THIS SPECIAL DAY

With a partner or in a group, each actor is to tell all that is known of this particular day. Note its importance to each individual, to the group, to the community, country and the world. Where have the noted details come from? They may have come from newspaper, television, family, friend, school or elsewhere.

Actors are to be encouraged to understand their relationship to all that takes place in life, near and far.

4.
A MOST INTERESTING PERSON!

Select any person in your life who has made an impact on you. You are then to inform the group all you know about that important person. Describe the human characteristics, the nature of the relationship, good and bad traits, details of the effect on you, etc.

5.
KEY SCENE

The director is to analyze the play to be produced in detail so that he may identify the key scene. Allow the cast to review the structure and details of the scene. After it has been thoroughly studied by the actors, they are to stage an improvisation of this key scene.

The improvisation of the key scene will heighten each actor's involvement in the event and will make the ultimate staging of the scene more dramatic, meaningful, and dimensional. Their new-found awareness of the key scene will bring the other elements in the play into sharper focus.

6.
I AM!

When assuming an acting role in a play, you are to create a complete biography of your character. Know everything about your character as well as you know yourself. Here are some of the facts you should know about your character. You will add other details, of course.

Who am I? What is my age? How do I earn a living? What schools have I attended? What is my training? Who are my parents? Who are other family members? What is my position in my family? What is the personal condition of my life? What is my disposition? Do I know my strengths and weaknesses? Where do I live? Do I live in a home or apartment? Do I reside in a town, hamlet or city? Who are my neighbors and friends; enemies? What is the design, structure, content of my room and home? What do I like to eat, and read and wear? What have I done in my life up to this event? What did I do yesterday? What has been happening to me up to my character's first entrance? What is my relationship with each character I deal with in the play? What is my goal of life in this circumstance provided by the playwright?

7.
FITTING IN TO LIFE SCHEME

To further develop an understanding of your character in the play in rehearsal, you are to know your position in relationship to all other characters in the situation in which you find yourself. How does your character fit into the major circumstance of the play? Know your needs, desires, obstacles, social condition, as well as your psychological condition. It is possible that your character does not know his psychological condition, but you the actor must be fully aware.

8.
THE EPOCH OF CHARACTER

The play you are performing is set in a period of time. As a living character of that period in time, you are to present to your director a thorough study of the historical, political and social climate of the period in which the play is set. Make the study as detailed as possible even if the study is never requested by your director.

9.
DEPTH OF THE PLAY

To penetrate the very depth of the play you are to stage, you are to write a thorough analysis of the play as interpreted by you. As you perform this task, you must, of course, have in mind the playwright's point of view. Be prepared to contribute your ideas at the early cast meetings when this subject will be discussed with the director. Your ideas may or may not be fully in harmony with the director's interpretation of the play. Adjustments may be required by you so as to be fully in agreement with the director's point of view. Quite often, an actor's astute analysis of his character and the play will be accepted and added to the director's view.

10.
YOUR LINE OF LIFE

You are to develop your inner line of life of the character you are to portray. This will consist of the series of events in the play which take you from beginning to end of your role in the circumstance of the play and how the events affect your inner life from moment to moment.

11.
DIRECTOR PROBLEMS

The director will employ every method possible to lead the actors into understanding every event of the play in rehearsal. He may consider inventing individual problems for each character, or group of characters, touching upon any event in the play. He may then encourage an improvisation of the particular problem. New dimensions of the circumstances will be discovered. There will be as much richness and variety as the director's imagination will allow.

12.
EXTERNAL EXPRESSION

Consider any beat or scene of the play in rehearsal. You are to find an opportunity alone, or with a willing partner, to move about the given space in which the scene takes place and explore every possible physical action as an external expression of your inner life, your inner rhythm, your inner monologue. Do this without dialogue if you are able. Free yourself to seek new levels of physical life even if prior blocking has been established. This may be done before, during or after a scene has been established in terms of movement and use of the space. Its objective is to discover new dimensions of your external expression. When witnessed by the director, he may or may not accept the new discoveries you have made, but the chances are that they will indeed be accepted and appreciated.

13.
COMPLEX GROUPINGS

In staging a play with a large cast consisting of villagers, walk-ons, soldiers, party guests, or other extras, scenes are often quite troublesome. The director will find it helpful to compose living units of people in groups of two, three, five, etc. Time will be productively utilized if each unit is encouraged to work first as an individual team, developing its actions, objectives, conflicts, resolutions and relationships. Dialogue may be permitted in an improvisation which they will create, which later may be allowed, reduced in volume, or mouthed with the physical actions discovered. Each person and each group is to discover the thread which ties them to the main action of the scene to be ultimately staged.

When each group has met with the approval of the director, all units will join the main action as active, motivated, exciting, living characters adding new dimension to the finished work.

14.
SKETCHING YOUR SPACE

Upon learning the life and problem of the character you are to portray, you are to conceive of the setting in which your character lives. Sketch such a setting by actively using your imagination. See your room, terrace, home, park, street, beach, boat or rooftop as vividly as your inner vision allows. As rough as it may be, draw the setting on a large sheet of paper. Add color and detail to excite your imagination. You may or may not have in mind the stage space in which the play will be performed. The value of the activity is to see it and sketch it to add dimension to your own character's life.

Ultimately you will view the design conceived by the assigned stage designer and director. You will enjoy comparing sketches. Such creations may not, but sometimes do indeed contribute to the final stage design for the production.

15.
DRESSING IN STYLE!

You will soon know your character well enough to conceive of personal tastes. You will know what food you enjoy, what kind of friends you attract, the books and magazines you read, and the clothing styles your character wears.

At the director's discretion, determine the scene to be rehearsed. Be then prepared to illustrate how you are to be dressed. You will find it helpful to sketch your costume and hair style, using cloth swatches and colors to suit the nature and temperament of your character. Should your costume room be well supplied, you may select from the supply on hand. If a full scale production is planned, the costume designer may invite your creative ideas for your character, or provide you with a costume selected by the director and designer.

16.
GESTURES

As you begin rehearsals, keep your gestures to a minimum as you avoid the use of any cliché action. Allow your inner life of your developing character to dictate a movement or gesture which will express the true feeling of the moment. Your gestures will then become as natural to your character as breathing for they will be justified.

Avoid over-use of any gesture. Should it become a mannerism, expect your director to notice its untruthfulness and be prepared for his rejection of the gesture. He will be seeking in you only natural and justified gestures which reveal new elements of expression. Your ideas, words and movements of the character will then be filled with truth and inner power.

17.
INTENSITY AND RHYTHM

Rhythm was a major element of importance for Stanislavski as he worked with his actors. He would observe the actors at work in the studio or in rehearsal and note if all his external actions, speech pattern, volume, tempo, were true manifestations of the character's inner rhythm and intensity and that they were in total harmony.

The director will assign a monologue or scene to be staged by the actors. Keen observation will be employed by the director to note your character's rhythm in all its visible manifestations. He will be seeking in you a perfect blend of inner intensity and outer physical actions. If effectively blended, you will have achieved the correct rhythm of the life of your character.

18.
DIRECTOR GUIDELINES

Stanislavski was as demanding of himself when he directed a play as he was with each of his directors at the Moscow Art Theatre. He met frequently with them during their directing assignments and grilled them thoroughly along certain channels. He demanded considerable work on the assigned script long in advance of casting and rehearsal. A thorough knowledge of the script was essential in order to understand the author completely, the theme of the play, and the characters in the given circumstances. The idea of the play had to be known so it could then be known by the actors and then by the audience.

The script is to be completely dissected into beats, objectives, super objectives, tempo-rhythm and preliminary movement. The inner rhythm is to be determined by understanding the inner life and intensity of each character and inherent in each scene. The social, political and historical elements of the period must be known. Only by adhering to these guidelines, would the director be privileged to assume the responsibility of leading a cast of actors.

19.
THE KEY IDEA

As an actor or director you must determine the key idea of the play you are to stage. The key idea is that which defines why the dramatist wrote it in the first place and why you decided it was fine enough to perform it. You will hesitate to begin work on a play without knowing the key idea. This is the idea you want to communicate to your audience because it is important to them. It will educate them and make them better, finer, wiser, more useful members of society.

When Stanislavski discovered the key idea of any play he worked with he wrote it in bold letters on the script to be ever reminded of it. He also wrote it on the board for all to see as a "banner."

Once you conclude what the key idea of your play is, write it in the front of your script so you will see it constantly.

20.
HIGHLIGHTS

As a character in a play to be staged, you are to note in your script each dramatic highlight of your role. Be guided by the theme of the play. Allow each highlight to guide you as you live the life of the character from beginning to end of the play. You may find it helpful to use a colored marker for this activity.

21.
DIRECTOR HIGHLIGHTS

The director highlights differ only in that he is to note every highlight of the script within the known theme of the play, rather than highlighting the actor's role. These noted points of significance will move the action along the through-line of dramatic content, from beat to beat, scene to scene, to the ultimate goal of the play.

22.
TEXT AND THOUGHTS

Select a short scene to explore this exercise, which includes two characters. Actor "A" is to speak the lines of the text. Actor "B" will speak the text as memorized in the scene and also speak all the thoughts of the character. They are to expect difficulty at times and encounter some degree of confusion for they find that they will be speaking at the same time. To minimize the difficulty, actor "B" will speak the words of the text with natural volume as he speaks his thoughts in a softer yet audible voice. Actor "A" will concentrate on listening to the text of actor "B" and avoid listening to the thoughts being expressed.

This exercise is used to expose the state of mind of the actor who is audibly expressing his thoughts. Actors "A" and "B" will take turns speaking thoughts of their character. When results are satisfactory to the director, the scene will be repeated normally.

23.
TEXT AND THOUGHTS - VARIATION

The prior exercise is to be repeated but with the inner thoughts of actor "B" being reduced to a whisper. The director, having already heard and approved the spoken inner thoughts of the actor, will permit the whisper so that the process is pursued, yet the softer level of speech will be less a problem for his partner.

The scene will again be staged. The director will allow their inner thoughts to be expressed soundlessly, using eyes and body to convey the active inner thoughts which were previously made audibly.

Each actor will take his turn performing the scene in this manner until the director is completely satisfied with active, truthful, meaningful inner flow of thoughts. The process may be repeated with every scene in the play, including those with several characters involved with dialogue and action.

24.
GROUP SCENE SUB-TEXT

To enhance group scene action in a play being readied for performance, the director will ask every member of the cast on stage to create an inner monologue for his character. The scene will then be staged as everyone will speak the inner monologue in audible volume. The actors must be disciplined not to react to any sub-text being spoken aloud nor to be confused by the many voices to be heard at any given time.

After being given the opportunity to be individually expressive, although a relatively minor character in the scene, the director will call for the scene to be staged normally. By keeping an active but silent sub-text, the scene will have gained truth, vividness, excitement as the minor characters contribute to the main action, relating to each other and to main characters in the scene.

25.
QUALITY OF VOICE

Stanislavski was sincerely fond of music and saw the relationship between good speech and fine music.

You are to choose a brief monologue to perform this exercise. You are to speak each word very slowly as you support your voice properly with your diaphragm. Sound roundly and fully each vowel and sharply articulate every consonant as you envision an image with each word. Give full treatment to the beginning, middle and end of every word. Sense the beauty and musical quality of your words as they are being spoken and truly penetrating to the very soul of each word of the monologue.

26.
SET CHANGES

It is not uncommon for the director of a play in rehearsal to initiate changes in the stage setting or altering the set pieces. The budget may be reduced or the play is to be staged in a smaller space than anticipated requiring changes in the initial plan. For creative reasons, it is also possible that the idea of the play as conceived by the director has become obscured by a setting and now needs adjustment or re-design. Actors face such challenges after a play has been blocked completely. The director may seek new dimensions with a changed design. It does happen.

You are to select a play with multiple stage settings. It may be Moliere's DOCTOR IN SPITE OF HIMSELF, or Chekov's UNCLE VANYA, Shakespeare's COMEDY OF ERRORS, HAMLET, and so on. Perform all the scenes of the play in one setting. Change from complex interior settings with couches, tables, fireplaces, french doors, wall hangings, to a bare stage with stools. Seek simplification to highlight inner life of characters or key ideas of the play.

27.
BLOCKING ADJUSTMENTS

The director will select a scene fully rehearsed and with established blocking. He will then make changes in the movements requiring each actor in the scene to adapt to the changes in the blocking.

The change by the director may be to emphasize a key point which had been unclear. A problem in the stage setting may have required change. He may have reconsidered the flow of movement as he seeks particular objectives. He may also simply wish to teach actors to face adjustments. There are, however, directors who refuse to lock in movements for creative purposes.

28.
RESTRICTED MOVEMENT

No one is to move during the entire scene! The director wishes you to improve your concentration by so doing. This no movement exercise is to focus your attention, to become more intent or more spirited. It may induce greater inner intensity of your inner life as you build to a point where you feel like bursting forth with a truly motivated movement not previously conceived. It may also be done to lend greater effectiveness to the words being spoken.

Stanislavski found this exercise to be very productive and used it often in rehearsals and in the studio sessions.

29.
FIVE BEATS

Plan to stage an improvisation on a given episode consisting of five beats. It may consist of arrival, problem emerges, situation builds, conflict develops, resolution or exit.

30.
EMOTION RESERVOIR

Actors develop a reservoir of emotions from which is drawn all that is required to stage a given scene. Any barrier to emotional expression will limit an actor's creative depth.

Each member of the acting ensemble is to be assigned a particular emotion to be improvised in a brief scene. The designated emotion will be the key feeling in the improvisation. Each actor will be given opportunity to stage his creation either alone or with a partner.

Although Stanislavski stressed that the character should build the circumstance that will result in a sincere emotion, this exercise was used in studio sessions as a drill. You are to be creative in your exercise to indeed establish the situation so that the given emotion will be the result of all that your character builds within the improvised circumstance.

31.
EMOTION RESERVOIR - VARIATION

Cards may be distributed to each actor in the ensemble. The cards will designate two, three or more emotions. The actors are to build an improvisation allowing for the expression of each emotion assigned. Try to allow one beat for each emotion.

32.
EMOTION SERIES

Director may select one or more actors to enter the stage to perform this exercise. One by one, he will call out an emotion to the actors on stage who must immediately put the emotion into an improvised moment. He may allow fifteen to thirty seconds for each emotional experience which must be completely justified. Sample emotions may include; sorrow, joy, broken heart, victory, defeat, reflective, determined, loss, disillusioned, contentment, weeping with joy, burdened, cheated, fearful, threatened, misery, fretful, despondent, anxious, gleeful, envious, loving, yearning, pity, injustice, resentful, and so on.

The adjustments by the actor to truthfully evoke each emotion will be the challenge. It calls for an extensive emotion memory bank on the part of the actor.

33.
EXERCISE IN DUALITY

Two actors will improvise a scene where it is known by the actor that the emotion in beat one is established before hand as is the final emotion in the third beat which is totally an opposite feeling. The opening emotion, for example, will be sadness, and the ending emotion will be joy. To exercise duality, the actor knows in advance each of the emotions, but his character must experience the first emotion without being influenced by the emotion which will end the scene.

34.
MEANINGFUL PAUSE

You are to perform a scene with a partner which is known to contain pauses stipulated by the playwright. When either actor is to include a pause, he will speak out the character thoughts which take place during the pause.

When thoroughly convinced that the pauses are filled with truthful life energy, the scene will be performed with silent pauses. The pauses, having been filled with expressive inner monologue, will have enriched the scene.

Those noted pauses in scripts have troubled some actors. Allowing the actor to understand the importance of filling such pauses with meaningful thoughts will erase any possible problem.

35.
STATE OF BEING

In a brief scene with a partner, you are to approach the event with the thought that this could indeed be happening to you. Free yourself to think, feel and act exactly as if it were happening to you.

By imagining, "What would I do IF what is happening to my character actually is happening to me?" The actions coming out of this form of thinking will generally be truthful and believable. This will lead you to the correct state of being on the stage. The correct state of being while on stage is the normal state of a human being in life. You must strive to place yourself in the given circumstances of the play. In so doing, you will discover that your psychological inner action will lead to external actions which will express the psychic nature of the character. This unity between the psychological and physical action is organic action on stage; a truly disirable state of being.

36.
FUSION OF ACTIONS

As you approach the scene to be staged, strive to act from your very self, using you as the foundation of your character.

Repeat the scene until you have achieved ease and flow of dramatic action as you become one with the newly created reality of your character.

Study the similarity of characteristics you share with the character you are creating. Note also the differences between you. Find all the causes for your character's behavior and then determine the justification for each of his actions. Approach the scene openly and freely allowing your similarities and differences to fuse creatively as you build the character. In time, your actions and character actions will blend in total comfort.

37.
SEEKING RHYTHM

After learning the scene at hand, define the inner life of your character. Study his inner intensity, excitement, energy, which form the life rhythm out of which we create the external dramatic actions. Perform the scene with an awareness of its life rhythm.

Rehearsal of these elements will lead to physical and psychological actions which are suited for the action and life energy of the scene to be performed in production as conceived by the director. The actor and director will work together to seek the proper inner intensity of the character. This constitutes the true rhythm of the moment which in turn will dictate the external actions and tempo appropriate for the scene.

38.
FLOW OF DAY

As you prepare to perform your scene on stage, begin to work on establishing your character's flow of the day. Be creative in imagining what your character did each moment since the night before. Review the events of your character's life through last evening, on into the night, this morning and all through the day until the moment of your entrance into the scene now taking place.

You are to penetrate deeply into each specific event of your character's day. Envision the people who shared experiences with you and the clearly defined places you frequented such as your home, bed, kitchen, park, office, prison, beach, and so on. What were the good and bad things that happened to you? What thoughts and dialogue did you have? Consider the reactions and all the significant elements which moved the action forward to this very event you are to experience in this scene. Then make your entrance a continuation of your flow of day as you are propelled into this event in your character's life.

39.
EPOCH OF THE PLAY

Should you be the director of the play to be produced, it becomes essential for you to know the epoch of the event. Learn what the distinctive characteristics of the time period are. Can the play be presented only in its point in time, or will it have its effect un-altered by up-dating it to modern times? There have been many failures as well as successes as producers have altered the play's epoch.

The time period may be stated in advance of the text by the author. Ideas are also gained by actions, dialogue, play title, list of characters and their station in life, description of clothing and hair styles, wigs, and so on. Props and setting with their furnishings will also reveal the epoch of the play.

You are to become thoroughly familiar with every aspect of the time period in which the play is set.

40.
CHARACTER QUALITIES

The director becomes familiar with the play, its theme, and its characters long before the cast is to be selected. He is to compare each role he is to cast with the qualities of the actor who will portray the character. His demands on an actor are to be guided solely by the qualities in the character created by the author. He is in no position to alter the playwright's conceived image of the character.

As the director, you are to strive to select the proper actor for each role. This may very well be your first approach to the staging of the designated play, yet it may very well be your most important action in terms of the success of the play. You are then to develop the inner qualities of the actor necessary for the qualities of the character. You are also faced with the responsibility of rejecting all the personal characteristics of the actor that are contrary to the character.

41.
CHARACTER PROPERTIES

As rehearsals take place you are building your character, conceiving his inner and outer life, his manner and behavior. The playwright may or may not have designated his personal props. Such stage properties should be an extension of the character you are portraying. You are to select for your scene several personal stage props for use by your character.

It is helpful to connect with the life of your character if some of your own personal objects become appropriate for the life action of your character. They may include wallet or handbag, kerchief or bandana, car keys, brief case, fan, cigar, cane, watch, lorgnette, monocle, bracelet, ring, and so on.

Allow the prop you select for your character to be significant to its life and not used to clutter the action or idea of the role. It should contribute to the development of the role and is a defined extension of your character.

42.
OFF STAGE

During the process of rehearsal, you as director will designate and provide areas off stage for actors to dwell in relative privacy as they carry on their created lives while off stage awaiting an entrance. They are to have a space where they can maintan their flow of day chanelled toward the next entrance. His inner monologue is to be continued in an uninterrupted manner through this off stage period. Whether his next entrance is only moments after his earlier exit or months later, his flow of day should allow him to fill every moment of lapsed time in the life of his character.

43.
THE RED THREAD

Stanislavski applied a term, the red thread, to the line of action which runs through the play and which provides the cohesive element that holds the play together. It begins at the opening of the play and travels through each scene and act until conclusion of the play.

You are to identify the red thread which runs through the play you are about to produce. You are advised to not begin directing any rehearsals until you have properly traced the play's red thread.

44.
ON SALE!

This exercise is for the theatre company which has an ample supply of set pieces, such as couches, chairs, tables, fireplaces, drapes, carpets, and so on. It will allow the actors to connect with the set.

The stage crew members are to display all items conceived in spaces where they can run a "sale" of all furnishings for a designed space in the play to be staged. They may, if space allows, arrange items in departments, such as den, living room, kitchen, patio, etc. The china may be in one area and the silver in another. Glass ware may be in a space of its own, and so on.

Cast members are to endulge in a shopping spree to "purchase" from the stage crew sales persons all items for their stage set "home." The setting may be a unit set, a multiple set, or a single room, so designated by the director.

45.
SKETCHING YOUR BEATS

You are to make the author's thoughts, images and words closer to your very own. Do this by selecting a short scene of three to five beats. Make a rough sketch of each of your beats. Try every possible variation of ideas you can conceive in each beat. You may determine the origin of the problem. You might probe the relationship with other characters. Or analyze your reaction to an incident. Seek also the root of your partner's behavior. You might consider how the beat would change if you altered an action or attitude. It might prove interesting to note how different the life of your character would be if you expressed your words with an entirely different feeling.

The sketch may include ideas such as noting what would be altered were you to enter five speeches earlier. Consider what would be done if you delayed your entrance by two minutes. Probe the beat thoroughly until you feel you have gone through the very process the writer went through when he conceived of the scene. You will be then as familiar with its inner workings as the author. It will widen your conception of the thoughts and actions of your role.

46.
OVER-PLAYING

In the process of preparation for a performance, over-acting at times is not only useful but necessary. It may result in finding new understanding of ideas, thoughts, events of the play and even allow discovery of emotional content not yet experienced. There are absolutely necessary conditions where some actors are holding back due to timidity requiring over-playing to release them from their restraint.

For such reasons, you are to over-play all dramatic actions of the scene. Strive for deeper feelings, more expressive physical actions, heightened emotions, louder voice projection, and break through established barriers.

Indeed, you may make new discoveries and experience greater dimensions not yet known. Become free enough to over-act for your own creative reason, and then free yourself to come down to a normal level when in performance, thus playing with more ease and confidence. It is to be used for exploratory reasons only and must not be used in performance.

47.
LIFE AS WE LIVE IT

You are to take the play which is in rehearsal and relate the subject of the play and its separate moments to real life as it unfolds today before your eyes.

See and hear all that constitutes life about you at this time. Appreciate all that is happening. Learn to love all that is life. Bring it into your art and into your vision of the role you are portraying.

As each rehearsal is being conducted in a creative atmosphere, it inspires you to create full-blooded visions of the role and to think of the events of the play vividly and to feel them strongly as they relate to the events of the world about you.

48.
UP-BEAT!

Select an appropriate scene that will allow an adjustment to an up-beat, brisk life energy. Heighten the tempo and all physical actions. Play the scene with brisk rhythm, sharp, clear-cut speeches, expressive and vibrant inner and outer life.

Try an impetuous and forceful entrance allowing one to burst through the door. Make the encounter dynamic. Justify broad, full movement about the space. Use props with a flair. Work the scene boldly and punctuate the ending with an expressive exit.

49.
SMALL OBJECTS

Stage a scene allowing the actors to employ the smallest objects with which to lend dimension to the life of the character in his given circumstances.

The action may require lighting a small birthday candle, examining a hair follicle, rolling a small wax ball from a candle, altering the signature with a pen point, removing a blemish on a photograph, studying a finger print, adjusting the tiny screw on eye glasses, cutting an aspirin into halves, extracting a dust particle from a partner's eye, and so on.

The action with the small object is to contribute to the scene and is to demand time and focus of attention. It is not to be employed as passive busy work by the actor.

50.
ETUDE

Taking the major plot of the play to be performed and with all its characters as conceived by the playwright, the cast is to create a major improvisation on the circumstances and situations of the play adhering to its theme.

The cast members are to be thoroughly familiar with their characters and the plot, and must understand their relationship with each of the other characters in the play. All lines will be improvised by the actors, allowing occasional words of the author where necessary, but kept to a minimum. The cast is encouraged to speak their inner thoughts of the characters, which will be helpful in maintaining their red thread, through line of action, in pursuit of their main objectives.

The exercise is a productive way to finding the true scenic atmosphere of the play to be staged.

51.
INTERVIEW

The director plays the role of a reporter on a small local newspaper. As rehearsals of scenes may be taking place in various areas of the theatre, he will move about covering the events taking place, writing down all he sees.

The director will make arrangements to interview each character in the play. Using his knowledge of the circumstances of the play, his probing interview will become enlightening for both parties. In addition, it will expand one's conception of his role. The actor or director may depart from the plot line of the script and cover elements relating to the private lives of each character. The exploratory route may indeed go in various interesting and challenging directions. Characters may be sitting by a fire, gardening, mowing a lawn, at work, and so on.

52.
LANGUAGE OF PROPS

Stage props have a language which they speak as they express ideas of the character using the prop. They speak often for the character who may indeed be silent at the time. A walking stick will often reveal much about its owner, being gay and cocky at one moment, sad and forlorn the next. It may hurry and run and skip along with its owner, or hang limply in dismay.

The monocle may come to life at an instant as its owner notes a brilliant idea, or all in dejection. The lady's fan snaps open with alertness and quickens its movement as it cools the mounting passion of its mistress, or it snaps shut with agitation or insult. A wallet flashes open with authority. The swagger stick slaps the boot of its officer with command.

Each actor is to select a prop which will be used in similar instances where it will express feelings and thoughts of the character employing the prop in a scene. It will add another facet to the life of the character. One may consider a parasol, letter, keys, duster, baton, tennis racquet, bottle, hair brush, and so on.

53.
NATURAL PHYSICAL ACTIONS

In rehearsal, you and the director must note the importance of a correct and honest expressiveness which has the power of an interesting physical action organically tied to an inner action and the actor's problem and which is not artificially invented by either the director or you. Make note of them so they will not be ignored, forgotten and thus remain unused in future rehearsals or performance. With proper justification, these unplanned physical actions may indeed be used in future instances to enhance the life action of your character.

54.
FIRESIDE

In countless classic plays, the fire place is the focal point of the setting, often a kind of family alter. The fire creates a warmth or unifying atmosphere. It seems to enhance any scene played by it. Props associated with a fire place may include old fashioned candlesticks, photographs, paintings as well as bear rugs, soft chairs, etc.

You are to create an improvised scene to be played by a fire place. It must be a contributing element to the scene in your own creative manner.

55.
SPECIAL CONDITIONS

Actors are to improvise brief scenes based upon a physical or psychological impairment. The character may be blind, crippled, deaf, insane, to a slight or major degree.

Consider visiting a veterans hospital or local mental institution. Special education departments of public schools may be visited to observe handicapped students. Reach for the inner lives of such human beings in order to avoid cliché imitation surface actions.

56.
CLIMAXES AND ENDINGS

When faced with an abbreviated rehearsal schedule, begin working on the endings of the play and each act practically from the first rehearsal.

Work as soon as possible on the major climax of the play and any conflict of major importance. Once these major events are refined, the channel of events becomes established. All else will require much less time and will blend quickly into the full picture.

57.
PARALLEL PATHS

As you approach the life of your character, you are to note if all the inner desires which guide you toward getting what you want in the scene are just as convincing to you as to the actual character you are performing. Indeed they must be if the role is to be portrayed truthfully. Be certain that you and the character you are playing tread the through line of dramatic action together.

58.
VALUED MOMENT

As soon as you become familiar with your new role in the play to be produced, you are to define the particular moment in any scene you consider the strongest, the most important, the most exciting for you.

The next step is for you to select the very sentence, the action, the phrase, thought or word in the text which is most valued by you.

59.
PARTNER'S MOMENT

Once you have defined the valued moments in your role as indicated in the prior exercise, you are advised to identify which moment in your partner's role is most important to your character. Note the action, sentence, phrase or word which affects you the most. Be prepared to explain to the director how and why you have selected the moment. Follow through with this activity in every scene involving your character.

60.
NAME THAT BEAT!

Having dissected your role into beats and objectives, you are then encouraged to apply a name to each beat to specifically highlight your dramatic action.

Examples: Help me! You lied to me! Take this! I want out!
You want to leave me. I want to kiss you.
I don't want your gift. You disgust me!
I need your support. I want you to be faithful.
I love you. Insulted innocence. Self pity.
Betrayed! Loser! I seek revenge! You must die!
Searching. Dethroned. Banished. Deceived!

61.
ADDING YOUR THOUGHTS

There is a point in rehearsal when you know your role thoroughly, you know your lines and your character problems and objectives. In addition, you understand the relationships you have with all characters in the play and you comprehend all your thoughts and the words you use to express them.

As an exercise for you to deal with dialogue and related thoughts, you will speak your lines as written in the text, but wherever you find it compelling to substitute for the words and phrases of the text, speak freely those words that express what is really on your mind. These words will be added to the text of the script. They reflect your related thoughts, what you think in relation to the characters involved with you and the problem at hand.

62.
SILENCE, PLEASE!

A well rehearsed scene is to be selected by two actors for this challenging exercise. It may be done with additional characters, but only after gaining comfort in the process.

The entire text of the scene is to be spoken only with your eyes. Perform the scene in silence, but think of each specific word in your mind with all its related sub-text and inner intensity as well as all appropriate physical actions as though the lines of the text were spoken aloud.

It is required that you focus intensely on each other to note each little nuance of the moment. Observe each other constantly and you will determine when your partner has completed the line in silence as you fire glances at each other, devoting limitless attention to one another.

63.
SILENCE AND RHYTHM

Scenic rhythm is the acceleration or diminishing of the inner intensity. It relates to the desire to realize the problem at hand and to execute the inner and outer physical actions of your character.

After gaining success in performing your scene in silence as stated in the previous exercise, you will be able to stage the next exercise. This scene will also be staged in complete silence as you direct limitless attention to your partner, piercing each other with your eyes as you speak each word within.

The new challenge is to tap your inner intensity with your hand to verify your inner rhythm, exhibiting any change in the rhythm whenever the inner intensity of your character changes.

Understanding scenic rhythm is a complex process since it has several facets. It is quite an individual matter but necessary for the actor to develop an awareness of inner stage rhythm and its affect on the life of the character and scene.

64.
INTONATION AND SILENCE

Intonation of speech is the emphasis of the key word in any sentence. The intonation may be colorful or pale, strong or weak, passionate, phlegmatic, tender or cold, hostile or loving. It will show your relationship to your partner, to the events of the play, to your own feeling, and to the convictions with which you color your thoughts and words.

As in the prior scenes, you will be prepared to stage it again. First, however, you are to mark your familiar script by underlining only those words that are absolutely necessary to the meaning of each sentence. Underline only the key words.

Stage the scene, letting your eyes do most of the work as you convey the text silently, but speak aloud only the words underlined. The intonation of these necessary key words will help to emphasize your feeling and inner intensity.

65.
PARTNER SUB TEXT

As you work with your partner in a scene, focus your attention on his eyes and physical actions. Strive to connect with his inner life action. Truly listen to his sub text as you establish this mind to mind connection. Opportunity will be allowed for each actor to reveal the sub text of the partner. This may be done by verbalizing the partner's inner thoughts during the scene in a soft voice or in a discussion following the scene.

66.
SKELETON OF THE PLAY

The scheme of the play, referred to as the "skeleton" by Stanislavski, is that which holds together the inner and outer actions of the play.

The director will allow the cast, when thoroughly familiar with the play in rehearsal, to select the leading facts and events of every scene of each act. An improvisation will be performed on each of these leading facts and events of each scene basing the activity on the author's theme and ideas. Having approached them in order, you will have then a chain of improvisations which will highlight the living skeleton of the play.

It is productive to improvise the entire play in this manner. In its skeletal form, the play may be improvised in a fairly brief period, revealing elements of great importance to actors and director.

> "Only in an atmosphere of love and friendship
> and of just criticism and self criticism
> can talents grow."

> Constantin Stanislavski

PART FIVE

THEATRE STUDY AND TEACHING SYLLABUS

SYLLABUS

This syllabus may be used for all actors, experienced and inexperienced, professional and non-professional, college and secondary school, and even middle school students under qualified instructors and directors. The chapters referenced are in Part One and Part Two of the handbook. Additional exercises may be used from Part Three. Part Four exercises may be used for very advanced students.

Week One Part One Chapter I Dramatic Quality

Discussion, lecture, exercises are used to illustrate the concept of an actor's dramatic quality. Such qualities include creative mood, appropriate attitude, achieving privacy in public and comfort, use of "fourth wall," etc.

Employ exercises from chapter one for groups or individuals.

Select only exercises deemed appropriate for class level and maturity of the students.

Assign partners to read a short popular comedy. Neil Simon comedies are suggested. They will be asked to select a segment of two or three pages and determine the central point or "main idea," as defined by Stanislavski. They will plan to stage a one to three minute improvisation of the scene based upon its main idea.

Week Two Chapter II The Art of Living the Role

Discussion and exercises are to illustrate the concept of truly living a role as performed by the actor so as to avoid mechanical, surface acting. The actor will learn how to give himself completely to what is happening in the circumstance.

Select appropriate exercises from chapter II.

Each team will present improvisation of assigned comedy. Encourage actors to use acting principles introduced thus far. (Mature groups may stage memorized scenes following the improvisation assignments.)

Week Three Chapter III Dramatic Action

Daily discussions and exercises will be selected to illustrate the concept of dramatic action. This unit defines the inner forces of the character, such as need, desire, objective, intention, and acting with purpose. The actor must know what the character wants at any given moment and to place great importance on the objective. It also defines the creative influence of pursuing objectives and the all-important "magic IF."

Partners are to read and select scenes from plays written by Tennessee Williams. The actors will build the improvisations on the "main idea" of the chosen scenes. Actors generally achieve comfort and confidence when they are led to improvise words and actions created by themselves without the use of any words of the playwright. They will build a foundation of dimensional inner life of the character in the given circumstance of the playwright.

Week Four Chapter IV Creative Imagination

Lectures, discussions and appropriate exercises are to illustrate the concept of creative use of the imagination.

Acting partners are to present all assigned improvisations of scenes from the plays of Tennessee Williams. Encourage the use of all acting principles studied thus far.

The first of three monologues is assigned to each actor. The monologues should be memorized and retained for common use for most auditions throughout the theatre world. They should be brief, eight to twelve lines, and varied, comedy, drama, classic Shakespeare. The memorized monologue is due for presentation next week.

Week Five Chapter V Focusing of Attention

Activities will be devoted to the principle of focused attention. The student will become familiar with the circle of attention, interaction, the fourth wall, etc. The concept by Stanislavski is that while performing the role of a character, there must be no awareness of an audience by the character. The character exists in a private space, as defined, with no audience in his life.

Present each memorized monologue. Stress the point that the character is in his private space. An audience does not exist in the life of the character, so it must not intrude.

Week Six Chapter VI Tension and Relaxation

Discussions and exercises will deal with the process of achieving comfort and relaxation on stage. Actors will select brief scenes from plays by Kaufman and Hart to be improvised. Student actors will strive to apply all acting principles studied thus far.

Week Seven Chapter VII Beats and Main Points

Lectures and appropriate selection of exercises are to acquaint the student actor with the process of dissecting scenes and acts of plays into beats, (as defined by Stanislavski) and their key points, or objectives.

The student will learn that the objective of each beat creates a spine, or unbroken line, leading to the super-objective of the entire play, consisting of the central theme that inspired the author to create the drama.

Assignment for the session will be the reading of plays by Eugene O'Neill. Acting teams of two will stage brief improvisation of selected scenes due the following week.

Week Eight Chapter VIII Scenic Truth

Class sessions will be devoted to achieving truth in performing the role of a character. Scenic truth is initiated by creative imagination, a newly created reality, and a sense of faith.

Appropriate exercises will be employed, followed by the improvisations of scenes from Eugene O'Neill plays.

Week Nine Chapter IX Recalling Feelings

Class activities will be conducted to show the value of all feelings, emotions and events students have experienced in their own lives. As a reservoir, they will be drawn upon to lend truth to moments in the life of the character being portrayed.

Assign five-minute memorized scene or short one-act play of choice by teams of two or more actors. Scenes will be presented week ten. Encourage the use of costumes, stage properties, proper blocking, sound effects, etc. A major factor will be the studied use of all Stanislavski acting principles thus far introduced. Class rehearsal time and supervision of each scene in rehearsal is to be considered.

Week Ten

Review Stanislavski principles from one to nine. Full dress rehearsal of all scenes as determined by instructor.

Present each memorized and rehearsed scene. The work may well serve as the quarter exam to evaluate progress of each student actor.

Week Eleven Chapter X Inter-communication

Class activity will deal with the valued acting principle of eye-to-eye contact, mind-to-mind and soul-to-soul relationship between characters in performance.

Assign reading of plays written by Thornton Wilder, such as "Our Town." Actors will select a brief scene for improvisation and then memorized and staged during week twelve.

Week Twelve Chapter XI Inner and Outer Adjustment

Discussions and selected exercises will disclose the method of adapting to circumstances of the play, harmony among characters, exploring the dimensions of the role, defining and penetrating the inner meaning of the spoken text, etc.

Rehearse and present memorized scenes previously selected.

Reading assignment of Arthur Miller plays. Select brief scene for improvisation followed by staging of memorized scene for week thirteen.

Week Thirteen Chapter XII Mind, Will and Feeling

Class sessions will be based upon study of inner forces as they influence psychological and physical life, and stir creative elements in the performing artist.

Reading assignment will be selection of plays by Irish playwrights. Sean O'Casey and John Millington Synge are highly regarded authors of popular comedies. Brief scenes will be improvised then staged following week fourteen.

Week Fourteen Chapter XIII Through Line of Action

Known also as the red thread or the unbroken line, this principle discloses the importance of the continuing line that ties past, present and future of characters in the circumstance of the play.

Actors present short memorized scenes from Irish plays. Assign two to five minute scene memorized for next session.

Week Fifteen Scene Study assignment.

Stage all scenes. Seek refinement of all aspects.

Week Sixteen Chapter XIV Creative Mood

Define the spiritual and creative instrument, psychological and physical elements, and heightening the private moment. Assign reading of play by Edward Albee or John Steinbeck. Present improvisations. Memorized scene due next session.

Week Seventeen Chapter XV The Super Objective

Analyze theme of play and its relevance in modern world. Stage memorized brief scenes as assigned. Select reading of play by William Saroyan or Lillian Hellman due next week.

Week Eighteen Chapter XVI Region of the Subconscious

Classes devoted to psycho/technique, living of the role and merging of actor/character to achieve artistic truth. Stage improv and brief memorized scenes. Read Wendy Wasserstein or David Mamet play for improv and scene due next session.

Week Nineteen

Stage improvisation and memorized scenes as due. Assign and rehearse three to five minute scenes due for mid term.

Week Twenty

Rehearse, stage all memorized scenes for mid term grade evaluation.

Week Twenty One Part II Chapter I Physical Qualities

Select exercises geared to building a character in physical terms. Assign reading of Ibsen and Strindbert plays. Choose brief monologue for next week. Assign scene-study partners.

Week Twenty Two Chapter II, III Costume and Physical Image

Students will note how fabric, color and style of costume reflect the psycho/physical elements of a character. Using appropriate costume for the character, stage monologues and memorized scenes from Ibsen and Strindberg plays.

Reading assignment will be Moliere, Ionesco, Beckett plays. With partner, find brief scene for next week. Appoint some students to direct each scene-study as a directing project.

Week Twenty Three Chapter IV, V, VI The Physical Instrument

Present exercises of three chapters and highlight aspects of how to develop and maintain character physical traits. Student-directed scenes are to be improvised and rehearsed. Each student director will stage assigned scene of the French playwrights and invited to comment about the scene.

Chekov, Gorki, Turgenev, Russian playwrights, will be next reading assignment. Appoint other students to cast and direct brief memorized scenes for next week.

Week Twenty Four Chapter VII, VIII, IX and XII Speech

Class activities will involve four chapters of valued material about clarity of speech, imagery, inner thoughts and feelings accompanying the spoken text. Activate the appropriate exercises to stress projection, articulation, voice placement, and musicality of speech. Student-directed scenes from the Russian plays will be improvised, rehearsed and staged. Clarity of speech must be enforced. Assign Molnar, Lorca, Pirandello for next student-directed scene.

Week Twenty Five Chapter X Actor-Character Duality

Discussion and exercises will illustrate concept of maintaining parallel lines of perspective as character and actor for the role being portrayed.

Select exercises, theatre games and improvisations to highlight all principles introduced thus far. Present student-directed scenes from European playwrights, Molnar, Lorca, Pirandello. Assign reading of the great works of early Greek writers, "Antigone," by Sophocles and "Lysistrata," by Aristophenes. Student directors will cast, rehearse and present short scenes week twenty six.

Week Twenty Six Chapter XI Timing and Dynamics of Action

Select exercises to introduce temp/rhythm, valued by Stanislavski, who firmly believed that variation of life-energy enhanced artistic beauty of performance. The Greek scenes to be staged are to be dissected into beats and performed with varied tempo and rhythm. Instructor is to examine each script to confirm accuracy of scene dissected into numbered beats, with main points underlined, tempo of each beat varied, and rhythm life-energy defined.

Assign Shakespeare readings of "Hamlet" and "Romeo and Juliet." Each student will present monologue next week. Brief scenes directed by students will be performed.

Week Twenty Seven Chapter XIII, XIV, XV

Discussion and exercises will cover personal quality of each actor, discipline, and the psycho/physical aspects of creative artistry. Present Shakespeare monologues. Rehearse and stage student-directed scenes. Assign plays by British writers, Shaw, Ayckbourn, Pinter, Wilde for following week.

Week Twenty Eight Chapter XVI Acting Naturally

Discussion and class exercises will stress the important element of acting naturally, living the role, and avoiding self-conscious, mechanical "acting" in performance. Stage all student-directed scenes from British plays.

Assign readings of plays by American playwrights, Renee Taylor, Elaine May, Christopher Durang, Elmer Rice. Self-directed, memorized, dissected scenes due next week.

Week Twenty Nine

Rehearse and stage all self-directed scenes. Instructor is to note that all acting principles are creatively employed.

Assign partners for mid-term scene study, which may be graded to evaluate progress. Scenes are to be five to ten minutes in length selected from classic or contemporary play, based upon theatre course objectives. Scenes are to be memorized and dissected scripts presented to instructor for evaluation. Appropriate costumes, stage properties and required effects are to be included.

Week Thirty Mid-Term Scene Study

Each scene is to be rehearsed privately in the presence of instructor, while other actors are rehearsing in other private spaces. Actors will strive to apply every acting principle studied during the semester. Instructor will guide actors as required, stressing articulate clarity of speech, focused attention, inner involvement, truthful living of the role in the character's private "space."

Presentation of all scenes will be made before class members. Positive comments from classmates will be encouraged.

Week Thirty One Actor/Playwright

Students will be assigned to write an original one-act play, two to ten pages in length, with a cast of two to five characters. They may be inspired to recreate a personal experience with creative embellishment, if so desired. They may also build on one of many improvisations presented during the semester, an excellent source.

Scenes will be read in class at the discretion of each student. Classmates will be cast in each play to perform the created roles. Each student may be in one or more plays. Each playwright will direct his own play. Time will be allowed in each class to rehearse and write. The staging of each play will take place during week thirty five, before an audience. Appropriate costumes, stage properties, technical needs will be provided by writer and cast members.

Week Thirty Two, Thirty Three, Thirty Four

Classes will devote time to writing, reading, rehearsing segments of each play in progress.

Week Thirty Five

Dress rehearsal of each original play will be directed and presented by the playwright before instructor. All other actors will be in rehearsal in private areas. Each writer is to accurately determine the running time of his play. The instructor is to be informed of the running time in order to establish a schedule of final performances, which may require several class periods.

At the established time, the group will gather to attend the performance of each original play.

Week Thirty Six

Two to five qualified students are to be selected to direct full one-act classic or contemporary plays for final project of the theatre term. Each student-actor in the class will be cast in one or more plays. The plays will be presented to an invited audience at a designated date during final week forty. If circumstances allow, the performances may be staged at evening time, to accommodate family members and friends of students.

Week Thirty Seven, Thirty Eight, Thirty Nine

Rehearse all plays. Each play will rehearse in the presence of instructor as required, while other plays are in rehearsal in other areas. The instructor is to note that acting principles studied during the semester are being artistically and creatively employed by each actor and director. He will evaluate each dissected script presented to him by actors and directors.

Prior to performance, instructor will require each play to be in full tech and dress rehearsal in order to achieve performance refinement. Each director will inform the instructor of exact running time of the play to allow proper planning of final performances.

Week Forty Final Performance

Present all student-directed plays before invited audience.

PART SIX

DIRECTING THE PLAY

Acting Principles At Work
And
The Dissected Script

DOCTOR IN SPITE OF HIMSELF

A comedy by Moliere

Scene One

A wooded area near the home of Silvester and wife Martine. He is a wood-cutter prone to drink.

Beat One	SILVESTER. I won't, I tell you I won't! When I say something around her, it's an order! And <u>a wife is supposed to obey</u>, Martine! (He follows her on hurriedly from off right.)
	MARTINE. (Crossing toward right of center stage.) And I tell you that I'll tell YOU how to behave!
Tempo-Rhythm	I didn't marry you in order to put up with your philandering tricks, dodges and carousing!
Fast	SILVESTER. Oh, a wife is a burden, a bother and a bore!
	MARTINE. And you're a bum, a boozer and a bastard!
	SILVESTER. I am not a bastard! Oh, how right was Aristotle when he said that a wife is worse than a demon!
Beat Two	MARTINE. What a smart fellow he is with his half wit quoting Aristotle! Hah!
	SILVESTER. Hah, yourself! I'm a smart fellow all right!
Medium Fast	Remember <u>I worked for a famous doctor for six years</u>, and I knew my First Latin book by heart when I was just a boy!
	MARTINE. <u>You're nothing but a woodcutter</u>, Silvester!

The super-objective of this Moliere comedy classic is marital harmony. This must be known by the director and the actors from the beginning. Martine seeks love and respect as wife. Silvester seeks dignity as a husband. These are the personal super-objectives of each actor in the role of character. All is achieved in final scene when he vows to mend his irresponsible ways. He promises to administer prescriptions of love instead of beatings. (Super-objective, Chapter XV).

Following the thru-line of action, (Chap. XIII) also known as the spine of play, leading to the super-objective, the director is compelled to sustain a brisk, spirited, and varied tempo and life energy, (Part II, Chap. XI) a necessity in comedy and farce.

A beat is distinguished by a complete dramatic action leading to a key point called the objective. (Chap. VII)

Martine begins beat one by entering as lights come up and crosses toward right-center in a haughty, arrogant manner. Their tempo-rhythm and life energy is fast and energetic. Silvester, angry and slightly tipsey, is in quick pursuit. She turns at right-center to face him and irately scolds him.

Beat two is triggered by Silvester as the thought of Aristotle comes to mind, reminding him, in his inner life, sub-text (Part II, Chap. VIII), of his past work with a doctor, and youthful study of Latin, a life more rewarding than present.

SILVESTER. And the best there is! I'm a champion at that!

MARTINE. A plague on the champion FOOL!

SILVESTER. A plague on the champion NAG!

Beat
Three

MARTINE. <u>Cursed be the day and the hour when I took it into my head to say "I do!"</u>

SILVESTER. <u>Cursed be the fool of a notary who made me sign my own destruction!</u>

Fast

MARTINE. It's a fine thing for you to complain of that affair! Should you let a single minute go by without thanking heaven for having me for your wife? Did you deserve to marry a person like me?

SILVESTER. I always wondered just that! What did I ever do to deserve such a demon wife!

MARTINE. It was an honor for you!

SILVESTER. Oh, you did me too much honor! And I had good reason to congratulate myself on our wedding night! Damn!

Beat
Four

Don't get me going on THAT topic. I could say a few...

MARTINE. And just what could you say?

SILVESTER. That's enough! We'll drop the subject. Just

Medium

remember that we know what we know!

MARTINE. Oh, heavens!

SILVESTER. <u>And heaven knows how many others there were before me.</u>

Variation in tempo-rhythm is a valued principle. His reflection of the past slows beat two tempo and life energy to medium-fast or medium. Each turns away to express private thoughts. Martine counters with sarcasm aimed at his low status as a woodcutter, exposition significant to establish their position in life. In weak pursuit of his valued dignity, his sub-text stirs him to self praise as a champion, which Martine, turning to him, scornfully derides.

Truly believing character and situation, they give themselves up completely and truthfully to what is happening (Chap. II). Their inner thoughts, feelings and actions are motivating the dispute stemming from disappoint-ment in their marital life.

The inter-action (Chap. X) is so intent that their "fourth wall" remains solid, enclosing them within their created space, maintaining their "pri-vacy" without audience intrusion (Chap. V).

Playing wittily on the word "champion," they face each other, fervently believing that superiority has been gained over the other in the exchange. It leads to a thought change to ending beat two.

Beat three is initiated by Martine, who's inner thoughts lead to the be-ginning of all her troubles, the marriage. She turns away and curses the day she married. The tempo-rhythm surges to fast. This outburst stirs Silvester's inner thoughts and images flash into his mind of the "conspiracy" obviously masterminded by the notary and Martine. With heightened self image, she haughtily states it was an honor for him to have her as a wife.

His inner thoughts of dis-honor of the wedding night begins beat four, slowing life energy-tempo.

MARTINE. <u>You bum!</u>

SILVESTER. <u>And you were damned lucky to find me.</u>
Gullible, innocent me!

Beat
Five

MARTINE. Lucky to find you? <u>A man who is bringing</u>
<u>me to the poorhouse! A drunkard whose</u> chief
occupation is eating everything I've got!

Very
Fast

SILVESTER. Not true!

MARTINE. When he's not drinking!.....

SILVESTER. I get thirsty!

MARINE.....And who sells off bit by bit everything in the
house so he can play poker and gamble!

SILVESTER. We mustn't let our possessions possess us!

MARTINE. And who has even got rid of my precious
alarm clock!

SILVESTER. So you won't wake me up so early!

MARTINE. ......And we're left with not one single piece
of furniture in the parlor!

SILVESTER. That makes your cleaning easier!

MARTINE. .... And who spends the whole day, morning
'till night, drinking and gambling and...

SILVESTER. I like to be active!

MARTINE. And while that goes on, <u>what do you expect</u>
<u>me to do with the children</u>?

Beat
Six

SILVESTER. <u>That's YOUR job,</u> mother!

He physicalizes his inner disturbance by turning from her and crosses left as he strains to drop the subject, but resentfully infers there were others. Pierced by the accusation, she weakly labels him a "bum."

Beat five is begun by him as he turns rapidly to her and states how lucky she was to have found an innocent husband, which causes Martine to turn and erupt in angered response. The tempo-rhythm surges from medium to very fast in a flaring exchange, with tight cues. The circle of attention is enclosing them firmly, for they are pointedly focused on each other's eyes, striving for mind-to-mind communion (Chap. X). Martine's sub-text is filled with his misdeeds and carousing. His rapid responses are comedic in nature, the flavor Moliere is seeking. With growing confidence, she pursues her objective with focused beratement, stepping toward him. His ineffective witticism instills in her a sense of victory in the interplay. She is convinced she is "reaching" him, thus achieving her objective.

Martine brings up a new issue of a sensitive nature, children.

Medium	MARTINE. The children are out of hand!
	SILVESTER. You don't discipline them enough!

Beat Seven	MARTINE. Oh, yes, and <u>you expect that things are going to go on forever, this way, you drunken lout?</u>
	SILVESTER. All right, calm down!
	MARTINE. And I'm to put up with your drinking, gambling, carousing to the end of time?
	SILVESTER. Let's not get excited!
Very Fast	MARTINE. ....And I won't find some way to make you behave?
	SILVESTER. Sweetheart, you know I am not very patient, and I have a good strong right! (Raising his right arm threateningly.)
	MARTINE. I'm not afraid of your threats! (A step to him.)
	SILVESTER. Oh, lollipop, (With sarcasm.) you're just itching for something, as usual, and one of these days!
	MARTINE. I'll show you I'm not afraid of you!
	SILVESTER. <u>I'll tan your behind!</u>
	MARTINE. Bum!
	SILVESTER. You're asking for it!
	MARTINE. Boozer! (Facing each other.)
	SILVESTER. I shall spank you!
	MARTINE. Souse!
	SILVESTER. I'll spank that little behind of yours! (Raising his arm.)
	MARTINE. Dirty no-good! (Stepping toward him with each piercing word.) Coward! Beggar! Waster! Villain! Thief! (Her voice reaching peak.)

This tempers beat six to medium tempo-rhythm. He faults her and dismisses his own responsibility by turning away, a fitting psycho-physical action. (Part II, Ch. XV)

Seeking change in their troubled martial life as her objective, Martine initiates beat seven with volatility. The sudden explosive force initiates a very fast life energy-tempo rhythm, similar to sforzando in music. We see that variation in tempo-rhythm is as essential in a play as it is in a symphony. The manuscript is akin to the musical score, with its allegros and andantes, dolce and scherzo, and the aria similar to the soliloquy.

Facing each other, their tight cues are sharp, as each tops the others last word in each speech. With passion, their voice volumn rises to make point and counter-point, mounting the emotional scale to the bursting point. The similarity to a musical score I again noted for it is in the mode of accelerando. With physical superiority, he threatens to beat her. She defies him and pierces him with stinging words to show her verbal superiority. He backs away and reaches for a nearby twig or branchlet to lash at her. She runs from him in fear as he pursues her. She screams.

Beat
Eight
	SYLVESTER. (Stepping back, he reaches for a stick or
	    twig to chase her.) That does it! You asked for it!
	    (Lashes at her.)

	MARTINE. Ohhh! (Screaming, she runs erratically
Very	toward down-right stage, then up-right and crossing to
Very	up-center.) Ohhh! (Tries to avoid the lashing.)
Fast	SILVESTER. <u>This is the only language you know to make</u> <u>you behave</u>. (Chasing after her.)
	MARTINE. <u>Spanking! Spanking! That's all you're good</u> <u>for! Wife beater!</u> Ohhh!

	(A neighbor, Monsieur Henri, enters down-left, shocked at the sight of the beating.)

Beat
Nine
	M. HENRI. Oh, Here! Here! What's going on here?
	    This is awful! <u>You mustn't beat your wife! Stop it!</u>
	    Silvester, stop it!

Medium	(Silvester moves away to right-center as Martine comes
	    to a halt at center and right of M. Henri, who is left-
	    center.)

	MARTINE. (Turns to M. Henri, hands on hips,
	    haughtily steps to him.) Now hold on there, you!
	    Supposing I want him to beat me! What's it to you?

	M. HENRI. (Retreating from her.) Oh, well....then....
	    uh....please go right ahead. If that's the case, Martine,
	    go right ahead! Sorry.

	MARTINE. What are you meddling for, M. Henri?
	M. HENRI. I'm sorry....

Beat eight inspires a very very fast tempo-life energy, which affects the mood of the actors as well as the audience due to the dynamics of the exciting beat (Part II, Ch. XI). The actors must be truthfully immersed in the lives of their characters, (Ch. II) to make the chase real and believable to themselves as well as the audience. Martine must fear for her welfare and Silvester must be emotionally driven to pursue her to chastise her and retain his superiority over his wife. This measure of creative reality is enhanced by a synchronized inner and outer adjustment by each actor to assure fine ensemble interplay (Ch. XI).

Beat nine begins with the intrusion of Henri from the left. The chase ends and the tempo-rhythm slows to medium. Silvester feels humiliation, so his physical action is to move away from Henri and is rendered speechless, a clear example of psychological and physical harmony (Part II, Ch. XV). She becomes defensive of her privacy and her marriage and so faces Henri stoutly at center. She chastises the neighbor who backs away toward left stage.

MARTINE. Is it any business of yours?

M. HENRI. No. Oh, no, indeed. Just being....
neighborly.

MARTINE. (Turning to Silvester to her right.) Take a
look at this intruder will you, who wants to prevent
husbands from beating their own wives! (Turning to
the neighbor, at her left.) That's a neighbor for you!

M. HENRI. I take it all back.

MARTINE. Do you have any interest in the matter?

M. HENRI. Why, uh, no. None at all.

MARTINE. Then why do you stick your nose into our
private business?

Medium   M. HENRI. Sorry. I'm sorry.

MARTINE. Mind your own business!

Fast   M. HENRI. I will indeed... If you say so.

MARTINE. I like to be spanked by my husband.

M. HENRI. It appears so.

Build   MARTINE. It doesn't hurt you any. (She reaches for a
To   switch.)

Fast   M. Henri. I don't think so... You're right.

MARTINE. <u>And you're a fool to come meddling in
things which are no affair of yours!</u> (She switches him.
M. Henri dodges her, backing from her, then moving
up-left, crossing right, toward center and moving
quickly toward Silvester. She pursues him.)

Moliere flavors the action with a behavioral adjustment. Rather than welcome the neighbor for halting the beating, she defends her husband and the lashing as she moves left to him. It startles Henri who is made to feel guilty for intruding on their privacy. Silvester now is experiencing an exciting inner life as humiliation is erased and manly pride takes its place with great pleasure and excitement. Thus, his inner life is pulsating at an exciting tempo, while his physical life is immobile. This should happen at the moment and not anticipated. Such moments of discovery are precious to truthful creative stage artistry as every moment should be.

The circle of concentration has now widened to include Henri in their space. Her defense of her husband, marriage and privacy impel her to drive him off and punish him for intruding. His movement to escape beating takes him up-stage, across to center and down to right-center where he encounters Silvester to end the beat.

Beat ten life energy-tempo does a crescendo to fast and very fast during the action. With bolstered confidence, Silvester emerges from immobility

M. Henri. (Left of Silvester.) Good neighbor, Silvester, I
ask your pardon. Go right ahead and spank your wife.
<u>I will gladly help you, if you like.</u>

Beat
Ten

SILVESTER. (Moving slowly toward him as Henri slowly
retreats.) No, I don't like. (Martine's unexpected
defense of him and his act has given him courage to
face the intruder.)

Fast

M. HENRI. Oh, well, that's.... allright.

SILVESTER. <u>I will spank her if I want to. And I will not
spank her if I don't want to.</u>

M. HENRI. Splendid!

SILVESTER. She's my wife. She isn't your wife, is she?

M. HENRI. No. No. She doesn't look a bit like my wife.

SILVESTER. You can't give me any orders.

M. HENRI. Oh, no. I agree. I agree.

SILVESTER. I don't need any help from you.

M. HENRI. None what so ever.

Very
Fast

You're doing quite well without me.

SILVESTER. (Stalking Henri left then up-stage, right
and down-right.) And you're an insolent meddler...
to come and interfere in other people's private affairs.
(He lashes Henri who retreats from him and escapes
down-left, followed by Silvester, who stops down-left,
turns proudly with a broad smile. He slowly moves

and assumes the manly head of household and steps toward Henri. The balance between his inner psychological action and his outer action renders his moment a purely organic response without over-acting, thus living the role truthfully in the moment, a principle all fine actors try to achieve. (Ch. II).

The rhythm of the dialogue is suited to the inner life process of each; Silvester's newly instilled confidence and Henri's guilt of intrusion. Moliere's flavor is not to be ignored as overly confident Silvester asserts that he will or will not spank her as he chooses. Henri agrees to this spiritedly, thus accelerating Silvester's inner intensity and increasing the scenic rhythm leading to the execution of the outer physical action, putting the twig to action which has been in his possession since beating Martine. His inner life builds to a heated level and Silvester pursues Henri about the stage, keeping him in range of Martine, undoubtedly to exhibit his daring and valiant deed for her benefit. This is inspired by his active inner life, for he is already anticipating his future action of reconciling with Martine.

Beat
Eleven

toward her, confidently recalling her defense of him and the lashing.) Well now, dear, let's make up, huh? (He reaches her and attempts to embrace her, but she evades him and steps right.)

MARTINE. Oh, indeed! (Turning to face him at her left.) After beating me that way!

SILVESTER. It's just to show you... I love you! (Again he tries to embrace her, but she moves right.) Come on! (Pleadingly.)

MARTINE. (Stepping away.) No. I don't want to.

SILVESTER. Oh, now give me a kiss.

MARTINE. No, I won't. I'm angry.

SILVESTER. But you told Henri it was all right!

MARTINE. That's different. I'm mad.

SILVESTER. For such a trifle?

MARTINE. You hurt me.

SILVESTER. Aww, I'm sorry. Will you pardon me? (Takes her into his arms.)

MARTINE. Oh, all right. I accept your apology. (She pecks him and crosses away, speaking privately so he won't hear.) But you'll pay for this. I'll get even with you. Mark my word.

SILVESTER. (Moves a bit toward left and then comes to her during speech.) You're silly to take the matter

This point is to illustrate that one action emerges from another. The inner thoughts, also known as inner monologue, when in character and living the role, are vivid with images, ideas, feelings, actions in multifaceted depth. (Part II. Ch. VIII).

This thought and Henri's quick departure initiate beat eleven as he confidently and proudly approaches Martine flushed with manly success. Here again, the playwright introduces the unexpected reaction. Martine, in pursuit of her super-objective; love and respect as a wife, is determined to teach him a lesson, which is her through line of action, (Ch. VII) leading to the super-objective. She rejects his embrace and moves away, to right. Like a film unwinding before her inner eyes, she, living the part and engrossed completely in the life of her character, recalls feelingly the mistreatment she has suffered by Silvester since their marriage. Her inner life is multi-leveled, rich and vivid with images of events which must be real happenings in the life of her character. This is conceived by the actor in creating a biography of the person portrayed.

Beat
Eleven

seriously. Those little flare-ups are sometimes necessary for a good marriage and just shows I love you. A few meaningless spanks between lovers just stimulates affection. So, pay no attention to it. (She pouts as he kisses her lightly on the forehead. He turns left to exit.)

MARTINE. And where are you going?

SILVESTER. I'm off to the woods.

Beat
Twelve

MARTINE. We are practically out of kindling in our home! And you have none to sell! You'd better work your head off!

SILVESTER. <u>I will bring in a hundred bundles of kindling wood</u>. I'm up for it. Mark my word.

MARTINE. You'll mark your jug of wine, most likely! One hundred bundles of kindling wood! Hah! You must be drunk already!

Very
Fast

SILVESTER. Well, I get thirsty when I work! (Moving left.) No harm in a drop or two to cool off when I work, is there!

MARTINE. Work! Hah! You mark my word! <u>You either bring home money today for our needs and kindling for our fire! Or don't you come home at all!</u> (He moves left.) Do you hear me?

SILVESTER. Oh, I hear ya all right! (Off left.) The whole bloomin' world can hear ya! (He is gone and Martine is down-center stage.)

The tempo-rhythm has slowed to medium from the prior beat of high life energy dealing with Henri. She pecks him lightly, to pacify him, then crosses right to unleash her private thoughts; to make him pay for the abuse.

Beat twelve is initiated by Silvester's turn to depart toward left stage. The tempo-rhythm builds to very fast as agitation again mounts to anger and frustration spurred by thought of no kindling fuel and no money in the household, harsh reminders of her awful condition. His guilt leads to defensiveness and sarcasm as he moves toward left exit. Their organic action is a true justification of their characters' psychological state, preventing any over-acting (Ch. XIV).

The life energy reaches a peak with her emphatic demand for money and kindling. She makes her point with deep emotional projection and achieves her objective, accented by his departure, to end beat twelve. She stands down-center stage, looking left infuriatingly.

MARTINE. Well. I will not forget this! (Looking after
Beat   him. Then, with determination, speaks softly with
Thirteen   angered passion.) <u>I'd like to find a good way to punish</u>
              <u>you for that beating, dear husband! No man should</u>
              <u>ever beat a wife!</u> I will teach you a lesson so it will
              never happen again!... Oh, yes, a woman always has
Medium   a way to take revenge on a husband. But, that's too
              dainty a punishment for that scoundral. It wouldn't
              be satisfaction enough for the way he has treated me! I
Fast   want a revenge he'll feel down to his bones! I just need
              to teach him a lesson. Those blows still smart! Darn
              it! I won't stand for it any longer! (With pride and
              anger, she exits right.)

End of Scene One

There is a pause, which accents her emotional state. The state of her inner being is felt deeply, for her super-objective is desperately wanted by her. It is a deep-rooted desire which fuels every moment of her unhappy marriage.

Adhering to her through line of action toward the established super-objective, she passionately voices her inner thoughts directed toward her husband. Her inner life is raging with images, feelings, actions, all leading toward teaching Silvester a lesson to improve their life together.

Moliere has given Martine the statement which may very well be his purpose for writing the play, the idea that "No man should ever beat a wife!"

Martine states her objective to seek revenge, ending the beat and the scene.

Scene Two
Soon after previous scene.
The setting is the same.

Beat
One

DULAC. By gum, Old Maurice will never marry
    beautiful Laurinda with her awful affliction. (As they
    enter up-left and cross down-left-center.)
VALERE. No. And how can we help if every doctor
    Geronte has brought in has given up? This strange
    illness of hers is a mystery to all of us.

Medium

DULAC. By jimini and by jungle, I've heard it said that
    for every cure, there must be an illness. Likewise

Fast

    and therefrom, M. Valere, it must be so that for every
    illness.... there must be a CURE! (This logic stuns
    Valere.)
VALERE. But Laurinda's illness is so weird!
DULAC. Thus... since two plus two equals a sum, <u>then
    what we need to find for this weird illness... is a weird
    doctor!</u>
VALERE. <u>I must help Laurinda.</u> Geronte is at the end of
    his wits!

(He notices Martine entering up-right to cross down-
    right.) Good day, madam.

Beat
Two

MARTINE. (Pauses.) Uh, good day, sir. (Edging toward
    down-right.)
VALERE. Are you from these parts?

Medium

MARTINE. Yes, sir. Over yonder by the river. You are
    strange to this area?

Valere is a gentleman. Dulac is a handyman to Geronte, the father of troubled Laurinda. They enter from left in an agitated mood with medium-fast tempo-rhythm to start beat one. Their circle of attention encloses them tightly, unaware of their surroundings. Their inner thoughts and actions are geared toward finding a solution to lovely Laurinda's strange ailment. Having to recall recent events which have altered their lives, seemingly a film of all the events, images, actions unwinds before their inner vision and engrosses them completely. The rhythm of their dialogue will thus emerge truthfully from their inner life process.

To bring about the required scenic truth, each actor must know the complete biography of the character being portrayed, and the relationship with all other characters involved. They are near stage center as Martine is noticed, which begins beat two. The life energy is slowed to medium. Martine is brought into their circle of attention. She, being surprised and cautious, exhibits a wary psychological and physical action (Part II, Ch. XV).

VALERE. Yes, I am visiting a dear cousin who's daughter is stricken with a mysterious illness.

MARTINE. What seems to be her problem? (Stepping toward center.)

DULAC. She has been attacked, m'am.

VALERE. An unusual disease has deprived her of all power of speech.

MARTINE. Why, I have an idea what you can do.

VALERE. You do? (Impressed.) Already?

MARTINE. Oh, yes, indeed, sir!

DULAC. (Excitedly.) You see, Valere, you can never tell what ideas can come out of the woods!

VALERE. What do you propose, dear lady?

MARTINE. <u>She should see a doctor.</u> (Pleased with her helpful suggestion.)

VALERE. ...Yes...of course. Several physicians have already exhausted all their skills on her. <u>But sometimes one runs across very unusual people who possess some wonderful secrets of nature, certain special remedies, which accomplish what regular doctors just can't do.</u>

DULAC. <u>That's what we're looking for.</u>

Beat
Three

Medium
Fast

MARTINE. Well! (She gets a sudden idea and turns away with a smile.) You could not have come to a better place for advice. <u>I know just the special person who can manage such a desperate case!</u> In fact he is good at absolutely NOTHING...but...the most desperate of cases.

DULAC. Oh, lordie! (Expectantly.)

She must genuinely discover them, without a hint of anticipation (because of frequent rehearsals) or over-acting. They, too, must not anticipate discovery of her. The physical action must be organically tied to their inner action and the problem.

Feeling more at ease, she steps toward the strangers in need of her assistance and offers her advice. Although the actress knows what is ahead, the character is totally unaware how they are to enter into her life and contribute to her super-objective. Thus, she moves in toward them to help. Her inner life is only concerned with the young lady in need of a doctor to cure her strange illness. The gentlemen are being polite and their inner lives touch only lightly on the possibility of finding someone special, in view of the failures of all the doctors thusfar involved.

Beat three is initiated when Martine gets a sudden inspiration which becomes her through line of action leading to her super-objective. This exciting impulse triggers a medium-fast tempo-rhythm. Her life within

VALERE. (Hopefully and with joy.) <u>Where can we find him?</u>

MARTINE. You can go along that path a few hundred meters. He is amusing himself by cutting wood.

DULAC. A doctor cutting wood!

MARTINE. Oh, think nothing of it. It's just a hobby! He's always cutting up... the wood, I mean. It relaxes him.

VALERE. Ah, yes, amusing himself by gathering herbs and medicinal roots and bark, you mean?

MARTINE. Oh, yeah, you might say just that! He's rather pecular in some ways. You'd never take him for the brilliant man he is.

DULAC. Oh, yeah, Val. <u>There are many brilliant doctors who deceive the people.</u> Oh, yes indeed. The more they deceive you, why the greater they are!

VALERE. Peculiar, is he?

MARTINE. Oh, yes! (Energized.) He goes around dressed in dirty old clothes, and sometimes he pretends to be ignorant...just to give his brain a rest, you see? At those times he keeps all his great knowledge hidden. There are long periods of time when he just absolutely refuses to exercise the unusual talents for medicine which heaven has given him.

VALERE. It's a remarkable thing how some very great men have some fantasticality, some oddity, mingled with their superior knowledge.

is now bursting with hopeful anticipation, which should not be conveyed to the strangers. She can only proceed with caution, providing them with one suggestion after another and sensing their response. Thus, her eyes are focused intently on their eyes as she strives to read their inner thoughts. They, too, are focused on her eyes, urging her to reveal more in the anxious pursuit of their objective. Their circle of attention has tightened about them, as they become close to each other, achieving total communion (Ch.X).

The tempo-rhythm surges within Martine as she senses progress in her remarkable pursuit of her objective. Her physical life approaches her bubbling inner life. Her inspiration leads her to describe the antics of this medical genius with colorful words. She must not appear to be glib. The words should emerge selectively from an active but spontaneous sub-text, even with hesitancy, for they must not appear to be rehearsed.

So focused is she on what they are saying, truly listening to each word, she picks up on "oddity" to start a thought.

DULAC. And some mingle their oddities so that you'd hardly notice!

MARTINE. This man's oddity is greater than you'd ever believe!

Beat   DULAC. How's that, m'am?

Four   MARTINE. Sometimes it goes so far that....(Inspired.) he...has to be BEATEN before he'll admit his great medical talents. (Restraining her glee.)

Fast   VALERE. (Incredulous.) Indeed?

DULAC. (Astounded.) You mean to actually give him a pounding on his noggin?

MARTINE. (With hidden joy.) Oh, yes! And I warn you that if he's in that peculiar mood, you'll never make him admit he's a doctor...unless you BOTH take sticks and pound him well until he finally confesses what he will hide from you at first.

DULAC. That's hard to believe!

VALERE. You can't truly mean that, begging your pardon, dear lady.

MARTINE. Oh, yes! That's what we do around here when we need his medical services.

VALERE. What a strange folly!

MARTINE. True enough. But afterwards, you'll see that he can do real marvels! His true genius is revealed at last!

Med.   VALERE. Remarkable! (Ecstatic with anticipation.)

Fast   (Glowing with inner joy.) His name is Silvester. It's easy to recognize him. He is this tall, and he talks rather queer, and he carries a little brown jug wherever he goes.

The new thought starts beat four and a heightened tempo-rhythm due to her mounting enthusiasm. She "discovers" the idea of beating, stemming from her own active inner life reflection of the recent and past beatings. This must not be planned by the actor, but is to be the result of true recall of her past life by living the part of the character. This inspired idea is immediately associated with her objective to seek "revenge" on her husband for the beating, and so states the need to beat him for them to achieve their objective. Further inspired by the reaction she sees and feels from them, her inner thoughts and feelings drive her to suggest they both beat her husband, and to do so without mercy until they gain results.

They ask his name and beat five begins. The life energy is a bit slower for success has been almost assured. Still bubbling within, a medium-fast tempo-rhythm is fitting as she adds dimension to his oddities and Silvester's favorite object, the jug. Objects are most often extensions of the character. Silvester's connection with his jug is certainly a vivid and deplorable

DULAC. A "jug," m'am?

MARTINE. Oh, he loves his little brown jug. He even talks to it.

DULAC. Talks to his jug, eh? He's a queer one, alright!

VALERE. But is it really true that he is so brilliant as you say?

Fast

MARTINE. (Inspired.) Why, he's a man who works miracles! Six months ago there was a woman here given up by all the other doctors. They thought she was dead, and were getting her ready for burial. They then brought in the man I'm telling about. They had to drag him in with force. He examined her, mixed up some herbs and colorful liquids and other secret things and administered her and pretty soon she got off her bed and started walking around the room as if nothing had ever happened.

DULAC. By golly! He's just the man we're looking for!

Seven

MARTINE. (Creatively unleashed.) Oh, yes, I'm sure he is. And only three weeks ago a young boy fell down from the church steeple and he landed on the pavement and broke his arms, his legs, and his head!

symbol of her carousing, wastrel husband. Dulac's inner life is set into motion with the oddities of this medical genius. He envisions rather remarkable images, a most valued acting principle, which give his character a rich organic life in the scene.

Valere seeks further evidence of the strange doctor's brilliance and so initiates beat six. She responds with creative enthusiasm and describes with colorful images, a miraculous event attributed to this great doctor. It must not appear rehearsed, for it is being created at the moment. The character must never know what is going to happen, even if the actor indeed does know. The story must have its flavor of newness for the actor, yet accurately recalled by the character, as if it did occur. Dulac voices their joy at finding their special doctor and achieving their objectives and ending the fast tempo-rhythm of beat six.

Martine is on a roll due to their acceptance of her fabricated miracle and can not resist the temptation to add another. This new enthusiasm causes a crescendo in the tempo-rhythm to very fast.

Very Fast Seven	Well, as soon as they dragged in this fellow, he rubbed the boy all over with his special ointment, and gave him certain herbs and liquids of various colors, and he stood right up, smiled and ran off with his scooter!

VALARE. Why, that is impossible to believe!

Very
Fast DULAC. Let's go git 'im, Val.

MARTINE. Oh, but remember the warning I gave you!

DULAC. Dad-burn and dad-blast! Believe me, if all he needs is a beating up, Laurinds is as good as cured! (Overjoyed.)

VALERE. (Expansively.) Yes indeed! And thank you kind lady!

MARTINE. (Thrilled with success.) Oh, don't mention it! <u>The pleasure is really all mine!</u> (Infused with joyful innuendo.) Ta, ta! (She turns away and flounces off down-right, <u>beaming with success</u>.)

VALERE. Oh, she is heaven sent! How fortunate we are! (Moving toward left.) Come. <u>Let's find this unbelievable doctor</u>, Dulac!

DULAC. <u>Yeah, let's go!</u> By gar! And By golly! (Exit left.)

End Scene Two

It must be a spontaneous response to her inner excitement; not pre-planned or anticipated due to prior rehearsals by the actors, for the character does not know that she will do this. Thus, beat seven begins with a telling of another great miracle by the great doctor who must be beaten to admit his greatness.

Dulac is inspired not only at the success in locating a great doctor to cure lovely Laurinda, but is inwardly anticipating with great pleasure the chance to beat up on a great medical doctor. His psychological and physical action is at a very exciting level.

Valere, too, is bursting with pleasure and gratitude as he thanks the kind lady who moves to exit, leaving them basking in the heated glory of success in finding their special doctor. They move to the left to exit with great excitement and joyful anticipation.

DROP ZONE

A drama by A. Pia

It is darkness before dawn, years ago at an air field somewhere in the south of England. The faint sound of aircraft engines is heard. The hurried patter of approaching footsteps is heard. A flash light pierces the darkness up right revealing some bunks and then briefly illuminates little toy ducks on the floor by a bunk.

Beat One	VOICES. You bastard! Turn off that light! Knock it off! Etc.
	CAPALDO. O.K. men, up an' at 'em! (Goes to each bunk.) C'mon, Lieutenant Hogan!
	Let's go, Tex! Hey, Yank! C'mon, Jake! Rosie, wake up! Let's go, Captain Mac!
Medium	VOICES. Blow it out! To hell with you, Capaldo! Who the hell sent you, Hitler? You rotten spy! <u>Get out o'here!</u> (He dodges a thrown shoe.) Guido, take off!
	CAPALDO. <u>Half hour to briefing!</u> C'mon Lieutenant Price!

Beat Two	ALAN. (In bunk, stage right, grabs Capaldo's legs.) Gotcha, Guido! (Rolls out of bunk sending Capaldo to the floor playfully.)
	CAPALDO. Hey, Lieutenant Price, le' me go! <u>I gotta wake up the other barracks!</u> C'mon!
	ALAN. <u>I got him, guys!</u> You workin' for the enemy, bastard?

For the director, a dissected script is a necessity. Thus, the main idea of the play, known as the super-objective, must be known by all at first rehearsal. This is an anti-war play showing horrors of combat. Also, each actor must know the biography of the character to be portrayed and the relationship with all other characters.

Beat one begins with Capaldo entering barracks. His purpose is to rouse the sleeping flyers for their combat mission. The life energy tempo is medium. Just as play is dissected into acts and scenes, scenes are further dissected into beats or units of action. It is a complete dramatic action with beginning, middle, end. Like a paragraph with its topic sentence, a beat has its main point or objective. When a thought or action changes, the beat changes. Significant objectives of beats adhere to the spine of the play, the through line of action leading to the super-objective.

CAPALDO. Who, me? For cry sake, it's half hour to briefing! An' I'm supposed to wake you up! Let me go!

TEX. (Up center bunk.) Hot damn, Capaldo! <u>Wake up the rest of the squadron first!</u> Sheee-it!

ALAN. So that makes you an ENEMY!

CAPALDO. Let me go so I can wake up the other barracks. The Sarge will have my can if I'm late again!

YANK. (Down left.) <u>We warned you every morning, Guido!</u>

ALAN. <u>What do we do with the enemy when he invades, men!</u>

VOICES. Shoot him down! Blast him out of the sky! Down in flames!

Three   CAPALDO. (On the floor.) Lemme go!

ROSIE. (Down left.) <u>Let's shoot him down!</u> IN FLAMES! (Getting into his flying suit, crossing.)

Very   We, the jury of the 304th Squadron, sentence you,

Fast   Corporal Capaldo, ENEMY FIRST CLASS, to be SHOT DOWN IN FLAMES! (Aids Alan.) All in favor? (Laughingly. Others join.)

ROSIE. Sentence is passed! (Cheers.)

ALAN. Sorry, Capaldo, you've had it!

YANK. (Joins.) Cleared for take off!

ROSIE. Roger! <u>(They lift Capaldo and carry him out in</u> an Air Force style "bum's rush" accompanied by chorus of "Off we go, into the wild blue...." Tex dances after them waving his pistol. At height of action out-side the barracks, we <u>hear a gunshot</u> and a scream from Capaldo. The men cheer. Capaldo's running footsteps are heard putting distance between himself and the laughing flyers, who now enter up stage right.)

Beat two is initiated by Alan who sends Capaldo on to the floor.

Tempo-rhythm burst to fast as other flyers playfully join the fray. As a symphonic score has its variations in tempo, mood, rhythm, dynamics, so does the play, which is akin to a symphonic score.

The flyers must truly believe they have been roused from a deep sleep and are reluctant to face the reality of a dangerous combat mission this day. Such truthful inner thoughts will lend deeper significance to their words and actions with Capaldo. They must not be surface actions timed in rehearsals by actors. They are now living the parts as combat flyers.

Alan, being inspired by his buddies joining in, triggers beat three with the thought of ousting Capaldo in grand style, for he is an enemy invader! This sparks the tempo-life energy to very fast. This act must be spontaneous and originate in his inner life as an outgrowth of beat two to have the correct organic action. It must not be contrived or anticipated by actors from rehearsals. These are real characters in a newly created reality, (Ch. II).

TEX. (Waving pistol.) Shot him down lahk a duck!
Texas stahl! Ahhh-haaa! (Vigorous Texas battle cry.
All laugh and ad lib to bunks to dress.)

Four

MAC. (Navigator Captain and leader.) Let's go, guys.
<u>Twenty five minutes to briefing.</u> (They dress and
disperse to latrine, off down left.)

Med.

ALAN. I can't figure it. Every day, I send in my
resignation. <u>They pay no attention! Like I'm nobody!</u>
JAKE. (Up right bunk.) That's right, Alan, <u>you're
NOBODY!</u>
ALAN. Screw you, Jake! (Exit latrine.)

Five

MAC. (Exiting to latrine.) <u>Move it,</u> Bill. C'mon, Rosie.
ROSIE. O.K. Mac. (Crossing.) The <u>trouble with dawn
is, it comes so early!</u> (Exits to latrine. <u>They laugh.</u>)
Med.
Fast
BILL. Yeah, Rosie! (Laughing.) <u>I'd like it better if dawn
came about noon!</u> (Applies cream and shaves.)
YANK. (Down left bunk.) On my next leave, I'm goin'
to London and I'm <u>gonna sleep for twenty four hours.</u>
(To latrine trailing wooden ducks.)
BILL. Alone?
YANK. Yep! (Smiles and exits D.L.)

Six

Fast

JAKE. (To Bill, who is shaving.) Instead of THAT map,
<u>go over your aerial maps so maybe we can find our
home base!</u> Looks more like you are off to the yacht
club instead of dropping paratroopers, rookie! (Bill
struggles to ignore comment.)

The objective is to get him out in memorable fashion so to impress Capaldo to waken them last in the future. Each flyer's inner life is in harmony with this intention and each contributes to the flavor of the action. The climax of the beat is the gunshot by Tex and Capaldo running.

Mac's sober note introduces a moderate life energy-tempo for beat four. Each flyer harbors his private inner thoughts triggered by apprehension, anxiety, fear or dread. Only humor can bury those horrible inner thoughts. Alan inserts a touch at this point, which only serves to invite Jake's cynicism as Alan exits to end beat four.

Rosie, Bill and Yank contribute to lighten the mood in beat five, which heightens the tempo-life energy to medium fast. It must be stressed that the interplay of humor can not be mere frivolity. It shields the multi-faceted inner life anxieties and fear. Inner visions of prior combat missions, burning aircraft, lost comrades, impending death stir their inner life, subtext and emotions. Yank ends beat five.

(Mac, entering, hears part of Jake's comment and stifles a response as he goes to bunk.)

TEX. (At bunk.) Some joke, man! That is CHICKEN!

Fast

MAC. Look, Jake it was his first mission here. You know damned well <u>navigating in Europe is different than in the States. Give him a break!</u>

JAKE. We don't give "breaks" in combat to snot noses just out of navigating school! This is for real!

MAC. You got another wild hair today, Jake? You've been on everybody's back for days! <u>GETTING CHICKEN ARE YOU!</u> huh?

TEX. Ah wish to hell ah were navigatin' that ship of yoahs, ah'd lose YOU but GOOD! Maybe then we'd have PEACE roun' heah!

JAKE. It is too much to expect a navigator to get me to home base after a mission? As for YOU, Texas, you couldn't have SEEN the map let alone navigate. I'll bet you didn't wake up 'til we hit the drop zone! Real BLIND flying!

TEX. (Resumes shaving. Laughs.) Shee-it. That's a real crock!

Seven

ALAN. (Entering.) How come you're shaving, Tex? A date?

TEX. Yeah! Ah heard Belgian girls are fine poon tang! <u>Just one lil ol' flak hole in mah</u> plane on the mission today, an' Brussels, heah ah come! Aaaa-haa!

Jake, motivated by his deep-rooted but suppressed fears, targets Bill to initiate beat six. His surging inner life builds the tempo-rhythm to fast. With insulting and piercing criticism of the young navigator, the major conflict within the flying team is exposed. Jake is emerging as a "chicken" flyer, a most degrading label, despite his excellent flying ability. Jake has begun to experience feelings of guilt instilled by his awareness of his opposition to this combat strategy to jump the Rhine River. The actor must truly find the source of these inner feelings of guilt, dread, fear, opposition by a thorough search into the history and biography of the Jake character. The lines of dialogue are not sufficient to organically portray this complex character. The actor's creative imagination (Ch. IV) must lead him to living the role truthfully in the correct state of being, proper organic action.

Alan launches beat seven on a lighter note to lower the tempo-life energy to medium fast as he teases Tex, who is quick to flaunt his greatest interest, women. It relieves the tension of beat six, Alan's intention. Mac counters

Med. Fast	MAC. (Delving into foot locker.) That was just a milk-run yesterday. If they don't change our route into Holland today, we'll have a helluva time with those anti-air-craft 88s. You can bet they didn't sit on their butts all night after we dropped those paratroopers yesterday.

MAC. (Delving into foot locker.) That was just a milk-run yesterday. If they don't change our route into Holland today, we'll have a helluva time with those anti-air-craft 88s. You can bet they didn't sit on their butts all night after we dropped those paratroopers yesterday.

ROSIE. Simmer saw supplies coming in late last night.

ALAN. Yeah, an' Bates said more paratroopers came in from 82nd.

MAC. It could be both. <u>They sure as hell need the support up there if they expect to cross the Rhine.</u>

TEX. I never saw such flak. (Exit.)

JAKE. I hope we drop supplies instead of troopers. <u>I don't want to be like sitting ducks!</u> (Exit.)

Eight

ALAN. (His small radio tuned to Armed Forces Network.) Ohh, listen to that Artie Shaw! To hell with the mission. <u>Let's go dancing!</u>

Med.

ROSIE. I'm with you! (Others agree.)

YANK. (Entering.) We're ready. (He goes to bunk with ducks trailing.)

JAKE. (Entering.) Another overcast! No fighter escort today! Damn!

YANK. <u>No protection again! Sitting ducks!</u> That's what we'll be!

Nine

MAC. Let's go before we lose out on those powdered eggs!

BILL. How long does it take to get used to that stuff?

with a sobering reminder of this day's mission and his sincere awareness that the route into Holland should be altered. His knowledge of combat strategy makes him wary of the impending briefing they are about to attend. Thus, his inner life is rich with images of flying routes into Holland by way of England and Belgium. The actor must perform an in-depth study of all elements of the character's life leading to this critical strategic plan to cross the Rhine River. (Its importance and questionable tactics led to novels and films such as "A Bridge Too Far.") Mac's inner concerns for his ideas, the lives of his comrades, unity, attitude are all filling his inner life and actions, establishing his harmony of psycho-physical response to the circumstance. Jake's fear is illustrated by stating as he exits that they are like "sitting ducks!" This ends the beat.

Alan again attempts to lighten the mood and starts beat eight with the suggestion to cancel the mission and go dancing. As Rosie and others agree, thus erasing the sober thoughts of prior beat with a more relaxed moderate

Very
Fast

JAKE. <u>Don't worry about it, "navigator," you won't be</u> <u>able to find your way to the mess hall.</u>

BILL. (<u>Charges into Jake</u> with fury, knocking him down.) Damn you! <u>I've taken enough of your crap!</u> (They tangle. Others rush in to part them. Mac pulls Jake aside as others grab Bill.)

MAC. <u>Damn it, Jake! Knock it OFF!</u>

ALAN. (Restraining Bill with Tex) All right, Bill! Settle down!

YANK. (Between them.) Drop it!

ROSIE. (Beside Bill.) Take it easy, Bill. Cool it.

TEX. <u>Damn it, Jake, you ah out of yo' mahnd!</u> Let's go, Bill. (They resume preparation for briefing.)

Ten

BILL. (Gets mail from bunk, now composed.) <u>You guys</u> <u>want letters mailed?</u>

MAC. Yeah, Bill. I have one. (Gets mail from foot locker.)

Med.

ALAN. Hold on, Bill. (He gets mail from bunk, goes to Bill.)

ROSIE. Just a second, Bill. Here. Imagine, Cathy will be holding this letter-and reading it to my baby who won't understand a word. (laughs softly.)

BILL. (Taking letter.) <u>How long is it since you have seen</u> <u>your wife and baby, Rosie?</u>

ROSIE. <u>Nineteen month...and six days. I've never seen</u> <u>my Herbie.</u>

ALAN. <u>Pretty soon now, Rosie.</u> (Pats him lightly on shoulder.)

tempo-life energy, a counter point of fear by Jake is introduced. The weather is to prevent fighter escort and protection. Yank's inner reaction of fear underlies his blunt statement of their condition; they'll be sitting ducks with no protection. Beat eight is ended.

Mac introduces beat nine with a need to depart, flavored with their joking pet peeve, powdered eggs. It backfires, however as Bill comments and exposes himself to Jake's insult. The life energy-tempo explodes to very fast as Bill, no longer able to restrain himself, lunges at Jake. It becomes a brawl. Bill's inner life must truly be truthful to avoid an anticipated, rehearsed and choreographed physical action. The animosity must be organic in nature, an outgrowth of the fear and anxiety all are feeling. They are parted, and beat nine ends.

Bill's composed offer to take letters to be mailed introduces a moderating beat ten. This leads us to see the painful private lives of those who have wives and children from whom they are separated, an unforgiving war condition. The inner lives of the characters must ring true as each is

TEX. <u>It won't be long, ol' buddy.</u>

YANK. (Crossing to Rosie.) This <u>Rhine mission will do it, kid.</u>

ROSIE. Yeah, (Nodding) this Rhine mission will do it for sure.

MAC. (Hand on Rosie's shoulder.) <u>Let's move it, guys!</u> C'mon, Rosie.

BILL. Any more mail to go? See you at the mess hall. (Smiling (If I can find my WAY! (They all laugh as they follow him out up right.)

Eleven   MAC. (As Jake lingers then moves toward exit) Just a minute, Jake. (Crosses to center.) Look, <u>we've had just about enough of your bull-shit!</u> What the hell is it with you?

JAKE. <u>I've been here two goddam years and I don't like having a rookie just out of navigation school on my crew!</u>

Fast   MAC. <u>Someone</u> had to take Bob's place on your crew, so I assigned Bill to you. Who the hell do you expect?

JAKE. Why a rookie? I have a fine crew. I deserve the best!

MAC. I checked Bill out with the Major and we believe he's going to be one of our top navigators. No one else will fly with you anymore! You ride their butts from day one! So, they want OUT!

JAKE. They can't do the job, so I chew them out!

MAC. What the hell are you talking about? Bob was a fine navigator! He stayed with you, dammit!

reminded of home and family. Rosie's personal situation becomes a touching symbol of all those young combatants taken from their loved ones to fight a war created by others. For the actor who must put himself into the given circumstance of the character and live the part, this scene becomes a deeply moving event. The inner feelings of all are at the breaking point. Bill lightens the mood playing upon Jake's words of being able to find his way to the mess hall.

Mac's need to assert his leadership and to bring about harmony, requires that he meet privately with Jake, not an easy thing to accomplish in a large barracks. This introduces beat eleven. Jake's psycho-physical action (Part II, Ch. XV) lends itself to the problem of the moment. His inner fear impels him to resist exiting. His guilt keeps him alienated from the others who have departed in a group. This hesitation is a highly important pause accent, a principle of major importance. Mac reads this psycho-physical action and uses it. He addresses Jake, needing to know his problem. Jake's suppressed inner fear makes Bill the target of weakness in his otherwise fine crew, which he feels he deserves.

And he's dead!

JAKE. We were shot down! WE WERE IN FLAMES FOR CRY SAKE! You blame ME? (Mac turns away.) The sons o'bitches! ALL BLAMING ME! (Turns and kicks bunk, then back to Mac.) You guys are all a bunch...

Twelve

MAC. (Cuts in angrily) YOU'RE A PAIN IN THE ASS, JAKE! You and your lousy disposition and temperment be DAMNED! You are intent on turning everyone against you! And you're succeeding! Only because Rosie is one hell of a guy do you still have HIM as co-pilot. Where the hell are you going to find another pilot with HIS loyalty?

Very
Fast

And you still have Clay, one of the best crew chiefs in the squadron! And you're BITCHING! You must be out of your mind, for CRY SAKE! If you like to pick on someone to satisfy that wild hair up your butt, pick on ME! NOBODY ELSE! Or I'll break your goddam back! Do you read me! (He is a tower of rage. He exits.)

(Jake stands still a moment. He moves toward exit, hesitates, retreats and sinks into chair at table, center. He lowers head to table. Yank, in the pre-dawn darkness of his corner bunk, had been an unwilling witness. He approaches Jake slowly and sits opposite. Jake, having sensed he was alone, is startled.

318

Mac, who's inner thoughts must be filled with facts of Jake's background so they become real living images, states bluntly that things have developed so no one wants to fly with him. The point is made and beat eleven ends and moderate tempo.

Mac launches into beat twelve with venom. The tempo-rhythm surges to very fast as Mac asserts his command and faults Jake for his antics and indeed challenges him with a powerful threat. This must come from profoundly active inner life to inspire the right mood and organic psycho-physical element. No "acting" is to be exhibited here, but truthful living of the role in harmony with the circumstance. Mac achieves his objective with his powerful assertion, turns and exits strongly, exuding personal strength and command. This ends volatile beat twelve.

Beat thirteen tempo-rhythm diminishes to slow. Jake is almost a broken man. This is manifested by his weakened movement into the chair where he lays his head on his folded arms, close to the fetal position without cliché.

YANK. (Softly.) It's okay, ol'buddy. I know how you feel.

JAKE. (Struggling for control.) Yank...dammit...(Lowers head.)

YANK. It's alright, Jake. I know.

JAKE. (Gaining control.) Yank, I don't know what the hell is happening to me....I've grown...scared. (Unbelieving.)

YANK. I am too, Jake... We all are.

JAKE. (Looking into his eyes.) I...never felt this way before...But...lately...since I lost Bob...How the hell do I deal with it, Yank?

Fourteen   YANK. (Shakes his head slowly.) I wish I knew...Accept it...I...don't know.

JAKE. Things are falling apart. I worked like hell to be a good pilot.

Med.   YANK. I know. You're the best, Jake.

Slow   JAKE. But...it all changed....since the crash....Bob didn't get out!

YANK. Forget it....You have war...you have death. What the hell else is it?... A game?

JAKE. I don't know. I've had enough! Enough of flak... and .... In this goddam war we live a whole life time. A life time of gambling.

YANK. Yeah, an' I was taught it was wrong to gamble.

Fifteen   JAKE. The world is crazy. People make a hell for each other...

It's easy for THEM to send kids out to be killed.

Med.   YANK. Well, I'm no KID any more! I've grown up in this lousy war.

Indeed, with all acting principles truly at work and living the part truthfully, the action could be a reflection of the creative mood in which the sub-conscious will function naturally in the believed circumstance (Ch. XVI).

Yank, unseen by Jake, moves from the darkened area of his bunk to the chair opposite Jake. His inner life is tempered to Jake's somber mood. His psycho-physical life leads him to the chair and is in complete communion (Ch.X) with Jake. By sitting, he puts himself on Jake's level to exhibit compassion for his flying buddy. With physical and eye contact, they understand each other and sense each other's feelings and trust due to mind-to-mind interplay, making the sub-conscious accessible, the highest form of creative artistry (Ch. XI).

The troubled inner life is brought to the surface as Jake, sensing Yank's spiritual communion, admits to growing scared. Yank easily admits his own fear, for his maturity and perception have brought all this to the surface. The psychological process must be thoroughly understood by the actor playing the role of Yank and living the part truthfully.

I see through it all and it sickens me....But...<u>we have to go.</u>

Jake. (Checks his watch.) Yeah.

YANK. Time to roll the damn dice.

Sixteen JAKE. <u>Seventeen minutes to briefing</u>. Let's get some chow. (He moves slowly toward exit.)

YANK. (Rising.) Yeah. Let's have some chow.

Med. JAKE. (Nearing exit, he turns to Yank.) Bring the ducks!

YANK. Roger! (Crosses to his toy ducks by bunk down left.) I won't go without them! (He leads the ducks toward exit as lights dim. The faint droning sound of aircraft engines drifts into the barracks as they exit. Blackout.)

End of Scene

Beat fourteen moves to a medium-slow life energy as they open themselves to each other. Their cues quicken as sub-text rises to the surface, exposing their private thought. Highly important elements are exposed. It is concluded that if you have war, you have death. War makes combatants age a life time.

A small, thus highlighted, beat fifteen brings out two vastly important statements for our world. People make a hell for each other. In addition, it is easy for those in power and who initiate war, to send young kids to be killed. This brief beat is performed in medium-fast tempo with sincere conviction.

Thus, it is their maturity that leads them to see negative aspect of war. It is wrong and inhuman. War means death. And death is to be feared and it is mature to admit it.

Their watch makes them face their commitment to war, thus introducing final beat sixteen with a moderate tempo and resigned life energy. They exit toward the beckoning and fearful sound of aircraft engines, with the ducks trailing Yank, a symbol of "sitting ducks."

ABOUT THE AUTHOR

Al Pia's involvement in theatre began as a youth in school stage plays as actor, director and stage technician, and through high school and college years. He earned his B.A. Degree and Masters Degree at the University of New Hampshire. Doctoral study at Harvard University was interrupted by recall to active military duty during the Korean War. When he later continued his doctoral study at Columbia University, it was interrupted by employment assignment to Europe.

He formed the Lancaster Community Theatre in New Hampshire, transferred to Connecticut and founded the Stamford Community Theatre. His administrative jobs then took him abroad. He worked in India and Turkey managing International Trade Fairs for the United States Commerce Department and in Munich, Germany with Radio Liberty, an international broadcasting firm for the U.S. Department of State. While in Germany, he acted in a film under famed director Gottfried Reinhardt with Sir Alec Guiness and Robert Redford. He and actress wife Betty formed The American Theatre Of Munich. They staged only great American classic plays in English, such as "Our Town," "A View From The Bridge" and others. They attracted highly talented actors from various countries. The Voice of America, impressed with their mission and success, aired some of their works internationally. They supplied actors for film companies on location in Germany and for film voice dubbing for famed Aventin Film Studio of Munich, several of which were directed by Al.

Upon returning to Connecticut, Al accepted the theater department position at the high school in Westport. At the same time, he founded a theater program for the City of Stamford and became the artistic director of The Sterling Barn Theater. He held the position for over twenty-five years. Their success earned accolades from the Stamford Advocate Arts Director, who stated: "The Sterling Barn Theater is the best little theater around." He ultimately departed to accept an appealing position as adjunct professor of theater at a regional university to teach and direct.

In his first year at the high school in Westport, Al directed a production of "Soldier, Soldier!" It was his full-length adaptation of the anti-war one-act play, "Bury The Dead." It won both Connecticut State Drama Association

Award and New England Theater Conference Moss Hart Memorial Award. He was then asked by the Dramatic Publishing Company to premiere new plays. Al directed their play, "Black Elk Speaks," at the high school. That very significant and powerful play won the New England Theater Conference Moss Hart Memorial Award, as did "Cabaret," "The Sound of Music," "West Side Story," and other major stage productions.

Upon retirement, a newly constructed studio was dedicated to his honor and titled Albert Pia Studio Theater in recognition of nearly thirty years of achievement in theatre arts at the Staples High School

Several full-length plays have been written and directed by Al at the Sterling Barn Theater. His drama, "Drop Zone," based upon his military career as a combat pilot in World War II, also won the New England Theater Conference Moss Hart Memorial Award.

The Town of Westport in 1996 and the City of Stamford in 1997 have honored Al for achievement in theater and cultural contribution to their communities. He was selected for admission to Who's Who Among America's Teachers Fifth Edition 1998 and Ninth Edition 2004-2005. Recently, he was honored by National Register's Who's Who in Executives and Professionals for appearance in the 2005-2006 Edition "for reaching a level of recognizable success in the field of theatre." In 1999 he received the Connecticut Critics Circle Award for Lifetime Achievement. The Westport Historical Society honored Al in 1998 for "Recognizing his gifted excellence in educating and preparing young actors for the professional theatre."

A novel was recently completed by Al entitled, "On Stage! The Communal Magic of Theatre." It is geared toward the organization and operation of community theaters, their cultural value and unifying influence in world communities.